T0246040

James Reaney on the Grid

Also by Stan Dragland

Wilson MacDonald's Western Tour

Peckertracks

Simon Jesse's Journey

Journeys Through Bookland and Other Passages

The Bees of the Invisible:
    Essays in Contemporary Canadian Writing

Floating Voice: Duncan Campbell Scott
    and the Literature of Treaty 9

Apocrypha: Further Journeys

Stormy Weather: Foursomes

The Drowned Lands

Deep Too

The Bricoleur & His Sentences

Strangers & Others: Newfoundland Essays

Strangers & Others: The Great Eastern

Gerald Squires

The Difficult

An Essay by Stan Dragland

James Reaney

ON THE GRID

The Porcupine's Quill

Library and Archives Canada Cataloguing in Publication

Title: James Reaney on the grid / an essay by Stan Dragland.

Names: Dragland, Stan, 1942– author.

Description: Includes index.

Identifiers: Canadiana (print) 20220468141 | Canadiana (ebook) 20220468184
	| ISBN 9780889844520 (softcover) | ISBN 9780889844537 (PDF)

Subjects: LCSH: Reaney, James–Criticism and interpretation.

Classification: LCC PS8535.E24 .Z65 2022 | DDC C818/.5409 — dc23

Published by The Porcupine's Quill, 68 Main Street, PO Box 160,
Erin, Ontario NOB 1TO. http://porcupinesquill.ca

The cover image is reproduced with the assistance of The Canadian County Atlas
Project, Rare Books and Special Collections, McGill University Library.

Represented in Canada by Canadian Manda.
Trade orders are available from University of Toronto Press.

We acknowledge the support of the Ontario Arts Council and the Canada
Council for the Arts for our publishing program. The financial support of the
Government of Canada is also gratefully acknowledged.

To the memory of my friend, Ben Basha

2000–2019

Contents

1. Introductory 11

2. English 138 23

3. A Living Chariot 33

4. Conscious or Instinctive 47

5. Backbones 53

6. Outreach 89

7. Farm Boy 93

8. Serenity 97

9. Lighting its Own Way 115

10. To Grumble 119

11. Anagogic 159

12. Angels 187

13. The Integral 205

14. Realism Reconsidered 227

15. The Book of Life 239

List of Illustrations 261

Acknowledgements 263

Notes 269

Index 313

Portrait of James Reaney by Barker Fairley, 1958.

[H]e has succeeded, as I think no poet has so succeeded before, in bringing southern Ontario, surely one of the most inarticulate communities in human culture, into a brilliant imaginative focus.[1]

— Northrop Frye

Where there is nothing to listen
to you, nor to listen to,
listen.[2]

— Robert Bringhurst

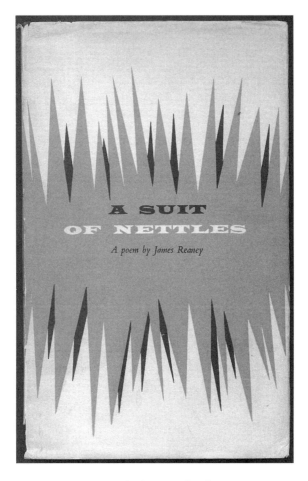

Dust jacket for *A Suit of Nettles*.

Designed by Allan Fleming. Macmillan, 1958.

Introductory

This started out as the tenth annual James Reaney Memorial Lecture. It was delivered in London, Ontario, on November 2, 2019. That version turns out to have only scratched the surface of what I've been finding to say about Reaney's literary career. As the talk grew into what it is now, it became ever clearer to me that Reaney's legacy includes one unmistakable masterpiece, the Donnelly trilogy, a play in three parts so magnificent that it stands, or ought to stand, with the work of literary greats anywhere. But there are many other works of real importance, plus a few that may perhaps be worth reading only to someone like me, interested in all of Reaney, because of what all of it has to say about the best of his work.

Before I met Reaney, I had read his *A Suit of Nettles* with pleasure and puzzlement. I had also heard that he was preoccupied with 'the iconography of the imagination.' A graduate student at the time, I was both intrigued and bewildered by that phrase. It was outside my frame of reference. I see now that I was right to be bewildered. I think I've come to know something about what Reaney meant by the iconography of the imagination, but it's not simple. It's not meant to be. So many of the pages that follow will be, directly or indirectly, devoted to trying to clarify the meaning of that phrase, and other complex matters, to the reader of modest competence I model on myself.

Newly graduated, I accepted the offer of a job at The University of Western Ontario, the name since shortened to Western University, where my education began in earnest. I learned from having to teach, and I learned from some of my colleagues, James Reaney chief among them, especially during the two years we were members of the same teaching team—see Chapter 1. For quite some time I was entirely under his spell. I spent my first sabbatical writing an article about his work. Later I edited and wrote the afterword for a collection of essays, *Approaches to the Work of James Reaney*. Toward the end of his life, I was the editor of his final book of poetry. By that time, though, our warm relationship had cooled. I have said elsewhere that he was to me a kind of father, a literary father. Any father-son relationship has the potential to be fraught. I was *with* Reaney for quite a few years, and I never lost my admiration for him and for his work, but I did come to realize that we were very different people and very different sorts of writer. Had we been intimate, rather than just friendly, I might have found out what he was thinking when he called me a 'post-modernist' just before I was to be interviewed for a documentary on his work in which I called *The Donnellys* 'Canadian Shakespeare.' I knew post-modernist was a bad word in the Reaney lexicon, but it's not something I have ever called myself. He seems to have thought I had gone over to the postmodernist critics who were stressing theory over literature, because I was nibbling at theory, trying to fathom changes in the literary zeitgeist that were happening at the time. I made the mistake, supposing I had wanted to be sure of staying on his good side, of citing some of that current theory in the afterword to *Approaches to the Work of James Reaney*. Or maybe he could just see that I wasn't turning into the sort of writer and critic that he valued. So there came to be some distance, some heat, between us: growing pains on my side, perhaps some disillusionment on his. We never worked that out.

Because of that unresolved conflict, I had some qualms about accepting the Reaney lecture gig, but my admiration for the work was too strong. One benefit of revisiting Reaney was to burn off pretty well all the negativity I had been harbouring. As I've read and reread the poems and plays and essays, written and rewritten what I found to say about them, the process has been to explicate, yes, but also to work out what I think and feel about many things, literary and otherwise. The result is personal, but, I think, not at all private. It reaches in directions and incorporates material that would never have come to light for me, and never would have come together, had I declined the Reaney lecture. I can hardly pay any higher tribute to my subject than to say how stimulating it has been to try to make my words worthy of his. I'm not going to get any smarter than I am now. This is it. It has taken everything I have to try to measure up to the phenomenon of Reaney. What more could a person want in a subject?

I'm not the only colleague, student or acquaintance of Reaney to have written about his work. To mention only books and monographs, there is *James Reaney* by old-and middle-English specialist Alvin A. Lee of McMaster University (1968); *James Reaney* by romanticist Ross Woodman of Western (1971); *James Reaney* by Reaney's son, James Stewart Reaney (1977); *James Reaney and His Works* by nineteenth-century specialist Richard Stingle of Western (1990); *How to Play: The Theatre of James Reaney* by modern drama specialist Gerald Parker of Western (1991); and *The Emblems of James Reaney* by Thomas Gerry (2013), a graduate student of Reaney's. Other colleagues and students of Reaney have produced anthologies, articles and interviews. He drew a number of us in, several from academic specialties other than Canadian literature. The list above is the iceberg tip of Reaney criticism, but the interesting thing about those books is that none of us who knew the man takes the same approach to his work. That's one way of saying there is a lot going on in it.

The books just cited are worthy works. With the exceptions of *James Reaney*, by James Stewart Reaney, who could hardly avoid mentioning that he is writing about his father, and Tom Gerry, whose friendship with the Reaneys appears only in his bio, none of the writers make anything of their personal relationship with the subject. This is quite proper. It's in the nature of most criticism: present your findings objectively, project an authoritative self, efface the authorial I. It's a good way to eschew any egocentric self-aggrandizement. I'm against that too. But the arm's-length approach precludes a level of personal engagement and knowledge that would sometimes be welcome. I knew Richard Stingle better than I knew James Reaney. There was only one office between his and mine on the lower floor of Western's University College. I knew that he and Jamie had been close friends since their undergraduate days at the University of Toronto. Stingle is acknowledged in the first issue of *Alphabet* magazine, though not by name, as the friend who, back then, showed Reaney a passage from Blake that helped him conquer a creeping nihilism and reaffirm his belief in metaphor as a way of knitting together a fragmenting world.

```
C G Y R S V K
D H Z S T W L
E I A T U X M
F J B U V Y N
G K C V W Z O
H L D W X A P
I M E X Y B Q
J N F Y Z C R
K O G Z A D S
A L P H A B E T
B M Q I B C F U
C N R J C D G V
D O S K D E H W
E P T L E F I X
F Q U M F G J Y
G R V N G H K Z
H S W O H I L A
I T X P I J M B
J U Y Q J K N C
K V Z R K L O D
L W A S L M P E
M X B T M N Q F
```

Front cover, *Alphabet 1* (1960). Designed by Allan Fleming.

Stingle told me that he saw Reaney's grit way back when others were taking him to be some sort of flower child. I would have loved to read a Stingle memoir of his Reaney days, but that was not his way. The man's intense loyalty came wrapped in a privacy. I'm not telling any secrets here—I don't know any—but I do mean to be up front about my relationship with Reaney. I suppose this is a version of the 'full disclosure' that is *de rigueur* these days, especially in journalism. Perhaps the approach draws my work in that direction, or else towards memoir. Well, any writing, no matter how cool and remote, is a kind of self-portrait of the author. It is so, at least, to any reader who attends not only to what is being said but also to the how of it—the style, the structure and all the rest—to everything that is literary in any prose argument, which is often most effective when it calls little attention to itself. Whether *behind* the technique, or *in* it, though, we are all particular people as we write. We have our own predilections and limitations. If a little of that is allowed to show, perhaps something of the subject's complex humanity will also show. Perhaps his or her work will feel like something intimately connected to a maker, rather than some remote, basically inert mass of material to be poked at.

James Reaney has said that David Milne wrote as well as he painted, and he was right. 'Feeling is the power that drives art,' says Milne in a 1948 essay called 'Feeling in Painting.' 'There doesn't seem to be a more understandable word for it, though there are others that give something of the idea: aesthetic emotion, quickening, bringing to life. Or call it love; not love of man or woman or home or country or any material thing, but love without an object—intransitive love.'[3] From the verbal field, from grammar in this case—an intransitive verb doesn't take a direct object—a visual artist draws a metaphor that helps him point to something ineffable that he knows by feeling. Perhaps, when the dust of a critic's reservations and grumbles has settled, it may be understood that he and his subject are linked by intransitive love.

A word about grid. As far as I know, Reaney used it only once in connection with his own work. He picked the word up from an alien context and used it in an empowering way, to say what he does with inherited literary patterns, especially archetypes. But think of what grid means literally. In the *Oxford Canadian Dictionary* it's 'a framework of spaced parallel bars,' 'a network of lines, esp. of two series of regularly spaced lines crossing one another at right angles.' Anything built on a framework so geometrical would be pretty stiff. The kind of grid that would better fit the best of Reaney's work would be more like a trellis. Set up a trellis for flowering plants to climb all over: it's there but unseen, supporting all that floral leaf-green beauty. Trellis, then, or perhaps—taking just 'network of lines' from the definition above—something more like the complex electrical systems also called grids. One sense of the 'on,' in 'Reaney on the grid,' is 'about.' He writes *about* rigid social or religious or literary grids or systems to oppose them. In his plays he will cross that sort of grid with looser, more tolerant systems, creating a sort of grid of systems. Inflexible grids are actually thematised in *The Donnellys*, while the structure of the trilogy is extraordinarily lithe. Some of the plays do edge toward the good-versus-evil grid, and some of Reaney's opinions are inflexible. His mind was wide open to many things and he was astonishingly creative, but he could close down. There will have to be a certain amount of play in the word 'grid' as used here, then, but I do want to hold on to it. In a way, everything I have to say started with Reaney's use of that word on an occasion when he suddenly turned into the prophet Ezekiel.

In what follows I quote Reaney liberally. That is one way of letting him speak for himself, if discontinuously, and that method differs from his. To note one large difference at a glance, you need only flip to the end of this book, behold the many footnotes, then turn to almost any one of Reaney's essays, or *14 Barrels from Sea to Sea*, his book about the national tour of *The Donnellys*, and see none—except in his one scholarly book, *The Donnelly Documents: an Ontario Vendetta*. As critic/essayist, even as poet, Reaney's way was to paraphrase the works of others. I do admire that. I even envy the capacity, in Reaney and others thus gifted, to digest any subject and make it their own. But I myself prefer to work up a kind of critical collage. If I seem to be leaning on the authority of those I quote, Reaney included, that's fine with me. I don't want my sources trimmed any more than they have to be when passages from them are plucked out and worked into an arrangement of my own. I have a warm relationship with most of these passages and the works of those who wrote them. A few are chosen merely to illustrate a point, some are to react to, but most, including most of Reaney's, are here because I admire them. Such quotation carries an unstated recommendation: if you like this, look up the source. Documenting with notes is a very tedious business, but it does show you where else to go.

Paraphrase certainly has its virtues. It's very effective in the hands of a writer like Reaney, who is so good at driving to the core of a subject and expressing it in his own words, often in metaphor. In a way, that's what his whole career has been about: taking in the external world, whether benign or threatening, and turning it back out in a creation that patterns and clarifies the 'chaos' of raw material. Only a powerful synthesizer can do that convincingly, though synthesis may leave the impression that the source materials are secondary to the argument being shaped, that the concerns of the shaper are paramount. There are times when it seems to me that Reaney is leaving out or glossing over or slightly misrepresenting some matters in the flight of his own polemic. Anyway, I want those I quote to speak for themselves. My labour is to weave their words, and in some cases pictures, into a design within which they remain themselves. Quote the good stuff then try to make your linkages worthy of carrying the golden freight.

Some words from Roland Barthes' essay, 'The Death of the Author,' came to me while I was thinking how to contrast what I do and what Reaney does with an essay. Barthes is postmodernist, so this, at least part of it, may make Reaney turn in his grave:

We know now that a text is not a line of words releasing a single 'theological' meaning (the 'message' of the Author-God) but a multi-dimensional space in which a variety of writings, none of them original, blend and clash. The text is a tissue of quotations drawn from the innumerable centres of culture.... [T]he writer can only imitate a gesture that is always anterior, never original. His only power is to mix writings, to counter the ones with the others, in such a way as never to rest on any one of them. Did he wish to *express himself*, he ought at least to know that the inner 'thing' he thinks to 'translate' is itself only a ready-formed dictionary, its words only explainable by other words, and so on indefinitely....[4]

Reaney's mentor Northrop Frye has said that 'Poetry can only be made out of other poems; novels out of other novels,'[5] so that much would pass; the indefinite regress of meaning would probably not. 'The text is a tissue of quotations': that touches a chord in me. But I choose and arrange and comment on my materials just like a live author—one all too conscious of shortfalls and incompletions in his writing, true—ready to take sole responsibility for what he finds to say. Reaney will embed the texts of others in his creative work, also consciously, just as though he too were still a live one, and not an Author, capital A, in Barthes's sense of an outdated authority that needs to be cut down to size. Reaney is in fact highly allusive. One example: he writes in *14 Barrels from Sea to Sea* about *The St. Nicholas Hotel*, middle play of the Donnelly Trilogy, being performed in the Salle Pauline Boutal, St. Boniface, Manitoba, 'home of the Cercle Molière, a local company with a long tradition just branching out into original plays on native themes. Their actors drop in and out of rehearsals and performances; since there is one quote from a Molière farce in *St. Nick* I keep looking at their faces to see if they'll get it.'[6]

Barthes is presuming to describe what writers can't help doing, because 'it is language which speaks, not the author....'[7] '[W]riting ceaselessly posits meaning,' he says, 'ceaselessly to evaporate it, carrying out a systematic exemption of meaning. In precisely this way literature (it would be better from now on to say *writing*), by refusing to assign a "secret", an ultimate meaning, to the text (and to the world as text), liberates what may be called an anti-theological activity, an activity that is truly revolutionary since to refuse to fix meaning is, in the end, to refuse God and his hypostases—reason, science, law.'[8] Reaney's rejection of such claims, though he has his own trouble with reason and science, appears in the third chapter of this book and surfaces in other places thereafter. Reaney will be joined by others who, in their own way, still believe in the pursuit of meaning, though they call for approaching it in a new way.

Barthes' intentionally provocative and rather paradoxical argument ('he is himself pre-eminently an author, a writer whose varied products reveal a personal style and vision'[9]) just grazes my thinking. As will emerge, I have much less invested in holding on to God than Reaney does. No doubt that helps to keep me neutral here. My own experience does show me that the writer is subservient to the writing. The writer I refer to is myself, but that self, that I, has to be made. That self is much more together than the one who struggled through draft after draft to give the other a presence, and something to say, with a modicum of gravitas, on the page. For me, there is no single moment of writing. Less and less, as I become older and simpler, do I feel any claim to own what I write. The I in what follows is me, then; it's also not-me. If that's a death, fine. And Barthes *is* on to something. The plainest and most elegant way of putting it that I know of is in Robert Bringhurst's poem, 'Sunday Morning':

> The loved is what stays
> in the mind; that is, it has meaning,
> and meaning keeps going. This
> is the definition of meaning.[10]

I have the feeling that Reaney's essays, especially those in which he writes about his own work, came much easier to him than essays do to me. I'm thinking now of a couple of his essays, essays that read as well as any of his others, but in them I find a self-reflexive remark suggesting that they emerged full-blown, in a single draft. 'But see here, *Brick*,' he says to Jean McKay and myself, editors of the magazine that published his play *King Whistle!*, 'I've been typing here for five hours trying to beat your deadline and now I'll finish.'[11] I'm astonished to think that anybody could write so quickly and yet so well. It helps me understand how the man could be so very prolific. Whether off the top or more considered, Reaney's essays are marvels of stylistic verve. His 'tone throughout these occasional ruminations on theatre and art,' writes Gerald Parker, 'shifts constantly, challenging the reader to sort through the cacophony of idealism, combativeness, fierce nationalism, satire, defensiveness, mischief, practicality, silliness, hyperbolic posturing, genuinely held convictions, and *reductio ad absurdum* asides and throwaways.'[12] That catalogue of tonal shifts shows why a reader has to be alert to Reaney's rhetorical wiles, though 'cacophony' isn't right; no single essay has all those shifts. And, at least as poet and dramatist, he was against anything dashed off. '[O]nce you have learnt how to build up verbal structures, each one of whose sounds has been weighed and patterned, you're never quite the same for other people's poetry again. I'm still constantly amazed at poets who expect you to read something they themselves have not read twice.'[13]

Elsewhere I have described myself as a meanderthal writer.[14] That has not changed. Consider just one roundabout excursion in what follows, on the subject of angels. Metaphorical angels are rampant in Reaney. They certainly have to be accounted for, but, strictly speaking, the discussion need not meander through so many of the angels I have met in other twentieth and twenty-first century art. Once I took that curve, angel after angel kept rising up out of my memory. Some of them are Reaney-related, others are tangential, but I really wanted to let them keep coming. I do sometimes think the blame, if blame there be, lies with the angels: they wouldn't let *me* go. Call it a draw.

I do want to obey, even honour, the quirks of a mind—my own and perhaps my reader's—that may tear off in any direction, but I still want to make a book that holds together. I want organic structure and I have two analogues in mind. I've held on to the first ever since decades ago I read it in Rosemary Sutcliff's historical novel, *The Mark of the Horse Lord*, set in what is now Scotland, north of Roman Britain. The Gaels, or Dalriads, of that place and time are horse people, and the kind of chariot they hitch up to is what I'm seeking in the way of design: 'It was a fine chariot that

Phaedrus found himself driving.... [I]t lacked all ornament that could add a feather's weight, but [was] ... finely balanced ... and like many British chariots, it was nowhere pinned or dowelled but lashed together with thongs of well-stretched leather, so that the whole structure was lithe and whippy, almost vicious underfoot, giving to every rut in the trackway, every hummock and hole and furze root when a stretch of track washed out by the winter rains turned them aside into the heather, like a living thing, a vixenish mare that one loves for her valour.'[15] That chariot, so finely responsive to the physical environment, seems well worth imitating in a mental environment.

The other analogue, or model, is Anna Lowenhaupt Tsing's book, *The Mushroom at the End of the World: On the Possibility of Life in Capitalist Ruins.* There will in fact be much more about mushrooms to follow than you might expect to find in a book that might simply be filed under literary criticism if it didn't meander so. But right now I'm thinking of the matsutake-mushroom-following design of Tsing's book. 'Unlike most scholarly books,' she writes in a preface called 'Enabling Entanglements,' 'what follows is a riot of short chapters. I wanted them to be like the flushes of mushrooms that come up after a rain: an over-the-top bounty; a temptation to explore; an always too many. The chapters build an open-ended assemblage, not a logical machine; they gesture to the so-much-more out there. They tangle with and interrupt each other—mimicking the patchiness of the world I am trying to describe.'[16] I had written most of this book before I thought to go back to *The Mushroom at the End of the World*, vaguely remembering the passage I've just quoted. That took me further back to *The Mark of the Horse Lord*. An open-ended assemblage, lithe and whippy: that sounds just right to me.

There is something else for me in Tsing's book, a warmer, more familial way of rendering Barthes' 'tissue of quotations.' 'Below the forest floor,' she says, 'fungal bodies extend themselves in nets and skeins, binding roots and mineral soils, long before producing mushrooms. All books emerge from similarly hidden collaborations.'[17] From here she moves into her acknowledgments. I thank my own particular helpers at the end of this book, but it's impossible to acknowledge *all* my hidden collaborators. They are my angels: silent others united in the multiform past-and-present sustaining surround of environment, community and tradition.

If you're partial to arguments that carry right on through, what follows may not be your thing. You might be better off with the likes of Reaney—forward momentum admirably sustained. What follows is always about Reaney. That's what holds it together, though the weave be loose. It's not some kind of scattergun hodgepodge. But I think it's only fair to offer a word about the procedure. If you're okay with argument as mostly placid winding stream with few rapids, many meanders and the odd oxbow lake where a meander got cut off (to meander on land is to stroll at random), then come on in.

English 138

In 1970, newly arrived at Western University, London, Ontario, to take up a post in English, I was assigned to teach a James Reaney-designed course called Canadian Literature and Culture. I was one of seven instructors, including Reaney. Team-taught courses in English literature were not unusual at Western then, but this one was. For one thing, half the syllabus was Québécois literature in translation. For another, the course scheduled an extra hour, in addition to the standard two lecture hours and one-hour tutorial, in which anything Canadian and cultural might be presented: films, poetry readings, discussions, readings of plays, performances of songs. In the two years that I was part of that team we brought established writers from across the country to read and/or talk to us.[18] The Canada Council was rich and obliging at the time. Something else that was unusual, at least in my experience, was the amount of nonfiction on the course, and it has only come home to me recently how much Southwest Ontario—Souwesto—literature was represented. Souwesto is the term Reaney says London visual artist Greg Curnoe coined, though I've also read that Curnoe credited Reaney.

Because of the Souwesto content—and here is something very distinctive about course preparation—instructors were able to travel to the nearby places where these books were set, photograph relevant locations, have the photographs made into slides and projected on the screen in Middlesex College theatre, while relevant music was also being played. Jim Good and I were photographers, Ernie Redekop was in charge of music. For visuals not directly relevant to the text of the day, the slide library of the visual arts department was an excellent resource. Each session, then, was a multimedia extravaganza. Lectures might involve all seven instructors on the same day, or maybe four, or two. Seldom one only. The many voices kept all this lively; a lot of careful collaboration and planning kept it from being confusing. It was a beautiful example of effective group action by a community whose members worked in concert toward a high-minded goal: sharing a deep interest in local and national literature and culture.

The course was an offshoot of Reaney's creative work. His aesthetic was anything but private. He wanted news of local, regional and national culture spread wide. In essays, poetry, fiction and plays, as well as in his teaching, he worked tirelessly to that end. The essays are extensions of the teaching. When Reaney found his mature vision, he was not content just to create a poem or a play; again and again, he also wrote about what he was doing, and why he was doing it. The flair and bite of those essays make them still pretty much the best—at least the most interesting—commentary on the Reaney vision and his ways of expressing it. A critic coming to it from the outside will of course bring some distance to his reading and thus find a different sort of purchase on the material.

I loved English 138, Canadian Literature and Culture. I especially loved listening to Reaney talk. He had a distinctive approach to any subject, also true of his writing, a way of cleaving to the core so as to break it right open, render it both clear and fascinating. I was in the presence of a mind and a voice that grabbed me like none other had before, and few have since. I was also part of a team that really worked, most likely because it was directed by a single, passionate intelligence, and involved much more than class time: meetings to discuss lecturing assignments, post-lecture coffee, the occasional lunch, and evenings entertaining our speakers at the Reaney house on Huron Street. That was where I met Reaney's wife, Colleen Thibaudeau, a poet who was to change my life in other ways than Reaney did. The two were on their own at the time, their children, James Stewart and Susan, having moved out and into their own careers.

Some specifics about a few of the Souwesto field trips. Everywhere we went, Reaney had been before, or had found out about, so he knew what to be looking for. We drove to Brantford to see and photograph the funeral home where the family of Sara Jeanette Duncan had once lived because we were teaching her wonderful 1904 novel, *The Imperialist.* We drove to Iona to inspect and photograph the setting of *The Scotch,* John Kenneth

Galbraith's memoir of growing up in that neighbourhood. Same with two of the other Souwesto books, Richard Maurice Bucke's *Cosmic Consciousness* and Orlo Miller's *The Donnellys Must Die*, but these books were especially and lastingly significant to Reaney.

In conjunction with *Cosmic Consciousness* (1901), we photographed a building at Oxford and Highbury Streets, once the London asylum where Bucke practiced as an 'alienist,' an early sort of psychotherapist. He was born in England, 1837, but came with his family to the London, Ontario area the following year. As an adult, before returning to London and setting up to practice there, he travelled widely, had many adventures, and became a friend of Walt Whitman, who once visited Bucke in London. (*Beautiful Dreamers*, a pretty good 1990 fiction film about that visit, has Rip Torn as Whitman and Colm Feore as Bucke.)

We also took our cameras to the house of a Western professor who had purchased Greg Curnoe's painting of the vision that inspired Bucke to write his book.[19] Bucke's description of that vision is written in the third person. It comes after a passionate endorsement of Whitman's 'Leaves of Grass' which, he says, 'contained, in greater measure than any book so far found, what he had so long been looking for.'[20] *Cosmic Consciousness* was on the course because Bucke was a Souwesto writer, a Londoner, and because he was important to Reaney for at least two reasons: as a visionary and as a progressive psychiatrist. He figures as the latter in Reaney's unpublished play, *Antler River*. Antler River is the English translation of Askunessippi, the Neutral First Nations name for the Thames River that forks (antlers) in London, so Antler River, here and in Reaney's novel *Take the Big Picture*, is a (decolonizing) name for London, Ontario. In *Antler River*, Bucke is superintendent of the London Asylum for the Insane who has instituted a 'music therapy orchestra' for the inmates; has hired 'one attendant to every four patients,'[21] so that patients will be supervised while out and about on the grounds of the asylum, 'freed of their restraints' rather than cooped up within; and has hired a farm instructor to teach patients farming. They are now, says one of the inmates, 'raising all our own food and selling the surplus at a profit as well.'[22] This is reminiscent

Greg Curnoe, 'The Vision of Dr Bucke, Nihilist Party Trilogy No. 1.'

Oil and collage on plywood, 122.7 cm. x 123.7 cm. Oct 1964–Dec 14, 1964.

of the social outreach of the Ontario sect called The Children of Peace, formed by David Willson, of which we will hear more later: 'without detailed or rigid doctrinal frameworks they were able to worship God practically with the fullest development of such diverse talents as music and cooking, economic cooperation ("a fund for the mutual benefit of each other"), and supporting a domestic science school for girls.'[23]

Like Willson, Bucke is one of Reaney's enlightened social activists, then, but Bucke's vision interested Reaney at a deeper level. Both were preoccupied with truly inclusive vision, rather than 'Single vision & Newton's sleep,'[24] as William Blake had it, but vision for Bucke was more than taking the big picture. It was spiritual enlightenment, insight into the workings of the universe. Here is how he describes its source:

It was in the early spring, at the beginning of his thirty-sixth year. He and two friends had spent the evening reading Wordsworth, Shelley, Keats, Browning, and especially Whitman. They parted at midnight, and he had a long drive in a hansom (it was in an English city). His mind, deeply under the influence of the ideas, images and emotions called up by the reading and talk of the evening, was calm and peaceful. He was in a state of quiet, almost passive enjoyment. All at once, without warning of any kind, he found himself wrapped around as it were by a flame-colored cloud. For an instant he thought of fire, some sudden conflagration in the great city; the next, he knew that the light was within himself. Directly afterwards came upon him a sense of exultation, of immense joyousness accompanied or immediately followed by an intellectual illumination quite impossible to describe. Into his brain streamed one momentary lightning-flash of the Brahmic Splendor which has ever since lightened his life; upon his heart fell one drop of Brahmic Bliss, leaving thenceforward for always an aftertaste of heaven. Among other things he did not come to believe, he saw and knew that the Cosmos is not dead matter but a living Presence, that the soul of man is immortal, that the universe is so built and ordered that without any peradventure all things work together for the good of each and all, that the foundation principle of the world is what we call love and that the happiness of everyone is in the long run absolutely certain. He claims that he learned more within the few seconds during which the illumination lasted than in previous months or even years of study, and that he learned much that no study could ever have taught.[25]

There was no return of the vision, but the one-time experience stimulated Bucke to study and write about what he calls 'a family sprung from, living among, but scarcely forming a part of ordinary humanity.... The trait that distinguishes these people from other men [they would of course almost all be men in 1901[26]] is this: Their spiritual eyes have been opened and they have seen.'[27] His book is a study of those men, beginning with Gautama the Buddha and Jesus Christ, and including William Blake and Jacob Boehme (he spells the last name Behmen, after the seventeenth century

English approximation of the German pronunciation)—four figures also important to James Reaney.

The ironic and skeptical among us, the materialists, might be inclined to discount Bucke's vision: too good to be true, not at all widely shared, certainly not sustained by the course taken by human affairs since his time. These days we don't hear much about assured happiness and there is reason to doubt that love is the foundation principle of life. Just consider what the wonderful grotesque paintings of Francis Bacon might be saying about modern life: 'Second Version of Triptych 1944' 'features three limbless figures with elongated necks and human mouths, teeth, and ears perched on wooden pedestals. Each figure is marooned in blood red-spaces. One mouth screams into the void; the other grins through clenched teeth. A third figure, on the left, feminized by pink washes and flowing hair, gazes vacantly beyond the picture plane. Interpreted through the exhibition's literary lens, this triptych distills the human condition in line with ancient tragedy: hope is foreclosed; free will is powerless against a predetermined fate; and that fate perpetuates suffering that can't be abated by the intervention of others.'[28] This might say more about the critic than it does about Bacon—it ignores the extraordinary artistry that captures such images—but nowadays we're more likely to hear such remarks about the human condition than anything about all things working together for the good of each and all.

And yet Bucke's vision somehow still carries power. Reading and rereading Reaney over the past year, I've been especially alive to the variations he plays on visions like Bucke's, often set up as creative alternatives to passivity in what he has called our 'Age of Dread.'[29] He called it that in 1967, when Dread was less prevalent, or perhaps less pervasive, its causes much less various, than it is now. I'm reminded of Sarah Milroy, writing about David Milne's 'series of mystical, wet-into-wet mineral-tones watercolours of still water edged in trees, pictures that offer sanctuary from mankind's modern fall from grace.'[30] Sanctuary is a good word for what Reaney was seeking. He found it in the symbolic architecture of David Willson's Sharon Temple and in the pacific vision of Willson's

Shaker-offshoot sect called The Children of Peace. 'Willson and the sect attract me,' Reaney writes in the notes about contributors to the ninth issue of his little magazine *Alphabet*, 'because in an era of so much fundamentalist squalor of the spirit, we find a group which has that priceless gift—sensibility—they are like a serene hallucination in the pioneer history of Ontario.'[31]

With composer Harry Somers, Reaney wrote an opera called *Serinette* contrasting The Children of Peace with well-to-do, respectable, narrow-minded bastions of early Canadian society. The serinette is a small, piping barrel organ imported from France for the purpose of teaching finches (*serins*) to sing tunes—Rossini and Donizetti in *Serinette*—rather than their native melody. The device becomes a metaphor for colonial interventions into local culture. A Reaney poem called 'Serinette' extends the metaphor's historical reach: long after pioneer times, domestic Canadian culture was devalued and suppressed in favour of culture imported from elsewhere.[32]

Reaney had his own uses for Milne. He was developing a new puppet play while touring with *The Donnellys*, 'the idea of which is supposed to be—better, more humane streets while its colour design is to be based on David Milne's painting "Billboards."'[33] I'll return to Bucke and vision later. First: *The Donnellys Must Die*, the other English 138 book of deep importance to Reaney.

The Donnellys Must Die is a balanced account of the feud along the Roman Line out of the town of Lucan, Biddulph Township, just north of London, that led up to the massacre of five members of the Donnelly family in February of 1880. Miller's book is an answer to Thomas P. Kelley's *The Black Donnellys*, which paints the Donnelly family as a group of low-life, pretty much subhuman cutthroats who terrorized the Lucan area until vigilante members of the community got fed up and took revenge. However this story is told, it carries great power (James Stewart Reaney calls it 'the greatest Souwesto folktale of them all.'[34]) On our field trips to the area I could feel an intense aura of fascination still emanating from the

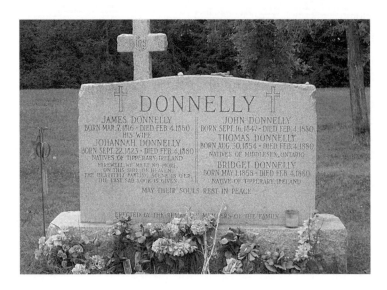

The newer version of the tombstone in Lucan.

locations where it took place. For English 138, we photographed the Donnelly tombstone in St. Patrick's Church, Lucan. The original 1889 stone read 'murdered' after the names of James Donnelly, Johannah Donnelly, Bridget Donnelly, Thomas Donnelly, family members murdered in their home, and also John Donnelly, who was murdered elsewhere on the same night. That stone was removed in 1964 because souvenir hunters were chipping off bits of the granite. The new stone was missing bits in the 1970s.

We photographed the Donnelly family farm. I wish I still had such field trip photos as the one of James Reaney holding up two fistfuls of soil from the Donnelly farm. 'This is what they were fighting for,' he said, echoing James Donnelly in *Sticks & Stones*, speaking of 'this earth in my hand, the earth of my farm / That I fought for and was smashed and burnt for.'[35] We photographed the Cedar Swamp schoolhouse where the vigilantes had met to plot their executions.

What makes all this so exceedingly fascinating to me, decades beyond the era of English 138, is that Reaney was writing his own Donnelly trilogy at the time. He had spent seven years researching documents having to do with the Donnellys and their times, delving in the archives of the Western library, in Ireland, from which the family had emigrated in 1842, and in Biddulph Township.[36] He visited Tipperary to look into the cultural context from which the Donnellys and their neighbours came. Standing with Reaney on the Donnelly property, I had no way of knowing that I was at ground zero of the creation of a masterpiece, but I was soon to find out. The original idea was to make one play out of the Donnelly material, but the full story was too complex to tell in a single evening; eventually it took three. The first, *Sticks & Stones*, premiered in 1973 at Toronto's Tarragon Theatre. The *St. Nicholas Hotel* followed in 1974, *Handcuffs* in 1975. I saw each of the plays, one by one, filled with wonder at how Reaney had created such capacious and flexible vessels to hold the power I spoke of, how, with the collaboration of director and actors, he managed to present the story in such grand complexity while keeping the plotline crystal clear. I saw all the plays in a week at the beginning of their national tour. This was September of 1975, in what was then the Drama Workshop in Western's University College. Then, at the finale of the national tour, in what might have been a once-in-a-lifetime opportunity, I saw the whole trilogy in a single day at Bathurst United Church Theatre in Toronto. There I was at the climax, though by no means the end, of Reaney's highly productive artistic career. *The Donnellys* is a tragedy nothing like any of Shakespeare's, but it's every bit as good.

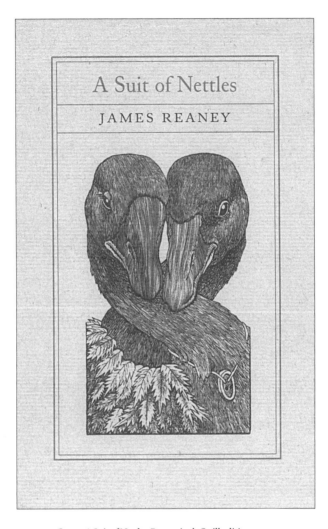

Cover, *A Suit of Nettles*, Porcupine's Quill edition, 2010.

Engraving by Jim Westergard.

A Living Chariot

Let's leap to 1984 and the so-called 'long-liners' conference on the Canadian long poem. A record of the proceedings is available in the Summer 1985 issue of Frank Davey's *Open Letter*. Reaney, a pioneering writer of long poems like *A Suit of Nettles*, had been listening to various presentations on the long poem, some of them based on what was called the absence of contemporary 'grids of meaning' sponsored by then current poststructuralist theory and taken to heart by certain postmodernist writers. A presentation by Roy Miki, for example, cited Jacques Derrida, theorist of deconstruction, on the disappearance of the 'transcendental signified' which had once held everything together. This was part of the orthodoxy of the time. It may be still, for all I know, so distant from Western University and its Theory Centre as I am now, but Reaney was never orthodox, and he wasn't having it.

In his play, *Gentle Rain Food Co-op*, he was later to create a cynical Professor who taunts his gullible students: 'you young, stupid punks—easily misled by any shiny new jargon'[37] like the 'earth-shaking theory of deconstruction. Harass the subject—find out what it's really like—give it a hard time....'[38] Asked by Wanda Campbell about postmodernism, which he tended to conflate with poststructuralism, he said 'Deconstruction—forget it! A disaster. As Frye said before he died, a plague of darkness. Really disintegrative. It's not what we need to do. What we need to do, he said, is worry about how we're going to survive. Thinkers should come together on that. They shouldn't come together on figuring out that Shakespeare meant the very opposite of what he seems to mean, which is quite often what they do in those critical things.'[39]

If plague there was, it will have been the hordes of critics who glommed on to Derrida's theories and worked over any text with them, as though you could ever be cutting edge while adopting and applying someone else's theory, as though you couldn't just as well start in from scratch—depend on yourself—and get the goods. Well, nobody with any kind of education and research capacity is a blank slate. I'm drawing here on many different thought companions, none of them prevailing, a procedure Reaney would not have endorsed. But some things Derrida has said when speaking more off the cuff than in the dense and diffuse jargon of his written discourse, suggest that *he* was not the plague. 'I behave—well, it depends on the moment, on the place—with this guiding principle: that we should question, that we shouldn't sleep, that we shouldn't take any concept for granted.'[40] Responding (a bit laboriously) in English to a question about the threat of nuclear arms he said, 'The only thing I'm sure of is a very trivial thing: that it's better to negotiate and to speak and to postpone the use of these weapons [he calls them "terrible toys"], and to analyze what these discourses—the political discourses—are, and to try to mobilize the people against what is threatening in this. What is the rhetoric of the politicians, the rhetoric of the military, of the scientists who work on this? You cannot separate, any more, some scientists, some politicians, some military decision-makers. One of the responsibilities of the university today is not to let those people do everything by themselves. This is *our* problem. We are competent. And if we are not, we should become competent on these questions and speak aloud. To make the conservation last.'[41] I'm not so concerned with defending Derrida—I'm no more his man than Reaney's—as with suggesting that there is more to him than Frye or Reaney see, or at least admit. In some ways, he is on the same page as they are. I'm working *with* Reaney, even when I'm resisting; I very seldom write *against*. I don't deconstruct, not as such. But I know that to confine oneself within the circumference of any other writer's world, no matter how capacious and fascinating, is to limit the capacity to think for oneself. I also know that no application of logic, no matter how rigorous, will dismantle faith. Reaney has his faith. And a line from one of his plays is a kind of core tenet: 'the integral versus the fractional life.'[42] He wanted things put together. Anything viewed as a disintegrative plague will naturally be anathema. I hear him saying such things, ponder them, often find myself thinking, Just a minute now.... To pay careful attention to Reaney is sometimes to find oneself thinking double. Yes, but. Or Yes and No. And sometimes just No.

At the conference, Reaney was indulging in his habit of sketching while others talked; to the published proceedings he contributed rough studies of other presenters. In his own talk, delivered in his characteristically vigorous and lucid way, he says 'there has to be … something outside of ourselves that inspires and orders. Even our past traditions revived might turn the trick.'[43] For him, this something outside may have been God. 'Jamie stopped going to church in his early adult years but later resumed,' says friend and collaborator John Beckwith; 'in an interview he said he wasn't sure whether he qualified as a bona-fide Christian.'[44] Attending church at all would mean compromising with what Northrop Frye, following William Blake, calls 'state religion,' but that only requires the doubtful Christian never to forget what Christ was all about, just as to survive in the university any true teacher has to hold on to the ideal of the university, no matter how perverted in a particular institution.

'The artist *qua* artist,' says Northrop Frye, 'neither doubts nor believes his religion: he sees what it means, and he knows how to illustrate it. His religion performs two great services for him. It provides him with a generally understood body of symbols, and it puts into his hands the visionary masterpieces on which it is founded: the Bible particularly, in the case of Christian poets.'[45] It sometimes seems, reading Frye on Blake, that he is so much inside Blake, 'speaking as far as possible from his point of view,'[46] that his generalizations about the poet assume Blake as norm and model for all poets. For throngs and hosts of good poets that is not so, but it certainly works for Reaney. In addition to the Bible, there was myth and written literature and all the other arts down through the centuries: an enormous fund of tradition to draw on. Northrop Frye qualifies—more on this later—as some*one* who inspired and ordered for Reaney, not as himself but with his powerful theorizing.

I like to think of Reaney reading Iain McGilchrist's *The Master and His Emissary: The Divided Brain and the Making of the Western World*, a book that appeared in 2009, after Reaney had died. McGilchrist was a teacher of English at Oxford before he trained to become a psychiatrist. Like Reaney and so many others, he decries 'the destruction and despoliation of the natural world, and the erosion of established cultures,'[47] blaming it on the modern ascendency of thinking located in the left hemisphere of the brain (more on this below), and, like Reaney and Frye, he holds that 'The 2,000-year old Western tradition, that of Christianity, provides, whether one believes in it or not, an exceptionally rich *mythos*—a term I use in its technical sense, making no judgment here of its truth or otherwise—for understanding the world and our relationship with it. It conceives a divine Other that is not indifferent or alien—like James Joyce's God, refined out of existence and "paring his fingernails"—but on the contrary engaged, vulnerable because of that engagement, and like the right hemisphere rather than the left, not resentful (as the Old Testament Yahweh often seemed) about the Faustian fallings away of its creation, but suffering alongside it.'[48]

Reaney's own long-liners presentation was so far out of the mainstream of skeptical thought being generally advanced at the time that he could actually call *Alligator Pie*, written for children, Dennis Lee's 'most effective poem.'[49] Dennis Lee was listening, somewhat ruefully I imagine, since the praise promoted a collection of lyrics to a long poem and whizzed over his adult poetry, including *Civil Elegies*, which we had taught in English 138. There was a Canadian long poem anthology available at the time of the conference (Michael Ondaatje's 1979 *The Long Poem Anthology*); Reaney doesn't seem to have consulted it. I see him, writer of pioneering long poems like *A Suit of Nettles, in* that company of long poem theorists but not *of* them, apart but standing firm for his own vision, which had much more in common with that of William Blake and Richard Maurice Bucke than with anything postmodernist/poststructuralist. I've become most interested in something Reaney said in the discussion that followed his presentation.

Asked where he stood on the matter of those so-called long-gone 'grids of meaning,' he offered this take on Jacques Derrida: 'The way I read Derrida is quite different. What Derrida is doing is he wants a reaction. He doesn't want you to agree with him, surely. No one could agree with that! [Laughter.] It's intended to arouse the old, whatever it is—the old Martin Luther, or something, or Ezekiel, or Isaiah, or those Old Testament prophet kinds of thing. Sure the role is absolutely all illusion. Nothing means anything; it's just a fog. But, by God, *I'm* not a fog. I see a living chariot with four wheels on it all covered with eyes! How about that?'[50] Death of the author? Not this one. The fog recalls the effect of 'a bird that eats my sun,' the metaphorical melancholy that afflicts Branwell In *A Suit of Nettles*. Branwell's friend Mopsus knows that bird. 'It made all life seem edgeless, blurred,'[51] he says. Branwell lacks definition. There was a time when Reaney also felt that he was drifting, but he had found his way well before the time of the long-liners conference.

Laughter followed Reaney's pronouncement. Some of it would have been provoked by surprise, maybe even admiration. Some was probably derisive. Here he was, funnelling Derrida's *Dissemination, Of Grammatology, Writing and Difference* and other influential books into a single exclamatory word: 'that!' But he was not joking. For by no means the first or last time in his writing and speaking life, he was channelling one of those Old Testament prophets—Ezekiel in this case. In this Reaney moment Ezekiel is really joined by William Blake and Northrop Frye, who says 'Blake's cosmology, of which the symbol is Ezekiel's vision of the chariot of God with its "wheels within wheels," is a revolutionary vision of the universe transformed by the creative imagination into a human shape. This cosmology is not speculative but concerned, not reactionary but revolutionary, not a vision of things as they are ordered but of things as they could be ordered.'[52] 'What is poetry-vision about?' Reaney asks in a *University of Toronto Quarterly* article: 'Joy and Fear: the reader can go to the height of joy with Ezekiel's vision of God on his chariot whose wheels have eyes; he can descend to the terror of a valley of dry bones or the demands of a God who seems to be asking him to eat his own excrement. All this in Ezekiel! And now, in our valley of dry bones—Canada!'[53]

'Sometimes,' Reaney writes in the Editorial to *Alphabet* 16, 'I think there's a chance all the children of Canada might become prophets the way Moses wanted and Joel dreamed: other times I wonder if the traffic isn't going to win out.'[54] The context for this is Vancouver's town fool, Joachim Foikis, being 'recently charged with disturbing the peace: beating a drum after a meditation meeting: "Streets are for people, not for cars."'[55] In 1960, Reaney was afraid that the traffic—and 'progress'—was winning. Thus the conclusion of a 1960 long poem of his own called 'A Message to Winnipeg':

> Leave the burning city
> > Leave this burning town
> Destruction cometh—a sucking cloud,
> > Your towers will tumble down
>
> Child's Restaurant will be consumed
> > Eaton's and Hudson's Bay
> Grass will grow on your neon signs
> > And the rivers dry away
> …
> Leave this burning city!
> > Will noone listen to me?
> Even now the doomfist knocks!
> It's the sound of our hearts, say we.[56]

Who is listening in 2022? Reaney's speaker might have sounded a bit hysterical to some readers in 1960, Reaney himself probably seemed out of date to many listeners at the long-liners conference of 1984, but what he was saying then asks to be heard, now, in the light of dire changes that were on the way in his time and are much worse now. 'There is … overwhelming evidence,' says Jan Zwicky, 'that our own species is, in gestalt terms, a bad idea. We have been unable to sustain stable internal relations to many other aspects of the biosphere, and we are set to take big chunks of it with us when we go. Why? What's wrong with us? My guess is that it has something to do with a lack of respect for, and denial of, human gestalt capacities. Those capacities tell us we're just one among many internally related aspects of the world. This is an inconvenient perception if you purpose dominion and control.'[57]

Winnipeg wasn't literally burning back then, and Winnipeg wasn't really what Reaney was exhorting people to leave; the urgency issued from all the sources of that metaphorical conflagration. Reaney built a literary career on proposing alternatives to science and technology, with its materialist philosophical underpinnings, which he thought was sending civilization into steep decline. He was offering stories intended to counter the dominant, ultimately destructive narratives of western civilization. In an essay about *The Donnellys* and what he calls 'a new theatre just being born,' he writes as follows:

[A]s [Northrop] Frye points out in his book, *The Critical Path*, all 'isms' come out of or go back into myths or STORIES, so why not present the concrete version of your favourite 'ism' rather than try to jam existentialism or Maoism or naturalism down your audience's throats the way ministers used to dose us with Calvinism. Maybe if we get used to seeing our society as being based on a story, we'll wake up and realize we can get a better story; I happen to think that with the Industrial Revolution we accepted the story of the successful magician who could do anything he liked with the world around him.... Well, listen to the story another way: Newton, Rousseau and Descartes were Sorcerers *Apprentices*, not the masters of their trade that the worshippers of Progress (another story) for so long considered them.[58]

'Plays,' he says elsewhere in the same essay, 'are supposed to change your life and your mental habits.'[59] When Reaney wrote 'Leave this burning city,' he was looking squarely at his own time and place—if symbolically—asking readers to look at it also, to register what is wrong, to consider what might possibly be made right, then to act. Those who he felt were joining him in that labour he called 'Identifiers.'[60] Identifiers make and live metaphor. Reaney is with Blake in wanting New Jerusalem to be

A one man band? Understand
& you can
This is a Man

James Reaney emblem poem: 'The Riddle',

from *Poems*, new press, 1972.

established, not only in England's green and pleasant land, but in Canada, starting with Souwesto, the territory he knew best and loved most. (I'll return to 'A Message to Winnipeg' later, when I've put myself in a position to say more about Reaney on the products of technology like the automobile. He never liked cars.)

'The most exciting thing about this century,' Reaney says in the Editorial to the first number of *Alphabet*, 'is the number of poems that cannot be understood unless the reader quite reorganizes his way of looking at things or "rouses his faculties" as Blake would say. *Finnegans Wake* and Dylan Thomas' "Altarwise by owl-light" sonnet sequence are good examples here. These works cannot be enjoyed to anywhere near their fullest unless one rouses one's heart, belly and mind to grasp their secret alphabet or iconography or language of symbols and myths. A grasping such as is involved here leads to a more powerful inner life, or Blake's "Jerusalem's wall." Besides which it's a hell of a lot of fun. It seems quite natural, then, in this century and particularly in this country, which could stand some more Jerusalem's wall, that there should be a journal of some sort devoted to iconography. After all, Ernst Cassirer defines man as a symbol-making animal.'[61]

For Reaney, Jerusalem's wall is a metaphor for a standing, permanent value, a standard of meaning, and an imaginative approach to making meaning in a place that needs it badly. He is not a biblical literalist. I'd like to rescue a remarkably lovely, poignant remark that touches on this from where it's buried in the discussion following his paper at the long-liners conference: 'I've been rereading the New Testament,' he says, 'and I can see how Jesus did it. I think he got the feeling that he would do, that he was the person that Isaiah was talking about.... I think that this poor boy went ahead with the whole thing. And he did it; he transformed the world. Simply through metaphor. By saying "I'm it."'[62] This is the kind of thing I meant when I said that Reaney could blast a subject open and show it in a whole new light. I've read nothing about Jesus that made me feel so much for him. This remark leaves aside a great deal of theology, to be sure, but I love the idea of Jesus mulling it all over, seeing that *someone* was needed for the role of Messiah and accepting the job because he understands the power of metaphor. Maybe he *was* chosen, but how much more interesting to think that he *still* had to choose!

All of Reaney's work is pushing for as much Jerusalem's wall as can be established in this polite, provincial, prudish place. At least that's how Souwesto and Canada looked to Reaney when he began writing. 'Having been brought up in the region where the [Donnelly] vendetta explosion took place, I have to say that the usual effect of the area is one of almost stupefying blandness and a so-called normality that was rife in the pages of the London *Free Press* from its inception in the late 1840s.'[63] 'This dull township,' he called it in a poem from *The Red Heart* called 'The Upper Canadian,' 'Where fashion, thought and wit/ Never penetrate....'[64] Here it is again, Mrs. Gardner's front parlour in Reaney's play *The Killdeer*, as described by her (s)mothered son Harry:

> Oh gosh! This room! This front parlour of yours!
> I think I'll go mad if I don't get one day
> Of my life when I don't come home to this....
> This room! This room!
> These brown velvet curtains trimmed with
> One thousand balls of fur! Fifteen kewpie dolls!
> Five little glossy china dogs on a Welsh dresser!
> Six glossy Irish beleek cats and seven glass
> Green pigs and eight blue glass top hats and
> Five crystal balls filled with snow falling down
> On R.C.M.P constables. Two little boys on chamber
> Pots: Billy Can and Tommy Can't. That stove—
> Cast-iron writhing and tortured curlicues!

'This is your room, Mother,' he goes on. 'Your mind is like this./ It's where I've spent most of my life and it's not/ Real pretty.'[65]

No wonder Reaney embraced stories of great dark energy like that of the Donnellys, John Richardson's *Wacousta* and Ann Cardwell's *Crazy to*

Kill, all later to be retold in Reaney scripts. '*Crazy to Kill* rather bowled me over,' he says in the Introduction to a reprint of Ann Cardwell's novel. '[I]t worked as an ingenious puzzle that enchanted me with the hidden horrors that lie just underneath, not only genteel surfaces, but also surfaces of dreariness and desolation beyond belief.'[66] In an unsigned review of Norval Morrisseau's *Legends of My People, The Great Ojibway* (*Alphabet* 13), he refers to the 'wealth of cultural experience in Canada,' meaning especially the Indigenous, elements which have 'never found their way into the "official" traditional culture of English-speaking Canada, a culture which seems to have been created by a branch of the Civil Service.'[67] He wrote those words before the rise of concern about appropriation of voice and culture. Some of the Indigenous content in his writing may seem vulnerable on that score, but any reader should be able to see that, early on, he was tuned in to the value of Indigenous cultures that he knew to be 'civilizations,'[68] and that he deplored the effect of colonialist depredations. At any rate, what Reaney was saying about the culture of Canada in which he grew up sounds very like what Germaine Greer had to say about the culture of Australia when she was growing up there. All British colonies had to find ways out from under the colonial mentality which so often took the form of lionizing and imitating British culture. 'Barry [Humphries, creator of Dame Edna Everage]', says Greer, 'I think was the best critic of the Australian way of life and it was *utterly* bleak.'[69]

Here is a simpler way of putting what Reaney was working towards, something he says in *14 Barrels from Sea to Sea*: 'I wonder if there's some sort of special firewater you could feed people in this country just to get a more loving feeling started?'[70] One way to do just that, to administer 'medicine' to those people (that's from the Invocation to *A Suit of Nettles*[71]) is to see the artistic possibilities of certain flexible, inherited grids.

During the Ottawa stop of the national tour of *The Donnellys*, Reaney found himself reading about 'Vatican II's pronouncements on loosening up Holy Church: "dogmatic theology must be firmly rooted in the very structure of reality, since after all it is an attempt to reconstruct the great architecture of divine wisdom, a sort of sublime Poetique in the sense of

Claudel." Oh Amen,' Reaney responds, 'for this sounds like Frye's "verbal universe"; anything to get away from the theology fights about "isms" that give us bishops instead of prophets, abstractionists instead of concretists. Half the difficulties we're in come not from stupid people, but clever ones who get tangled up in systems....'[72]

And there you have the basis for the vast majority of Reaney's drama—the conflict between those who demonize, exclude, persecute and even murder people who don't fit into their systems, whether Protestant or Catholic, liberal or conservative—any either/or rather than both/and. Reaney had some either/or opinions himself (he thought literary realism was no good; more on this later) but his plays feature latitudinarian nonconformists, men and women of the spirit, rather than the letter, people of vision: David Willson of the Children of Peace; William Dale in *The Dismissal*, who pushed for the hiring of Canadians in the closed shop of 1890s University of Toronto; the union leaders of *King Whistle!* who buck unfair labour practices in the factories of 1930s Stratford; the teachers in *Three Desks* who love literature and pass love and knowledge on to their students, as opposed to those who want the academic system to serve them only; the visionary Indigenous characters of *Wacousta!* rather than rigid British imperialists like Colonel de Haldimar, who releases in the title character a gigantic power of hatred and vengeance; Dr. Troyer, the scryer in *Baldoon* who represents vision, generosity and love, contra James McTavish's Scottish protestant grasping and emotional thrift.

Baldoon features contrasting Protestantisms, the free and the oppressive. 'As the company enters from the back of the theatre,' goes the first stage direction, 'they should be singing Tunkard, Mennonite and Shaker hymns; there should be a great feeling of bells, wind instruments—joy in God, the easy attainment of His light, joy in His creation. This should be a contrast with the more austere, bleak music of the Presbyterian Psalmbook which we'll use at the beginning of Act Two.'[73] Here is 'Simple Gifts,' the Shaker hymn that opens and closes *Baldoon*:

'Tis the gift to be simple, 'tis the gift to be free
'Tis the gift to come down—where we ought to be
And when we find ourselves in the place just right,
'Twill be in the valley of love and delight

When true simplicity is gain'd,
To bow & to bend we shan't be a-shamed
To turn, turn will be our delight
'Till by turning, turning we come round right.[74]

'To bow and to bend.' A version of this is spoken in *Serinette* during a Sharon Temple service of The Children of Peace: 'While lines of division are so distinctly drawn/ A Saviour's absent and he's gone.'[75] Sharon Temple is a lantern of light and openness. The contrasting church in *Serinette* is St. James Cathedral in York, Upper Canada, its windows so narrow, and candles not allowed within, that the choir can't even see to read their parts.

Flexibility of thought and behaviour is a defining feature of James and Judith and Will Donnelly, and, tragically, it's also one thing that their *idée fixe* neighbours can't abide about them. Donnellys don't take sides in local disputes. They are, according to their enemies, renegade be-by-themselves. Perhaps another way to put all this, a more capacious way, is to quote Reaney on the gyroscope which gives the title to one of his best plays, because it prescribes movement and the embrace of opposites, of others and otherness, even in oneself, as an alternative to becoming stuck in system: 'Gyroscopes,' he says 'keep their balance under the most adverse circumstances.... Yes, the gyroscope idea applies to souls ... in the following ways: if you keep spinning, that is, moving from where and what you are now to the opposite of that and then immediately to the opposite of that, then you have power, flexibility, love, energy, community—in short, BALANCE—even in our absurd world where the real horizon is often obscured.'[76] 'You achieve balance,' says Jung, just before he goes on to assert the feminine in the masculine and the masculine in the feminine, 'only if you nurture your opposite.'[77]

To turn, turn, will be our delight. 'The hardest and most rewarding lesson,' says M. C. Edwards in her book called *Centering in Pottery, Poetry, and the Person*, 'has been to learn to experience antipathy objectively, with warmth. For antipathy follows a gesture of separating, and the goal, which is to be both separate and connected, requires that one move inwardly in opposite directions. Toward self-definition and toward community. Toward ethical individualism and toward social justice. It is this fusing of the opposites that Centering enables.'[78]

There are times when I'm more convinced by what Reaney says about what he's doing than by the play in which he lays it out, so taken am I with his prose apologias, but not in this case. *Gyroscope* is a comic working out of an issue that goes way back with him, and in which he was ahead of his time: the complexity and fluidity of gender identity. Someone should take up this theme. A good place to dive in would be the more serious, darker version in 'The Ditch: First Reading,' a story collected in *The Box Social and Other Stories*.

There is also, in Reaney, the complexity of identity itself, as in plays like *Colours in the Dark* and *The Donnellys*. A stage direction in *Colours*: 'The whole play is going to be like this—six actors playing many different roles—suggesting how we are many more people than just ourselves. Our ancestors are we, our descendants are us, and so on like a sea.'[79] 'Any national identity,' he says elsewhere, 'any identity is a web of adjusting visions.'[80] Maybe this all goes back to 1962 and Reaney's motto on the coat of arms of the Avon River in *Twelve Letters to a Small Town*: 'One of my earliest wishes / "To flow like you."'[81]

Conscious or Instinctive

Let me now return to Reaney in the question period mentioned above. '[T]he way Derrida works for me,' he went on in the discussion following his talk, 'is that I merely react—not necessarily in a positive, optimistic way, but with images and metaphors; and to hell with it, I don't care whether they're "grids of meaning" or not; I'm going to grid away.... It makes me feel happy.'[82] When I imagine Reaney looking like a literary throwback to his peers at the long-liners conference, the image has pathos. That view of him and his work might seem confirmed by such things as the fact that he never modernized his verse, but kept right on capitalizing the first letter of each line, kept on rhyming too, and sometimes went for strained inversions to make a rhyme work. His three Governor General's Awards (1949, 1958, 1962) were now decades behind him.

But I knew the man and he was anything but pathetic. He was his own man, always, and whether or not appreciation for his vision and his accomplishments had declined over time, he continued on with great force. His gridding linked material from the here and now with archetypal patterns intended to read that material and clarify it. 'Is there any difference between the two worlds—one real, one legendary,' he asks in the Editorial to *Alphabet* 2. 'Not really. The story of Dionysos is every child's story only heightened, polished and scrubbed so that we can see its significance more clearly.'[83] The relevant question here is not whether this approach and procedure is dated, but whether it can still be made to work. The answer, a resounding yes, is *The Donnellys*. Nothing else Reaney wrote rose to that level of sublimity, but the trilogy is only one good reason to be taking him seriously now.

I want to show what Reaney was gridding away with, literary theory for one thing. But first it might be well to say that, theory of any kind aside, there are other legitimate and productive ways to work. Some ways quite eschew theory. Immediately following a *Poetry* (Chicago) review in

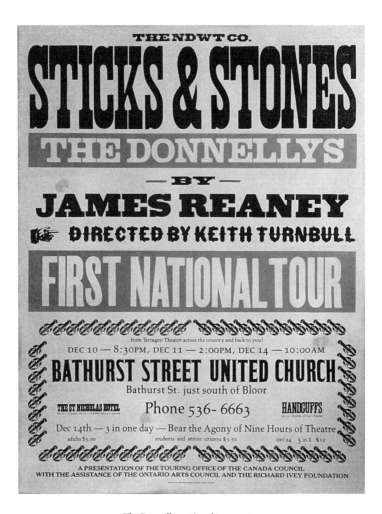

The Donnellys national tour poster.

which James Reaney extolls the criticism of Northrop Frye, Margaret Avison (Western's first writer-in-residence and a poet Reaney esteemed) writes that 'Part of the delight would fade from Canadian poetry, I suspect, if scrupulous editing and carefully formulated critical theory and appropriate niches in Dominion Post Offices and the like were to replace the unpredictable tussling murmurous *sub rosa* life that is the poet's lot here today. Would we feel the need for "just appraisals" of our contemporaries anyway, if by some utopian *fiat* poetry could be banished from the academies? Perhaps a poet in a more orderly culture might envy the Canadians their free range, their informality, their loquaciousness or taciturnity according to their natures.'[84] Avison prefers to be out on her own, 'out of range,'[85] as she puts it elsewhere. But the anti- or un-system writer handiest in present circumstances is Colleen Thibaudeau, who happened to be married to James Reaney. Same loving household, same leftist politics, very different poetics. Here is Colleen talking about Jamie's grid work and respectfully distancing herself from it. This is from a special Thibaudeau issue of *Brick*, part of Jean McKay's 'biographical sketch' of Thibaudeau, incorporating an interview conducted with Colleen by Jean, Don McKay, Peggy Dragišić (Now Roffey) and myself: 'People were always asking me about the archetypes and things,' says Colleen. 'Well, I never studied the archetypes, and they're a little bit mentally beyond me. I mean if someone explains it to me I can remember it for a while, but I can't work that way. Like he [Reaney] will draw it all out, and he knows from which column he's drawing his images … and I think that's good, to be conscious of what you're doing, but with me they either seem to come instinctively from the right area, or … It certainly expands your world.… It also gives you pegs on which to hang your thought. It makes your mind tidier, and so on.…'[86]

In 1957, writing in an essay called 'The Canadian Poet's Predicament,' Reaney seemed to be split between the two approaches to writing manifest in the household at 276 Huron Street, London, Ontario: the instinctive or the conscious. '[N]o one seems to know, no one seems to be able to tell you, whether you should be self-conscious or unconscious about the craft of poetry, whether you should really tackle literary criticism as a help or intuitively arrive at the same goal.'[87] Reading that today, I'm inclined to respond, of course no one *knows* which way to go, because there *is* no one way. I also wonder about that 'should.' Reaney eventually accepted the external authority of Northrop Frye, but not because Frye said anything about what he *should* do. One chooses, if the need arises, on the basis of what and who one is and needs to become. The authority is oneself, in other words. Whatever you do, however you do it, you have to be true to yourself. '[T]he pupil has to fend for himself to honor the professor,[88] writes Guy Birchard, truly. Reaney fended, so did Thibaudeau.

Though, if to be instinctive is to go inward and to be conscious is to go outward, we might be able to recast this contrariety in the terms Reaney himself employs in *14 Barrels from Sea to Sea*. Attending a meeting of the League of Canadian Poets concurrent with the Vancouver stop of the sea-to-sea Donnelly tour, he remarks on the difference between that sort of company and the kind he has lately been keeping: 'I had forgotten, being so much with actors lately, how different poets can be from actors: the lyric ones, and the League contains mostly lyric ones, are churning inside with their private oracle cauldrons and lonely triumphs; by the way of contrast, actors are always trying out new persona masks, and when they get drunk are apt to be heard from immediately. Buy lyric poets drink and they murmur for quite a long time before erupting.'[89] Reaney began as a lyric poet, if the term is applied to writers of miscellaneous short poems churned out their own entrails. When he grew out of that isolation, as he would put it, when he turned toward longer forms with archetypal backbones—turned outward—he became something of an actor himself, especially in *One Man Masque* ('I particularly enjoyed directly attacking an audience with my poetry rather than getting at them privately and secretly in a book'[90]), and as an activist playwright bent on developing community. He was anything but private for the latter part of his career. Well, neither Jamie nor Colleen was an introvert—presumably a synonym for lyric in this scenario—and the either/or breaks down by looking just at the two of them.

Some have called Reaney's play *Gyroscope* autobiographical because in it a man whose wife is a poet decides to become a poet himself, which occasions an exchange of identities between them. But there is nothing particular to Jamie and Colleen in the relationship between the main characters in *Gyroscope*; neither is the poetry they write characteristic of either Reaney or Thibaudeau. Colleen was a member of the London Poetry Guild, where she was content enough to consort with writers of lesser stature. The idea for the play probably started at home, but Reaney was never interested in being merely representational. The germ may have been in the domestic scene. If so, it diverged right away.

If I were here to discuss Colleen Thibaudeau, I'd go on to demonstrate why she is much more diffident about her own process than she needs to be. Marshall McLuhan was the supervisor of her University of Toronto M.A. thesis. She is a wonderful poet, and still too much in her husband's shade. I identify with *her* stance, in fact, because I too have the untidy mind. I come at Reaney ardently, but from something of a distance. He goes out; I go in. More on this later. But I'm not interested in taking sides. After all, no matter how anyone works, whether by instinct or according to plan, results are what count. Jean McKay and I, at *Brick* magazine, admired both Thibaudeau and Reaney. *Brick* 5 was the Thibaudeau issue. *Brick* 8 was the text for Reaney's play *King Whistle!*, with all sorts of context for the play, including an explanatory essay by the author. Brick Books was equally impartial, though we didn't become Reaney's publisher until 2005, when we brought out *Souwesto Home*, his last book of poems. By contrast, Colleen Thibaudeau's chapbook *Ten Letters* (1975) was the first publication of what became Brick Books—a poetry publishing house I kept on with for forty-odd years—and we published two more Thibaudeaus thereafter, *The Martha Landscapes* (1984) and *The Artemesia Book* (1991), the latter being a selected. With Michael Ondaatje, for Coach House Press, I also edited *My granddaughters are combing out their long hair* (1977). When in 2000 I assembled a Brick Books twenty-fifth anniversary anthology, I drew the title, *New Life in Dark Seas*, from 'The Glass Cupboard,' a Colleen Thibaudeau poem.

Before I leave this section I might say that Colleen Thibaudeau may be the poet nearest to James Reaney who follows her own muse, rather than Northrop Frye or anyone else, but she and Margaret Avison are not the only ones. George Johnston, who might actually be called a mythopoeic poet, at least in his first two books, was a student of Frye's who later became a friend but not a follower. Frye 'loves systems,' Johnston says. 'This was one thing that attracted him particularly to Blake's prophetic writings, and for my M.A. year I did my best to follow him into this territory, but my imagination is not systematic.'[91] Unlike Reaney, Johnston 'began a Ph.D. thesis [with Frye] on Blake and Yeats but soon abandoned it.'[92] He acknowledges the strong effect of Frye on other Canadian poets, though, some of it negative. 'For a while he was thundered against in Canada because he was considered to have a low opinion of the importance of direct personal experience in poetry.'[93] It wasn't all thunder. Sometimes the resistance was considered and generated a good poem. R.G. Everson's 'Report for Northrop Frye' contains the Frye line that caused so much furor:

Opening with dynamite blast
we grope in underground workings
to tunnel Labrador granite

I find no fossil in igneous rock
no curious paintings on broken walls
no lock of hair or mythical token

Nothing ever alive precedes man here
If 'poetry can be made only out of other poems'—
in new space to what may I refer?

We bring our own light to a dark place
Crowbar, sledge hammer, pick
pound Labrador granite

We make sounds from Arctic silence
Life is here and now—we bring it
We bring men's laughter and good sense [94]

Backbones

Now what about Reaney's grids? I've been paying special attention to them in my recent reading, doing so according to a principle something like the one that underpins Reaney's little magazine, *Alphabet*: the strategy of juxtaposing documentary and myth in that distinctive magazine of ten year's duration: '[T]ake the face cards out of a card deck; then put a circular piece of cardboard near them. Curves and circles appear even in the Queen of Diamonds and the Knave of Spades. But place a triangular shape close by and the eye picks up corners and angularities in even the Queen of Clubs. What every issue of *Alphabet* involves, then, is the placing of a definite geometric shape near some face cards. Just as playing about with cubes and spheres can teach an artist and a critic a better sense of composition, *Alphabet*'s procedure can have the same result with iconography and symbolism.'[95]

That *is* grid work, of course, and grid is, metaphorically speaking, the geometric shape that I'm putting near Reaney's work to help show what it's about and what it does. 'Grid' is not Reaney's own word, as I've said. He picked it up from others at the long-liners conference, and the literal meaning, with all those right angles, is not the perfect image for what he does. He'd be more likely to say pattern, or formula, or catalogue, or paradigm, or list. Also backbone. 'Word-lists as backbones for plays,' he offers in 'A Letter from James Reaney,' '(see my sixties *Alphabet* for the concept of BACKBONES which Sheila Watson helped me to see at Toronto grad school).'[96] I'll keep on with grid here, but really list is the better word. 'There is something about lists of things that hypnotizes me,' Reaney says in the introduction to 'Catalogue Poems,' a section of his book called *Performance Poems*. Now watch how he goes on to slide things together in metaphor: 'I think this fascination is connected with our joy in the rainbow's week of colours, in the 92-element candle you see in a physics lab at school, but then see all around you like a segmented serpent we're all tied together by. Our backbones, with their xylophone vertebrae, are such sentences; lists of symbolic objects in some sort of mysterious, overwhelming progression I have elsewhere called the backbones of whales, and indeed they are, for they are capable of becoming a paradigm ... used as a secret structure.'[97] His play, *Canada Dash, Canada Dot* is built on lists of various sorts. So is *Colours in the Dark*. See for example the list of CN and CP railway stops in Scene 10, the list of writing class students in Scene 11, the list of 'Sailboats that brought ancestors' in Scene 12. In fact, lists or catalogues appear everywhere in Reaney's work, including *The Donnellys*.

As you can tell from listening to Reaney's turn as Ezekiel, and this is confirmed by a reading through his work, the Bible is a frequent reference and a rich source. His first writings, the poems of *The Red Heart* and the stories eventually collected up in *The Box Social and Other Stories*, were apostate—there was a time when he was writing, rather bitterly, in unfaith, and troubled by what he has called 'the flood of bitter ink/ Flowing from the divided boy long ago,' the boy whose parents divorced[98] and the family was reconfigured to involve an uncongenial stepfather—but he returned to the Bible as a source of archetypal stories and as a comprehensive pattern that carries a reader from Genesis to Revelation, alpha to omega, a 'grid,' if you like, that answered a growing need in him for large, overarching and containing pattern. Of course he had the Bible early on, owing to his upbringing in a series of evangelical churches,[99] an influence he was obliged to modify so as to hold on to the spiritual essence of religion while repudiating doctrinal rigidities and splits that fractured 'organized religion' into a babel of competing sects. The twain of Protestant and Catholic are never supposed to meet, for instance, at least never to marry, in the schismatic world of *The Donnellys*.

Large pattern was one of the things Reaney also took from Northrop Frye, first from *Fearful Symmetry*, Frye's book on the poetry of William Blake, and then from the giant *Anatomy of Criticism*, a book that grew out of lectures on literary symbolism in a course that Reaney took as part of his work toward the Ph.D. His thesis, 'The Influence of Spenser on Yeats,' was supervised by Frye.

Reaney was already a writer when he came under the influence of Frye, but felt that, for want of a sustaining grid, he was flailing and needed guidance. The University of Toronto he had attended as an undergraduate, taking a degree in literature with a minor in classics, was mostly committed to the history of ideas, an approach to literary content that he found uncongenial. In an essay paying tribute to Frye as mentor, he says, 'How on earth did I ever escape from the notion that poetry provides only a false front for philosophy and a verandah for her very fat brother—History.'[100] In this you can hear something of what Reaney was later to resist in poststructuralist theory that, according to him, 'think[s] … philosophy's bigger than literature. I don't.'[101]

'I don't know if anyone quite understands,' he goes on in praise of Frye, 'what a torture to a would-be poet the whole problem of "ideas" and "philosophy" can be. Here I was, at the end of my freshman year, with notebooks filled with metaphors; … but what I wanted to know was [now he comes to the grid]—what backbones and what galaxies do these lists belong to and in. In his first lyric phase, an artist can coast for a long time on childhood and Biblical paraffin, but already I was conscious of needing the patterns for longer poems than lyrics.'[102] The solution came from Frye on Blake. 'Once I absorbed both Frye and Blake on "Poetry is allegory addressed to the intellectual powers" what happened was that I was finally able to stand in the house of literature and close the door on philosophy, theology and history until I needed them. In short, you can explain literature in terms of itself, something that is so obvious in mathematics and music, but seemed so difficult in my first years at Toronto.'[103]

The definition of poetry is Blake's, quoted in *Fearful Symmetry* from a letter Blake wrote to Thomas Butts, and may need some of the annotation Frye gives it. First, a little more of the Blake passage: 'Allegory address'd to the Intellectual powers, while is it altogether hidden from the Corporeal Understanding, is My Definition of the Most Sublime Poetry….'[104] The corporeal understanding, Frye says is literally 'bodily knowledge: the data of sense perception and the ideas derived from them. From this point of view *poetry* is something to be explained, and the notion that any kind of commentary will ever explain any kind of poetry is of course vulgar.... The "intellectual powers" go to work rather differently: they start with the hypothesis that the poem in front of them is an imaginative whole, and work out the implications of that hypothesis.'[105] A plainer version of allegory appears later in *Fearful Symmetry*: 'universal significance in the artist's creation of particular things.'[106] The remark that Reaney appears to be going on, above, may well be this one: 'The allegory that is addressed to the intellectual powers ... is a literary language with its own idioms and its own syntactical arrangement of ideas.'[107] The basic idea is that a complex poet like Blake can be interpreted 'in terms of his own theory of poetry,'[108] and without bringing to bear some outside framework. Further, 'the interpretation of Blake is only the beginning of a complete revolution in one's reading of all poetry.'[109] So it seems to have been for Reaney: reading about a revolutionary revolutionized his writing.

Anatomy of Criticism was yet to come. About that book, Frye is modest as only a genius can be. 'The gaps in the subject as treated here,' he says in his introduction, 'are too enormous for the book ever to be regarded as presenting *my* system, or even my theory. It is to be regarded rather as an interconnected group of suggestions which it is hoped will be of some practical use to critics and students of literature.'[110] I seem to hear in Frye's insistence that he has *not* exhausted the subject, that others should not think it has been and should therefore continue to think for themselves. 'He was not one to have disciples,'[111] says George Johnston, so what do we make of something Reaney said in an English 138 lecture: 'I've sold my soul to Northrop Frye.' Who is he in this moment, Faust or Robert Johnson? More like the latter, I'd say. The devil taught Robert Johnson to play blues like nobody else, so goes the story, without exacting much in return. What I make of Reaney's remark is: one genius employs hyperbole to pay tribute to another. Others have taken that kind of statement, and Reaney's mythopoeic poetics, as evidence that he was a derivative writer, one of the so-called Frygians like Jay Macpherson, maybe even one of the so-called 'small Frye.' Such reductive labels are handy for dismissing writers of uncongenial and competing ideology. Reaney calls these antagonists 'the anti-symbol, anti-anagogy gang.'[112] I'll let that word 'anagogy' gather some meaning from context until the time comes to offer a definition.

There is huge pattern, or grid, to *Anatomy of Criticism*. In his third essay, to simplify a work that is anything but simple-minded, and beautifully if densely written, Frye divides the types of literature into four modes: the mythos of spring: comedy; the mythos of summer: romance; the mythos of autumn: tragedy; the mythos of winter: irony or satire. These are not watertight compartments; they leak into one another. But they offer a huge, shapely design into which any work of literature may be placed by those who wish to do so. This kind of synoptic mapping of the verbal universe was heartening to Reaney. In a sense, it underwrote everything he did from then on in. However, in actually looking at what he wrote, other than the essays, you would most likely find it difficult to detect any very direct or literal influence. At least not often.

One thing I have been able to trace directly to *Anatomy* showed up in the production of a loosely structured dramatic presentation called *Souwesto!* This was presented in Western's Drama Workshop by student amateurs. There doesn't seem to be any extant text or script for this show, which may have been partially created by students. I vaguely remember that there was a stereotypical villain who swooped around in a black cape emitting snarls of evil laughter. The Souwesto anthem, however, appears in Reaney's *Performance Poems*. It was composed by Reaney and James Stewart Reaney, 'remembering the hurt we had suffered when a European neighbour had laughed at our region for being so flat.'[113] 'Do not call it flat,' the students sang, with enthusiasm in *Souwesto!*, 'not where God hath sat/ With holy bottom fat.' I remember the song after over thirty years. I never laughed at Souwesto for being flat—nothing wrong with flatness to a prairie boy—though I remember being taken to see the hill just out of Leamington. It had about as much elevation as I do. The laughter also stung Reaney into a poem called 'Souwesto,' which offers more detail about the physiography of the region:

Souwesto! Souwesto! Is where God hath sat

With holy bottom fat

Leaving ups and downs, villages and towns,

Eskers, kames and moraines, municipal drains

Dingles, dells, ravines,

Berms and muddy streams, Niagara Escarpment![114]

All right: the Niagara Escarpment is a dramatic eminence. That settles the issue.

One segment of the *Souwesto!* variety show whirligig was a clock drawn right out of *Anatomy of Criticism*. The minute hand was an actor who revolved with arm and finger pointing by turns at four other actors at north, east, south and west, each of them representing a Frye mode and each displaying a brief action appropriate, respectively, to the spirit of comedy, romance, tragedy and irony. The tragedian stands out in my memory: every time the dial hit him he doubled over and screamed in pain. Round and round turned the wheel of modes in one of the most hilarious scenes I've ever witnessed in the theatre. I'm sure I would have found it funny even if I didn't know I was watching, in fast-forward capsule form, 'Archetypal Criticism: Theory of Myth,' Third Essay in *Anatomy of Criticism*.

In 'July: Catalogue Poems,' the section of *Performance Poems* about 'lists of things'[115] that Reaney says fascinate him, with suggestions for how to make a list into the backbone for a poem or a story, he says 'Further ideas revolve around the lists to be made of commedia types of characters in Frye's *Anatomy of Criticism...*,'[116] and that appears to be fleshed out in an essay in honour of Frye called 'Some Critics Are Music Teachers':

In the rehearsal hall, let us go through the following modulatory etude, basing our exercise on a passage from *Anatomy*: 'For children's drama or romance—you can be a Knight, you a Dragon, you a helpful Dwarf, and you a Witch.' Change the focus to comedy, and the Witch who supported the Dragon becomes: 'a Churl. You who were the Dwarf become now a Buffoon, you who were a Dragon become the Self-Aggrandizer, and you who were the

Knight become the Self-Deprecator with the Buffoon on your side.' Change the filter to tragedy and: 'you who were the Knight now become the Villain.' This last part of the role-playing game is very important because it reminds the participants just how closely they are related to their opposites. Without a Dragon there'd be no Knight. Without Malvolio, there'd be no Belch, Aguecheek, Maria, and Feste; they'd have nothing to do but laugh at Sir Andrew, which doesn't take long. No Malvolio, no clown. To my mind this kind of groundwork in convention produces a more buoyant play, partly because the actors now know what the other actors are thinking. [117]

That is just a sketch, notes for what might be made out of the Frye modes, whether by Reaney or his reader.

Richard Stingle, another student of Frye's and a long-time friend of Reaney's, does point out that the wheel of modes may be traced as they turn through *A Suit of Nettles* and *The Donnellys*, and there is 'Anatomy of Influence: The Decisive Effect of Northrop Frye's *Anatomy of Criticism* on James Reaney's Donnellys Trilogy, as Directed by Keith Turnbull,' an M.A. thesis by Teri Rata Loretto. Well, these critics might have been taking off from something Reaney said himself, about *Anatomy of Criticism* having 'finally opened out the verbal universe for me':

There's something finally enlightening about those paradigms in *Anatomy* where you're invited to play 'Animal, Vegetable, Mineral' with the imagery of literary works. Forming sets of image-ladders that extend from heavenly ones down through middle earth to chaotic ones you can play games with Shakespeare plays in which you watch modulations as the genre is shifted a nuance this way or that. Then there are the pages in *Anatomy* where these vertical ladders as they are absorbed into literary works, modes, genres begin to turn on what I would like to call Wheels of Life down from epiphany into elegy, the dens of irony, up into satire, comedy and back to epiphany once more. Watching these various wheels—this is it; you could build a theatre that looked like this wheel of life and write Commedia plays using *Anatomy*'s lists of the basic dramatic characters. [118]

It should be noted that *A Suit of Nettles* was finished in Winnipeg, before Reaney had the full Frye experience, including *Anatomy*.

Certainly, the Frye lens is useful, but the modes and the rest never overtly shape works like *The Donnellys*. The backbone of large pattern is just palpable, yes, but it doesn't feel imposed from without. It supports from within, like the skeleton of that other organism, the human body.[119] '[I]t would not be going too far to say,' writes Craig Stewart Walker, 'that a full critical understanding of Reaney's work without recourse to Frye's would be extremely difficult, if not impossible.'[120] Full understanding? Maybe not, but a solid critical understanding of any writer worth his or her salt, without recourse to theoretical grid, has to be possible. It would be silly not to factor Frye in, but if Reaney were simply applying what Jay Macpherson calls the 'Fryekit,'[121] he wouldn't be up to much.

Macpherson used that word in an article in which she uses the kit herself to analyze Reaney's *One Man Masque*. She doesn't care that using the word might mark her and Reaney as derivative small-Frye. The irony, for me, is that her 1957 poem sequence, *The Boatman*, quite as Frygian as Reaney (and nothing like him), would be intelligible to a reader quite innocent of Frye, though a literary education—from Greek mythology to the Bible to nursery rhymes to Blake—would certainly deepen the experience. In his own brilliant essay on *The Boatman*, Reaney mentions Frye (never far from his mind) only three times. Neither reference has anything at all to do with his interpretation.

Reaney and Macpherson were friends and mutual admirers. Reaney performed *One Man Masque* for Macpherson's University of Toronto classes, and Macpherson came to Western to read and talk to Reaney's classes. When she visited English 138—which is where I met and fell in love with *The Boatman*—she made it clear that her poems typically came while she was lying down, listening for patterns of rhythm that would eventually coalesce in words. Yes, Frye was important to her conscious, thinking mind, but her 'writing' process was sub-verbal, bardic. A waking dream, a summoning of visitation. As she paced back and forth across the stage of Middlesex College in 1972, *The Boatman* well behind her, and what was to become *Welcoming Disaster* (1974) resisting all her efforts to coax it out, Macpherson's lengthy dry-spell frustration was palpable. If the Fryekit were all she needed, she would never have had to suffer so over what she told us she lived for: creation, Poetry.

Barker Fairley taught German at the University of Toronto and was a founder of *The Canadian Forum*, an influential magazine of the humanities 1920–2000. Reaney was published in the *Forum* early in his career. Fairley was also a visual artist. In a book about his life and art, the portrait he made of Reaney in 1958 has a one-sentence remark about the subject: 'James Reaney I regard as a genius with the unique ability to write innocently about things not innocent.'[122]

That would have been a response to the early work. Something Fairley says elsewhere, not about Reaney but about painting, touches what I'm writing about here. 'Theory is not enough to produce great art. It is only one side of the story and the other side is some objective world in which the theory can lose itself, dissolve itself. Call it what you will. The place for theory in the finished work is that of the skylark that loses itself in the blue, heard but not seen, forgotten yet flooding the air with melody.'[123] Melody, design, inspired flight over a fully-realized objective world: *The Donnellys*.

Three things, then, about Frye and Reaney:

1) the mythos grid is a starting point; what any true artist makes of it depends on their own creative imagination.

2) Defending his push for native drama and nationalism in general, Reaney says 'I don't believe you can really be world, or unprovincial or whatever until you've sunk your claws into a very locally coloured tree trunk and scratched your way through to universality.'[124] 'The idea behind the whole 3 parts [of *Canada Dash, Canada Dot*] is that you see the whole world in a local grain of sand.'[125] That local tree trunk / grain of sand is not only Souwesto, Canada; it's also highly particular and detailed knowledge of fact and event drawn from widely scattered areas, set into tensile relationship and urged into motion to make what Reaney called, in one place, 'a complex web of little and big sounds,'[126] and in another, 'an organism, a pulsating dance in and out of forms &c.'[127]

3) Greeting the publication of Reaney's collected poems, and deploring the fact that his reputation was 'in its slump phase,' Margaret Atwood, another student of Frye, says that anyone who actually reads Reaney poems will surely understand that 'there is nothing else *like* them.'[128] Well, that is true of all his writing. '[W]hat became clear to me during a chronological reading of this book' Atwood goes on, 'is that most commentators—including Reaney himself, and his editor and critics—are somewhat off-target about the much-discussed influence of Frye on his work. I have long entertained a private vision of Frye reading through Reaney while muttering "What have I wrought?" or "This is not what I meant, at all," and this collection confirms it.... The influence of Frye ... was probably a catalyst for Reaney rather than a new ingredient....'[129]

Amen. Frye came up immediately when I thought to follow Reaney's gridding, and Frye does have to be mentioned, but no, the sources of much of the gridding lie elsewhere, and are myriad, complex and often interlinked. It's worth remembering, too, that Reaney endorses Frye as a social as well as a literary thinker (Frye's *The Modern Century* was on our English 138 course) and never merely as some acolyte writer kowtowing to his guru.

Besides, Reaney's 1954 essay, 'To the Secret City: From a Winnipeg Sketchbook,' written well before the immersion in Frye, already sounds a note that will resound again and again in his work. You find it in Frye, too, but here it must be Reaney on his own. 'To draw a map of a city like Winnipeg,' he writes, 'is sometimes the beginning of understanding it and sometimes the end. In the following scenes I have attempted a different sort of map, the map that sees the city as having a human form, a map which guides the onlooker to some of the different limbs and organs of the city's body.'[130] So the essay begins, and here, by sketching a number of walks in which Reaney tries to find the 'soul or uniqueness'[131] of Winnipeg, is where it's heading:

It has been this walk where, as the images flew thick and fast of birth, dying, rebirth, the bridge, heaven, hell, the three old women, the two rocking chairs, one became aware of some other world behind this world of appearances, a world that if you asked it enough questions sometimes revealed for a few moments its possible golden order to you as it had to me, really not in just this last lucky walk, but in all the walks. Because if the city had on all my exploration of it been wonderful at all, it must have been because beneath its *mask* of disorder and disconnection there lay somewhere a poetic city, a possible New Jerusalem, sometimes breaking through to whatever part of one's mind catches such messages. [132]

This is the only Reaney essay I have read in which the writing is often clunky—he hasn't yet found his breezy mature style—but in it he has already formed a humanist approach to reading the mythic or symbolic or archetypal real behind the apparent real that he will employ for the rest of his life.

Well, the grids are everywhere, sometimes left as lists to be later annotated or fleshed out, or to become a backbone or 'secret structure' of a fully-formed work. When so deployed, encyclopedic and dynamic, as in *The Donnellys*, then they embrace the whole of experience, light and dark, Heaven, Earth and Hell, and they convey a reader or viewer through the whole multifarious, multi-levelled world. The list of lists I'm about to offer was gathered together by combing through just about all of Reaney. If Jamie were here, he'd say grab hold of one or two of these grids, head home right away and build something on them. And look around you. Which are the unnoticed grids that have you in thrall, which are the benign grids that hold you up and keep you safe? 'A great many people go through life without questioning the sanity of the way our genetics and our society and our minds arrange things....' [133]

To make your own grid:

One valuable source of public poems you put together on your own, perhaps as a consciousness-raising project for your community, is a collage of excerpts from the local writers and artists; the history of your apartment building before it became one; a report from Overhearing Oswald (the auditory equivalent of a Peeping Tom) who combs the shopping malls with a tape recorder for absurdist dialogue.... Apply the techniques available in my *Donnelly* trilogy or *Colours in the Dark* and you're away.... Keep a record of yourself and your community, a daily record. One day, take a look at what you have been collecting, be it weather or passersby on the street, or a review of all the clothes you have ever worn—the passage of the angel of time[134] ensures that what once seemed so banal and commonplace will quickly become that magic thing; the past, remembered and organized by the humblest of formulas—the patient daily record.[135]

    Performance Poems is a prime source of lists. It's an agreeably shaggy 8 1/2 x 11 inch miscellany of materials, some of them quite drafty, but there is an organizing principle. 'For this collection's format,' Reaney says, 'I have adopted something much looser than the conflicting gyres of life and death chosen for *One Man Masque*; I've grouped the poems and prose-poems into a calendar.'[136] A reader might also trace the format of *Performance Poems* to the calendar cycle in *A Suit of Nettles*, there being twelve sections, each named after one of the months, many of them also under the umbrella of a Greek/Latin title: January: *Ethos* (spirit of culture); February: *Dianoia* (perception and experience), March: *Melos* (melody); April *Opsis* (spectacle, the visual); May: *Facta* (acts or deeds); June: *Poetics*. That system lasts for the first six months, after which English titles begin to appear: July: Catalogue Poems; August: Private Public Poems; September: *Mythos* (body of myths); October: Halloween Conceit; November: Images of War and Peace; December: *Summa* (summing up). Each month has its how-to introduction, *Performance Poems* being a do-it-yourself manual for poetry and drama.

    Okay: lists, some of them here 'dehydrated',[137] requiring moisture from the imagination to plump them into something poetical. First, poem 'u' of an alphabet of poems in *Souwesto Home* called 'Brush Strokes Decorating a Fan:

A Useful list:

Hermes

Hera

Apollo

Zeus

Venus

Vulcan

Mars

Athena

Vesta

Hades

Poseidon

Ceres.

Useful for what?

Well, I don't quite know yet,

But I swear that as an infant,

Born near the Little Lakes,

I met them.

Every morning in our house

Vesta used to light the stove[138]

Vesta is the Roman goddess of fire and the hearth. Her name has appeared on Swan Vesta 'strike anywhere' matches since 1906.

Performance Poems has 'a refugee from an unfinished suite of mine called *Collegiate Olympus*, in which the poet sees his high-school teachers as the twelve Greek gods....'[139] Also barley, buckwheat, oats and wheat,

ancient & curiously differing seeds

Each of whose advents changed lives.

Caused armies to march, towers to be built,

Empires and kingdoms to rise and fall:

Powerful vowels in the human printing press.[140]

Swan Vesta matches.

Further lists: the six senses; the parts of speech; parts of the body, with matching animals, and the twelve signs of the zodiac; 'the twenty-seven words that one uses At Home;'[141] the sun, the moon and the seven planets; 'Professor Sheldon's list of the various kinds of male body shapes photographed in his *Atlas of Man*'[142]: ectomorph, mesomorph and endomorph, with associated psychologies[143] (the types show up in *Three Desks*); the conjugation of a verb as backbone for a poem, like the one about Granny Crack in *Twelve Letters to a Small Town*, *One Man Masque*, *Colours in the Dark*, and elsewhere; the nine muses; the furies; the graces; the four directions; four winds (in *Listen to the Wind*); the four seasons; the four elements ('In fire or flood or field or air where we wander now' says Tom Donnelly about the afterlife of the Donnellys[144]); 'the Celtic system of dividing a kingdom into four parts, each with its separate caste: … Ulster—warriors, Munster—farmers, Connaught—priests and Leinster—poets—and—musicians. There is also a fifth class of tinkers and untouchables';[145] the days of the week; the twelve months of the year, also the Indigenous twelve moons; the constellations; terms for the elements of a coat of arms; the four floors of a department store in a poem called 'Department Store Jesus'; the Ten Commandments (at least once called 'an alphabet'[146]); 'phonetic symbols from Pike's *Phonemics* arranged in a circle;'[147] the *Ontario Tree Atlas*; saints' days of the church.

Here is Polly accounting for Bethel's seduction of Polly's bishop father in *The Easter Egg*: 'You knew he liked his Anglicanism high off the incense stick so you put on a regular circus for him. You memorized all the saints' days, your accent changed, on St. Cecilia's Day you sang, on St. Lawrence's Day you made griddle cakes, on St. Andrew's Day you played noughts and crosses and on St. Sebastian's Day you shot a bow and arrow. And on St Valentine's Day—you moved in for the slaughter.'[148]

There is also the book about Elgin County wildflowers that inspired 'The Wild Flora of Elgin County,' one of my favourite list poems, plumped with names, in *Souwesto Home*:

On the roadsides & verges, ditches, ponds, & streams
Of Elgin Country,
There are more than 100 families of green persons.
So say those wise guides to the *Flora of Elgin Country*,
Messrs William G. Stewart & Lorne E. James,
Of St. Thomas well remembered.
E.g., they invite you to meet Miss Buttercup,
Of the Crowfoot family.
She has a brother named 'Cursed Crowfoot'
Who lives in a wet ditch at Kipp's Corners,
Concession V, Yarmouth township.
Miss Buttercup, by the way, lives on a dry clay roadside
And her first name is 'Common.'
Relatives are Miss Hepatica Americana,
And the Windflowers who live at Carr's Bridge,
Two miles south east of Sparta.
Calpa, Miss Marsh Marigold, again at Kipp's Corners,
Stands in peat in the water of a ditch,
And the Red & White Baneberry girls can poison you—
Over in dry sandy Springwater woods.

Now, William Blake says that plants & trees,

That—in other words—'Flora' are

'Men & women seen from afar.'

So all these plant families are people,

People you should know,

And become more serene & thoughtful

In doing so. [149]

Serene and thoughtful—and protective. Other people of our acquaintance, members of the family, include trees. 'I want to remind you,' writes Diana Beresford-Kroeger, 'that the forest is far more than a source of timber. It is our collective medicine cabinet. It is our lungs. It is the regulatory system for our climate and our oceans. It is the mantle of our planet. It is the health and well-being of our children and grandchildren. It is our sacred home. It is our salvation.' [150] '[W]e are a nation with an intensely lived past and our minds are the better for trying to contact it,' says Reaney elsewhere. 'Well, for one thing, the contact teaches you not to be bored with your surroundings, for example to love them, and that is the basis for all civilization as far as I'm concerned.' [151]

Alphabet 9 has an article by Ralph Cunningham about David Willson, who formed the Children of Peace after he was 'formally expelled from the Yonge Street Meeting [of the Society of Friends] on 15 Oct. 1812,' [152] and who had his Sharon Temple built to a symbolic grid:

In the medium of architecture, Willson, an unlettered man who left a number of published works, gave his revelations the striking form he could not give them in his writings.

The Temple's square plan symbolized the ideals of unity and justice; Willson is supposed to have said that the square base signified that the Children of Peace meant to deal on the square with all men. The three storeys represented the Trinity. The door in the centre of each side, at the cardinal points of the compass, indicated that the people were to enter from every direction, and on an equal footing. The equal number of windows in each side were to let the

Sharon Temple. Photograph by Bruce Forsythe.

light of the gospel fall equally on all assembled. The lanterns at the corners of the three storeys represented the Twelve Apostles. Inscribed with the word *peace*, the gilded copper ball suspended among the topmost lanterns proclaimed peace to the world. Inside, the twelve columns forming a large square under the base of the second storey stood for the Twelve Apostles. The four columns forming a small square in the very centre stood for faith, hope, love and charity, the foundations on which the Temple was built. Arches linking the four columns represented the rainbow.

On a square altar among the four columns stands the ark, a miniature temple in which the Bible was placed.[153]

For one section of *Canada Dash, Canada Dot*, a play built on lists of Canadian things, humble and otherwise (as is the children's play, *Names & Nicknames*), Reaney draws on this description, adding a few things. The rainbow is Noah's, he says, and he mentions the three thousand panes of glass that bring all the light in, as well as the 'One hundred and sixteen candles placed in the windows' 'at their feast of illumination in

September.'[154] Having more respect for Willson's writings than Cunningham does, he folds lines from Willson's hymns and other writings, including a bit of the holy vision that got him going, into the story of his life and work. (See below, page 207–08.) The symbolic architecture of Sharon Temple is more implicit in *Serinette*, which actually premiered *in* Sharon Temple in 1990, the only time I've been in that remarkable building, now a National Historic Site.

In 'Topless Nightmares, being a dialogue with himself by James Reaney,' it's possible to see his play *Wacousta!* being generated out of various lists. '*Could I see the script?*' asks Reaney of himself. 'Well,' he answers, 'right now it consists of the melodrama version plus lists of things I've made after carefully reading the book [John Richardson's novel *Wacousta*] through twice.' First, there is 'a list of things you hear which could be the beginning of a new script….' 'And here's a list of unusual words & phrases which could be used in choruses….' 'I've also made lists of costumes….'[155] For details, see the essay itself; right now I'm just concerned with showing something of the Reaney process, beginning, as it so often does, with lists.

We could also go to *Names & Nicknames*. In a note for the play, Reaney says, 'Many of the choruses … are taken from the suites of words used in a speller that my father learned to spell out of in the 1890s at the Irish School near Stratford, Ontario; scenery choruses came from such word lists as "In the Yard" and "On the Farm." The great monumental lists of boys' and girls' names in this book gave me the idea for the climax of the play.'[156] *Canada Dash, Canada Dot* is another play made out of lists like the names of stops across Canada on both Canadian National and Canadian Pacific Railway lines. For Reaney, as might be expected, trains are more than trains, and the listed stops are interleaved with other lists, in speeches that unite narration and stage direction (while the passages below are being said—they occupy one column of three on the page—two columns worth of names are simultaneously being recited). It should be remembered that the script of *Canada Dash, Canada Dot* is the libretto for a play set to music. Words and music together are meant to tell a story in counterpoint:

Between the Red River Lowlands and the Rocky Mountains
lie these names of railway stops you hear.

Between the lowlands of the present, our present time, our present selves,
and the giant mountains of the ancestral past lie lists of names,
stops on the railway of the mind.

The names of the kings and queens who have ruled over Canada.
Governor generals—governors general—and lieutenant governors.
Passenger lists on boats that flew across the Atlantic with white wings.

Lists of names in graveyards. On war memorials.
Lists of names in old directories. [157]

Canada Dash, Canada Dot is the only Reaney text that has to be printed
sideways on the page to accommodate its three (sometimes two) columns,
and that leads me to say that making one of these plays or operas is never a
simple matter of listing. The lines in this play, things to be said, are sometimes bare-bones plain, columns of numbers and nouns only, at one
point; sometimes they are bunched up simultaneously to create a multifarious aural effect. And lists in no two plays or poems are used in the
same way.

One interesting way to approach all the Reaney grid work is to follow his
championing of traditional education programs against the so-called
'progressive education' that infiltrated educational institutions at all levels
during his time as artist and educator. As he saw it, such retrograde
reforms meant, at best, teaching only what was deemed to be useful—certainly not poetry—and, at worst, offering a student only what he
or she might chance to be interested in. Traditional education, by
contrast, was a discipline rooted in basics and rounding out a verbal and
numerical universe to ground everything else a student should go on to
find out and build on. Reaney would know about this severe and thorough

discipline because he was sent through it at Stratford Collegiate and Vocational Institute, his high school, and later at university: 'a product of the Honours English course at University College, Toronto, taught since I was twelve by products of that institution, I have no doubt been brain-washed into seeing a tradition where poets and others keep aping, in one way or another, their literary ancestors.'[158] 'Because educational theory has forgotten,' he says in the same article, 'that at the centre of our genuine culture is some verbal DNA called a Bible and its assisting verbal chromosome—Homer and Greek Myth, the essential nourishing connectives are lacking and the will-o'-the-wisp of what people like in mass entertainment flits here and now there.'[159] In high school he took Latin and Greek, French and German. (These subjects, plus mathematics and art are taught in *One Man Masque*'s Prince Rupert School.) He had a 'crackerjack teacher of biology and natural sciences' and access to 'an excellent [school] library.'[160] Extracurricularly, he studied piano 'with a Stratford musical legend, Cora B. Ahrens.'[161] His mother and father put on plays.

I have been wondering if the wasteland that was my own elementary and high school education in rural Alberta brainwashed me into rather unsystematic improvisation of my further education. It's one possible reason I approach Reaney from a distance. No high school Latin and Greek for me. I did get the whole of *Anne of Green Gables*, read aloud to the class by Miss Hansen, in grade six. I've always been grateful for that reading, that novel, and was delighted to find it on the course list for English 138. But one loved book does not a tradition make. Wondering about my own 'educational' background is a way of pondering a more general matter: how much of anyone's approach to many things might be explained by the example of early exemplars, whether structured or haphazard. Maybe I shouldn't complain. 'A schooling that is not too strict, and is actually what many people would call a bad one,' says Jung, 'is in my experience the best.'[162]

For me, the question—which approach, disciplined or unstructured, is best—is not an idle one. Had I read through Reaney at the time we were both members of a committee to consider possible changes to

Western's Ph.D. comprehensive reading list in Canadian literature, I might have understood why we found ourselves on opposite sides of the issue, Reaney for less and I for more individual choice. I'm also asking myself, really for the first time, whether the way I went about teaching, the way I still go about learning, maybe even the way I write, were all more or less determined in my youth. I don't think I can just blame uninteresting teachers and stale curriculum, though I have been inclined to. After all, why was it that, music lover though I was and am, I quit piano lessons as soon as ever I could, while Reaney stuck it out and really learned how to play?

Can I blame athletics? Other than reading for myself, sport was the only thing that really interested me until I reached university. It would not have deflected Reaney. I see no sign anywhere that he took the slightest participatory interest in sports. Once, in a pickup softball game, he demonstrated that he didn't know which end of the bat to hold. In *Take the Big Picture*, he has his five-year-old triplets playing hockey for their school at the age of five. No, sir. Some research would have helped there, as it did for the convincing NHL hockey section of *Canada Dash, Canada Dot*. Reaney did have physical stamina, it seems, as demonstrated at the annual Nihilist Picnic, 'an artists' tradition in London, held out at the village of Poplar Hill and at which I once won the Bill Exley trophy for the longest, continuous jumping.'[163] (The Nihilist Picnic figures in 'Jumping Contest,' Scene 6 of Reaney's play, *Antler River*.)

Since a real nihilist (not funny) shows up elsewhere in this book, I should perhaps explain that a group of serious London artists united under the nihilist banner as a way of declaring their anticorporate outsider or underground identity. Associated was the Nihilist Spasm Band, a so-called improvisatory London, Ontario noise band, with vocalist Bill Exley, Greg Curnoe on homemade electric kazoo, Murray Favro on homemade alternative electric guitar, and others, all with improvised instruments good for making antimusic. I see an equivalent spirit manifest in the Rhinoceros Party founded in Quebec by writer Jacques Ferron. Like the London artists, also quite serious about their art, the

Rhinoceroses stood outside the mainstream in an entity—an actual political party in their case—thought up for satiric purposes. The party reached outside Quebec. I voted Rhinoceros myself once, in a London civic election when it was quite clear that Jane Bigelow, my actual candidate of choice, was obviously going to win.

Reading Reaney on educational theory, I almost always find him coming down on the side of structure, though there is some interesting nuancing of that position in the children's play, *Ignoramus*. The play begins with a debate between traditionalist Dr. Hilda History and progressivist Dr. Charles Progressaurus, whose saurian name says what Reaney thinks of *his* approach. Here it is in a nutshell: 'No child should be forced to learn what he doesn't want to learn.'[164]

The upshot is an educational competition.[165] Mr. Frothingale, a wealthy brewer with philanthropic instincts, has just adopted 'TWENTY ORPHANS AGED TWENTY MONTHS MADE HOMELESSS BY FLOOD.' He offers to lodge ten orphans with Dr. History and ten with Dr. Progressaurus for seventeen years, an examination to be administered after that time to see which group is the better educated. (Those new to Reaney may find their eyebrows rising at this experiment in social engineering, so it may be well to say what he was going for: 'I have always wanted to try an Aristophanes Old Comedy type of play where you have lots of comic chorus work and grotesque farcical combats.'[166]) The odds would seem to be stacked against Dr. Progressaurus, given that Reaney is ideologically in the camp of his opponent. Dr. History is modelled on Dr. Hilda Neatby, author of a critique of progressive education called *So Little For the Mind* that Reaney admired. (She also inspired the July eclogue of *A Suit of Nettles*.) So how is it that the competition ends in a draw? It's because the one-size-fits-all method looks like brainwashing (conformity-making in this context) to the Governor General of Canada, arbiter of the challenge, and he sees that the do-whatever-you-want method has not prevented those who really want to learn from finding a way. If I were taking all this personally, I'd be pleased to find a kindred spirit, an ardent individual actually able to recover from benign educational neglect. This one instance of nuancing aside, though, that is not where Reaney stands.

The conflict between traditional and progressive education shows up again and again, in Reaney's essays, in other children's plays like *Geography Match,* in the long poem, *Imprecations: The Art of Swearing,* and in my favourite source, Reaney's first long poem, *A Suit of Nettles.* The general principle lies in something Granny Delahay says in Reaney's novel, *Take the Big Picture.* Granny D enjoys being stretched by a story with some mystery to it: 'things *should* be over people's heads,' she says, 'or how in Tophet are their heads ever going to get any higher?'[167] (Saying Tophet instead of hell—see Chapter 23:10 of the Book of Kings—keeps Granny clear of profanity.) Naturally, Granny is also down on an educational outrage that Reaney returns to in several different works, *Ignoramus* included: 'stunting children's minds with Dick, Jane, and Puff pap.'[168] She is referring to early readers starring two kids: Dick and Jane, and their pets, Spot the dog and Puff the cat. I myself was introduced to those flat, insipid characters. Having learned to read before I went to school, I could already handle sentences more complex and more interesting than 'See Spot run.' Reaney denounces 'this famous primer pastoral, bland and pastel, suburban and cunning, telling no story, proferring no metaphors, completely utilitarian, materialist, devoted to teaching us how to read traffic signals and cereal boxes and not much else.'[169]

Before I get to *A Suit of Nettles,* let me turn back to an illustrative parable at the beginning of Reaney's tribute to Northrop Frye: 'Northerners up here in Canada,' he says, 'keep hearing a story about the rock star Jerry Lee Lewis; it is said that his career started when his father brought him home a piano, told him it was his and, not being able to afford lessons, also showed him where middle C was.'[170] That story was probably meant to illustrate a marvel: no lessons and yet look what Jerry Lee Lewis could eventually thump out on those keys! But Reaney was not so impressed. 'Now suppose,' he goes on, 'there had been someone present who was not only able to show Jerry Lee Lewis where middle C was, but, instead of leaving the boy to his own devices, had proceeded to show him all of Middle C's relations, enharmonic aunts and uncles, the twelve families of twelve, etc., in short—the road to *The Well-Tempered Clavichord.*' [171] Theory proper to the discipline, in other words—just what Reaney is about to go on and say, in this essay, that Frye offered him. But Jamie, I have to say, *The Well-Tempered Clavicord* is a hell of a piece, but does anybody dance to it? If Jerry Lee Lewis goes the way of Johann Sebastian Bach, what about 'Whole Lotta Shakin' Goin' On'? Whither 'Great Balls of Fire'?

I am being serious—somewhat—but I also give Reaney his analogy. Here's one of mine: nobody gifted with athletic ability gets very far in any sport without first mastering the fundamentals. That takes years of physical and mental work with coaches who know how to bring a young athlete along by stages. Thinking like Reaney, I note archetypal possibilities lurking in that sentence: *Bildungsroman, Künsterroman,* Sports-roman—apprenticeship, initiation. Also, as I already mentioned, Reaney was not, like me, a piano lessons dropout. He followed the Toronto Conservatory program to grade eleven, became proficient enough to play duets with composer and collaborator John Beckwith. This is the Reaney who sits at a piano to be recorded for an Ontario Institute of Studies in Education (OISE) tape on which he plays an assortment of keyboard pieces—hymns, ragtime, classical—between a selection of his poems from *The Red Heart* to *Colours in the Dark,* the Reaney who worked with Beckwith on a children's musical about competing bands called *All the Bees and All the Keys.*

It's the Reaney who incorporated music of all sorts into his plays and wrote librettos for operas. He had, and he used, the bones of musical theory and practice—that grid—before and after he got the Frye grid for literature. One of his essays, another of his tributes to Northrop Frye, is called 'Some Critics Are Music Teachers.' Largely about good and bad productions of Shakespeare plays, this essay graces the material with musical metaphors. An example: 'With plays, all is lost unless the director makes the mechanism or organism in front of us move at the correct tempo—with, naturally, the nuances, rallentandoes and rubatoes that make the noting of "correct speed" more than just the results of buying a metronome.'[172] (Rallentando: gradual decrease in speed; rubato: tempo-rary relaxation of strict tempo for the sake of quickening or slackening, usually without altering overall pace.)

The initiation Reaney wanted for his literary compositions would not be quite right for most of your rock 'n' roll composers, of course, and his missionary thrust should be acknowledged. He was a man of great generosity and dedicated outreach. He wanted better for everybody and, naturally enough, he created the shape of that better in his own image. By the way, though Reaney was not much interested in most pop music, he did respect Bob Dylan and The Beatles. *And* his editorial to *Alphabet* 17 somewhat surprisingly opens with a plug for a rock 'n' roll pioneer: 'went to San Francisco last Easter [1968]. Chuck Berry at the Fillmore West. He was good but how interestingly bad the light show was.'[173]

A Suit of Nettles is a beast fable about geese in a Souwesto farmyard. It's also an extraordinarily sophisticated sampler of poetic forms, grid after grid after grid. Reaney had known the alphabet since he was small and the alphabetical list of epigraphs about geese that opens *A Suit of Nettles* is an early manifestation of what was for him a frequent backbone. He had also lived by the calendar, as we all do, and *A Suit of Nettles* turns, month by month, through a whole rural year, one of its structural models being Edmund Spenser's 1579 *The Shepheardes Calendar*, which itself drew from Virgil's pastoral eclogues. Other grids or models for parts of the poem were the blazon, the sestina, the Spenserian stanza, Anglo-Saxon alliterative verse, the history and geography of Canada, the history of phi-losophy and the course of myth as derived from Frazer's *Golden Bough*. Too much to lay out here (but see 'This Tottery Dance,' the very helpful second chapter of Alvin Lee's book, *James Reaney*), all of it handled with a firm and gentle touch, some of it quite funny, some of it really poignant.

But I will bring in Ross Woodman's helpful remarks about the 'fram-ing vision' of *A Suit of Nettles*. This is 'a version of the four-fold Christian cosmos that defines, or helps to define, the literary tradition connecting Spenser, Shakespeare, Milton and Blake. There is at the top the divine order centred in the Christ-child.... Immediately below the divine world

Branwell, an engraving by Jim Westergard
from *A Suit of Nettles*, Porcupine's Quill, 2010.

is the visionary world … a world imaging as in a dream the divine one entered by faith. It is, in other words, the poetic counterpart of the religious one.… Below this visionary world is the natural world to which man in his fallen or unimaginative condition is bound. … Finally, below the realm of nature (including fallen human nature) is the demonic world which seeks to destroy the other three by denying the creative force at work within them.'[174] This scheme, in whole or in part, underlies a great deal of Reaney's writing. Making it thus explicit helps a reader to know what is intended even in poems like this little big one in *Souwesto Home*:

> I know a book that opens up people
> And reads them,
> Spreads them out, pleat by pleat,
> Till they see as far up as up,
> Till they see farther far than down.
> It makes so sharp their eyes
> That East or West
> They can spot Nobody coming up the Road.[175]

I want to spend a little more time on the debate between a goose called Anser, current liberal-minded master of the gosling school, and a goose called Valancy, who remembers the very demanding curriculum of a previous generation under a disciplinarian called Old Strictus. Anser is named for his genus, grey goose; Valancy is named for Isabella Valancy Crawford, one of Reaney's favourite Canadian poets. Reaney's naming usually tells you something.[176] Anser is who he is, that's all; Valancy is a poet. Well, says Anser, 'whatever did that pedagogue of such renown, Old Strictus, teach you as a gosling?' 'When I was a gosling,' Valancy responds, 'he taught us to know the most wonderful list of things. You could play games with it; whenever you were bored or miserable what he had taught you was like a marvellous deck of cards in your head that you could shuffle through and turn over into various combinations with endless delight.' 'Well, well, well,' says Anser, 'Might I ask just what this reviving curriculum was.' In response, Valancy's voice elevates from the demotic to the magisterial as he relays a poem, a litany of grids, some of which have structured Reaney plays or poems:

Who are the children of the glacier and the earth?
Esker and hogsback, drumlin and kame.
What are the four elements and the seven colours,
The ten forms of fire and the twelve tribes of Israel?
The eight winds and the hundred kinds of clouds,
All of Jesse's stem and the various ranks of angels?
The Nine Worthies and the Labours of Hercules,
The sisters of Emily Brontë, the names of Milton's wives?
The Kings of England and Scotland with their Queens,
The names of all those hanged on the trees of law
Since this province first cut up trees into gallows.
What are the stones that support New Jerusalem's wall?
Jasper and sapphire, chalcedony, emerald,
Sard, sardius, chrysolite, beryl, topaz,
Chrysoprasus, hyacinthine and amethyst.[177]

One appearance of the four elements is in the second verse of a poem called 'Near Tobermory, Ontario,' in which the speaker looks 'upon a blue cove,'

And I look upon the sisters four
Blue sky & blue water
　　Rock, pebble & earth
And the light I see it with.
　　　　…
But Light, you're quite another thing.
　　Indeterminate,
You hold all yet let them slip
　　Into themselves again. [178]

'What do we say when things turn out right?' asks the schoolteacher Miss Beech at the end of *The Shivaree*, and she answers herself: 'Love Triumphant! Oh, Victory of Light!' [179]

'The Kings of Britain' appear in a section of *Alphabet* 2 called 'Icons,' [180] and as an 'initiation rite' [181] in *Three Desks* by which, when he memorizes and recites the list, an alienated student is readmitted into the honours program at the small liberal arts college in that play. 'The influence of the Brontës [on *Listen to the Wind* and especially on *Zamorna! and The House by the Churchyard*] is pronounced.' [182] The various ranks of angels, from Seraphim to plain old angels, are listed in *Performance Poems*, [183] where Reaney also says 'Quite a bit of the catalogue philosophy invades my mental-landscape play *Colours in the Dark....*' [184] Here, for example, are framing stage directions, lists of associated visuals and music, for opening and closing Scenes (5 and 21):

White suggests Sunday, Alpha, White Trillium, Harmonium, the Sun, 'Shall We Gather at the River', 'The Big Rock Candy Mountain'. [185]

Black suggests Some Day, Omega, Indian Pipes, Z, the Earth. Back at the opening Birthday party.[186]

About Valancy's program, really a tight version of Reaney's own, Anser exclaims, 'My goodness, how useless so far as the actual living of life is concerned. Why we have simplicity itself compared to what that maze of obscurity was. I mean since our heads are going to be chopped off anyhow we only teach the young gosling what he likes.'[187] Now there's a defeatist attitude; there's a disheartening diminishing dead end. I regret to say I feel it pulling at me now when once I just dismissed it. Death is still the standard fate of every individual, yes, but—talk about 'Age of Dread'!—the slow death of the biosphere ('the Earth's collective network of ecosystems'[188]) and human life, the so-called sixth extinction, is now in view. The decline Reaney was cataloguing and resisting is so far advanced that to keep on with cultural work in the face of it sometimes seems futile. In this day and age of dread, what we need for encouragement is a book like Robert Bringhurst and Jan Zwicky's *Learning to Die: Wisdom in the Age of Climate Crisis*. Even anticipating the global and cosmic chop, they say, it makes no sense to seize up and lie down. Let's go down singing, they say, if go down we must.

Reaney's 'Author's Notes' for *Baldoon* follow a play about an early nineteenth century haunting caused by witchcraft and the magic powers that explain and oppose it. While strolling past the location near Wallaceburg, Ontario, where the haunting was said to take place, he encounters some present-day skeptics. ' "Surely you don't believe all that about the Baldoon mystery," one of them said. "Why, around here we call it the Baboon Mystery." '[189] Reaney doesn't take these people on, just laughs, keeps walking. But what emerges privately as he goes, at least what he writes out for his readers, is a credo. 'Yes, I do believe all that,' he writes. 'I believe that there was an old house here besieged by demonic phenomena.... I refuse to believe all materialist explanations....'

I want to believe too that Dr Troyer the famous witchfinder of Long Point on Lake Erie did have magic beneficent powers and could with his scrying stone see a great deal farther into the levels of existence above and below our modern, natural one than TV aerials even manage. When McTavish and McDorman make their epic journey from Baldoon to Long Point pursued through the Longwood by witches I believe that too. I believe principally because it's a great deal more interesting to, than not.[190]

'[O]ut of the past,' he goes on, 'comes a world where the laws of atheism, progress and materialism suddenly break down. Surely it is a good thing that they do break down occasionally to let in some terror and some mystery. This is a story from our deep past and our own Lake St Clair fen country which should add a feeling of there being more depths and heights to existence than our present day usually discovers.'[191] This is Reaney in familiar territory, Northrop Frye territory also, looking to see any particular time and place in terms of a vertical dimension—those 'depths and heights'—that widens and mythologizes it. I don't know how many times I've read this particular polemic, actually enjoying it more than I enjoyed the play, without feeling disappointed. What I've come around to being disappointed by is that 'interesting.' 'Interesting' is far too casual to be a firm basis for belief. The credo would have been much stronger without it. I have the feeling that Reaney is doing what he can here to reel in the skeptics. To get such folks *interested* might be to crack open a window in the materialist mind. Reaney himself was not just *interested* in belief; he was a believer. His faith was a spur to discipline, to learning, to analysis—ultimately to making. Grounded in something as simple as natural childlike play, his faith is a complex, dynamic source. For my money, there are few richer models for the sort of singing recommended by Bringhurst and Zwicky than the committed creative life and work of James Reaney.

Variations on the education debate are repeated in other Reaney works. In *Geography Match*, as I've said, the contrasting approaches to education just advanced are put to the test with two groups of students under the tutelage of a traditionalist and a 'progressive.' They are embedded in two plays about academic life, *Three Desks* and *The Dismissal*, as well as in *Gentle Rain Food Co-op*, and they are explicit in *Imprecations: The Art of Swearing*. This is a long poem which begins with actual curses Reaney heard at home, as a boy, before shifting to the sort of cursing that is actually spell-casting. I can't resist introducing some of the swearing before moving on to a curse directed at those responsible for dismantling Old Strictus-style education.

'[A] lost skill?' Reaney says about cursing. 'Perhaps I, a non-swearer, can revive the art./ Then we can teach it at Western: Swearing 22.' 'My own father never swore,' he begins, 'except—"the dirty beggar!" '

> Never *bugger*. *Beggar*—as damn becomes darn, and God
> Is always Golly where the bright angel feet
> Of Elwy Yost have trod,
> But my stepfather was quite another story:
> 'Great Judas Iscariot—that fart in a windstorm!
> Get off my toes, you bloody cocksucker!'—to a horse.
> 'Son of a sea-cook' was his mildest imprecation.
> On a daily basis *shit-ass* and *piss-willie*
> Were levelled at neighbours, relatives, those
> Who deserved this, those who did not.[192]

Elwy Yost was the ebullient host of a film series on TV Ontario. Howie Meeker, once a colour commentator on the Hockey Night in Canada broadcast, must also have trod with angel feet since 'By Golly' was one of his standard expressions.

Now here is a curse on what Reaney calls 'the lighter side,' one of three levelled at progressauruses. These curses are meant to be amusing, and so they are, though the target, educational reform, is not, was not to him.

Oh ye hippies and merry draft dodgers who in the sixties
Came to University College stampeding my dear old professors,
Mobbing them till they scrapped the old Honours English Course,
And gave you the anything at any time:
No down payment on Emily Brontë; Virginia Woolf now,
Beowulf later on, a literary cafeteria for
Academic piggies. Communitas delenda est!
May you in Heaven be presented with harps tuned in this order:
A 2 octaves below Middle C, next F natural 5 octaves above High C,
Next ... and may your conductor Saint Cecilia shout:
Saint Saens' *The Swan* by sight or OUT!
Having failed the harp test, may you fall into Hell
Where the only pitcher of water
Stands at the top of a staircase whose steps
Can only be climbed in the following manner:
Step #102 first, then step #3, then step 52, then 7 ...
Yes, in precisely that order, you mental grasshopper,
Or no water![193]

So an unstructured program of education is a wasteland: my own 'education' until, by the skin of my chinny chin chin, I finally got to university
and started figuring out how to learn. *Communitas delenda est*: community must be destroyed. Community *building*, now a remedial effort, was
Reaney's admirable lifelong work.

As I have shown, the kinds of grid that Reaney finds to use for either
content or form are many. They draw from diverse disciplines, some of
them traditional and archetypal, some more particular and local. He was
always drawing on what he called 'the imaginative force which sees ways of
making more meaning out of the world, finding the clue that joins up the
different mazelike levels of our inner and outer worlds.'[194] In his play *Listen to the Wind*, according to Jay Macpherson, 'while the outer story [of
four children play-acting in a Souwesto farmhouse] is slight, gentle, and

touching, the inner one [the romance Saga of Caresfoot Court] consists of a series of explosive confrontations, which unlike the outer events are distanced from us by the conventions of English landed-gentry setting and melodramatic plot mechanics.… The balance of the two stories conveys the relationship between life and creative dream.'[195] What makes this play so poignant and endearing is that young Owen, the principal dramaturge within the play, is ailing physically and emotionally. His parents have split, but agree to participate in the play. He hopes thereby to bring them back together. Win or lose, though, the Caresfoot Saga embodies his desperate and sometimes savage thoughts.

Reaney's research brings sometimes obscure or arcane knowledge into the reader's or viewer's ken, information that thickens up the texture of this poem, that play, the works, until the Reaney oeuvre comes to seem almost encyclopedic. There is a loving intercultural exchange of lists in *Wacousta!* between Charlotte de Haldimar (British) and Le Subtil (Cree). She offers him a tour of the guitar with nomenclature that might surprise many players of the instrument: 'The back, the side, the neck, the rose, the belly, the bout, the purfling, the peg, the bridge …' Ellen Holloway, also present, finishes up: 'the nut, the strings'[196] A linguistic exchange follows:

Charlotte	Le Subtil
Teach me Le Subtil. We call this the crystal flood, but you call it	nespi
the chequered shade	agoowastew
tree bole	mistik
a birch tree	waskuay
the earth	uskes
radiance, light	wasteo[197]

'With the knowledge of the locale and the historical period he had acquired,' says John Beckwith, Reaney's collaborator on *Taptoo!*, 'Jamie's libretto contained numerous quotations from writings and proclamations, and similarly my score quotes from over twenty musical sources—military tunes, tavern songs, hymn tunes, patriotic numbers of the period [which] resembled the mix of drama and familiar tunes found in the eighteenth-century form of the ballad opera....'[198] *Taptoo!* is 'based on events surrounding the establishment of the town of York, Upper Canada (now Toronto) ... 1780 to 1810.'[199] One of my favourite examples of Reaney research is in Scene Three: 'How to Play the Drum.' (Two of the main characters are drummer boys, one honest, the other devious.) I've removed all stage directions but one from the Drum Major's instructions, directed at apprentice drummer Seth Harple:

> The first thing
> previous to a Boy
> Practicing on the Drum
> is to place him perfectly upright!
> Left heel in the hollow of the Right Foot.
> Then put the Drum Sticks into his hands
> Secondly, let the Boy's Drum be slung on the Neck
> The Drum bearing on the left thigh so that ...
> Thirdly, previous to commencing to learn the Long Roll ...
> Don't hit your knees, Master Harple.
> Try to hit the centre of the drum!
> (*Eventually Seth plays a perfect long roll.*)
> Well, now then, today, now that we've learnt the Roll! The Open Flam! The Ten-Stroke Roll! The Close Flam from Hand to Hand! The Drag! The Drag and Stroke! Let's try the Eleven-Stroke Roll![200]

I never saw *Taptoo!*, would have loved to hear as well as see it, but I found even reading these words fascinating. They show how Reaney's research hauls up specific grid information that is both instructive and dramatically usable. This particular research also helped with *Wacousta!*, where a stage direction says '*All the commands are given by different sequences of drum taps.*'[201]

The passage above comes from the 'outer world' of percussion that is part of the soundscape of the opera, but military drumming, when mastered, is like other kinds of drumming in many cultures. When Seth knows his language, he can speak with it:

> After many months of practice
> when I finally, finally,
> could play for real soldiers
> marching, marching,
> I felt so close to our Commander.
> There were no written orders.
> We drummers and buglers were
> extensions of his mind.
> We were his voice, his thunderous voice,
> commanding, commanding.[202]

This is a language of the 'inner world.' 'Our inner ear,' Jan Zwicky says, 'gives life to the music of the human mind.'[203]

Now let's go back to the list of grids in the curriculum of Old Strictus. It ends with all the jewels set in the walls of the New Jerusalem in the biblical book of Revelation. We are back to prophecy. And from there it's a short leap to the early (1960) poem called 'The Alphabet,' which links the creation of those walls with rounding up the whole alphabet of letters. One of the impressive and educational aspects of this poem is its demonstration that *saying* the letters creates a soundscape. This may not be heard so much from the vowels, though on Reaney's page, like all the consonants, they are spelled like proper nouns, with a capital letter up front. A is Ay, for example. We are in the region of phonetics, without any fancy symbols for the sounds of terms (plosive, fricative and so on) for the way they are made. Just listen to the sound of consonants pulled out of the imperative sentences that make up the poem:

Ull Mm Nn Rr and hisSsings
Wuh and Yuh
Puh, Buh, Phuh and Vuh
Huh, Cuh, Guh and Chuh
Tuh, Duh and Thuh!
Juh, Quuh, Zuh and X [204]

Each letter has a solid name, as well as a sound. Groupings of letters are pounded into the wall, along with the precious stones, to create a page version of New Jerusalem. This one hearkens back both to Revelation and to Blake, whose New Jerusalem, as I've already mentioned, was invoked in the editorial to the first number of *Alphabet* and whose symbolic universe Northrop Frye was the first to map. I'll have more to say about Reaney's poem later.

Outreach

None of the later Reaney plays were merely sent out into the world for director and actors and all to make of them what they could. Reaney went out with them, sometimes to collaborate in their development, sometimes to help spread the message of the finished play. Especially with the NDWT Company that was formed to stage *The Donnellys*, author, director and actors charged out into classrooms and community halls with workshops designed to advertise the plays, yes, but also to wake audiences into the feeling that they too could be creative. *They* could be actors and sound effects people. *They* could make up their own plays. Reaney especially loved addressing himself to children, the open-handed, open-minded ones least likely formed within some ideology or script or grid. He wanted to show that their creativity, like his, could be rooted in their own locale, core of the universal.

Here is Reaney in Timmins, northern Ontario, with a production of *Wacousta!*, workshopping with what he calls 'the "Alphabet," a "Reaney game" where, by using the letters of the alphabet, bits and pieces of everyday home-territory scenes and awarenesses, snippets of (in this case) Timmins consciousness are given expression in poetry, in mime—in theatre. What to the young people of Timmins had previously been just plain old boring Timmins, Timmins to be avoided, Timmins to be forgotten, was thereby changed into something exciting and attractive, something to be truly appreciated. It seems to me that it is this sort of appreciation of one's own home territory, and the expression of it, that is so much the desired goal of a great deal of Canadian writing today, and not only of writing but of Canadian culture as a whole.'[205] I hope Timmins *was* transformed, and I hope the transformation had staying power. The evidence is not yet in.

But what kind of evidence should we be looking for? Robert Shipley, retired professor of environmental studies at the University of Waterloo, was 'bored, directionless and surly' as a London high school student.

'I had friends who were honing their B & E [break and enter] skills. I was a spark of trouble looking for a place to ignite.' Then his Westminster High School English teacher sent him to the Alpha Centre Listener's Workshop, where Reaney welcomed him and immediately directed him to impersonate a kitchen sink. 'I hesitated for just a moment but by then a girl was washing her hands with imaginary soap in the basin formed by the loop of my outstretched hands.' Right away, Shipley was caught up in the workshop 'forging Jamie's next play, *Colours in the Dark*.' Fifty years later, he still calls Reaney an 'inspiration. He taught me that my roots were in the soil of Southwestern Ontario, which was a rich and storied civilization. He invited all of us to be proud of our place in the world.' 'Reaney may not have saved my life,' Shipley concludes, 'but he certainly gave it direction at a critical moment.'[206] A university career beats prison all hollow. How many more such testimonials might be written?

I see what Reaney was trying to accomplish through the eyes of Del, narrator of Alice Munro's *Lives of Girls and Women*. As a girl, Del couldn't wait to get out of Jubilee, a fictional Souwesto town; the woman, now a writer, has a very different view, and her method of gathering material sounds very like that of James Reaney:

People's lives in Jubilee as elsewhere, were dull, simple, amazing and unfathomable—deep caves paved with kitchen linoleum.

It did not occur to me then that one day I would be so greedy for Jubilee. Voracious and misguided as Uncle Craig out at Jenkin's Bend, writing his history, I would want to write things down.

I would try to make lists. A list of all the stores and businesses going up and down the main street and who owned them, a list of family names, names on the tombstones in the cemetery and any inscriptions underneath. A list of the titles of movies that played at the Lyceum Theatre from 1938 to 1950, roughly speaking. Names on the cenotaph (more for the First World War than the Second.) Names of the streets and the patterns they lay in.

The hope of accuracy we bring to such tasks is crazy, heartbreaking.

And no list could hold what I wanted, for what I wanted was every last thing, every layer of speech and thought, stroke of light on bark or walls, every smell, pothole, pain, crack, delusion, held still and held together— radiant, everlasting.

At present I did not look much at this town. [207]

Munro stayed home; her local stories touched the world; there's universal for you. Londoners Greg Curnoe and Jack Chambers (Reaney calls them 'militant regionalists') were all for loving their region and making their art out of it. So was David McFadden, another regionalist and collaborator with Greg Curnoe. 'Since earliest childhood,' he writes in *A Trip Around Lake Erie*, 'I've felt that the further you get from Hamilton, Ontario, the less interesting things become, the less magic there is in the air.' [208] Some people, it seems, don't need to be workshopped into loving their own locale.

Artists with a bit of moxie will come to resent being told that where they live doesn't count for much. Reaney was part of a nationalist movement to shift the cultural centre from there—London, New York—to here, his country and his region. He would have liked Newfoundland poet Mary Dalton. She has published a book of essays called *Edge*, so is that where she's writing from? Some remote margin of Canada? No. 'There's a lovely map,' she says, 'called "the Newfoundland-centred universe." Mine is a Newfoundland-centred universe, so I don't consider myself as part of the hinterland.' [209] The edge in her title has been sharpened for anyone who would say otherwise. Wherever I am, the point is, that is the centre. (*Whoever* I am, whoever you are, that is also the centre; every *person* should be viewed and valued accordingly.) For poet Al Purdy, the omphalos of the world was Ameliasburgh, Ontario. There are many ways of expressing what Reaney wanted to accomplish with his outreach.

The drive to inclusiveness occasionally invited some chaos. 'My most scary time,' he says of one of the Stratford workshop sessions for *King Whistle!*, 'was handling a crew of roller skating toughie tykes who came, invited by me, to the daily workshop and rollerskated all over the school on those gleaming floors. They kept knocking each other over à la Roller

Derby movies, and some of them had those impervious faces that are the result of too many additives in too many Big Macs; slowly they faded, but we did have twenty little to small kids anyhow.'[210] (One of Reaney's bugbears was additives in processed foods.)

Whether or not additives in food are in themselves responsible for bad behaviour—the diagnosis may be suspect—such food issues are a small part of the many abuses Reaney blamed on progress, capitalism (money) etcetera, reasons why he periodically exhorted his audience to get their lives together and focus on what really matters. Research for *King Whistle!*, especially interviews with those who had been involved with the strike, showed Reaney

what our society could be like. Why isn't it as exciting and rich as these people should make it; well, money. The more research came in, the more I realized that those with the money make awfully sure there isn't enough of it to go around. But—it was no use trying to do away with money because it also seemed to focus people's lives in a good way.... One thing the research taught me was not to underestimate the effectiveness for social justice of the Christian Church as it existed in Stratford in 1933. A great many of the strike leaders belonged to churches—usually Baptist or United Church; their ministers supported them to the hilt, and the kind of society these people find possible is neither Marxist nor Capitalist, but what I would call pragmatic-Christian. In other words, religion not politics is the final way of controlling money—which even today seems like an uncontrollable demon in our society. In William Blake such a force is known as the Spectre of Urthona, the personification of our will to control the environment which often gets away from us and starts controlling us.[211]

Partly to spread that kind of thinking around, as well as to assert the importance and interest of local stories, Reaney wanted maximum inclusiveness in his workshops and plays. During the third Stratford workshop preparing for *King Whistle!* '85 showed up for auditions—we offered them all parts!'[212]

Farm Boy

In his James Reaney Memorial Lecture, John Beckwith says that Reaney adopted the persona of a farm boy. Reading that I thought, yes, 'persona' makes good sense, though Reaney was not always wearing it. He was a farm boy by origin, and he held on to the family farm for a long time. It was a spiritual centre for him, as well as a working farm and a dwelling place. That spirit of farm boy innocence, depicted and endorsed in Reaney plays and stories and poems, is not evidence of some sort of naiveté or arrested development, however it might read to a card-carrying sceptic. Even an admirer like Tim Inkster will say that 'Reaney was, I suppose, somewhat naïve, and remained unapologetically so throughout his career. I have, for example, a butterfly he made as a party favour for his own 21st birthday celebration—conclusive evidence, I would imagine, of a man "sadly out of touch with reality" but not so distantly removed from his own imagination.'[213]

Perhaps Inkster was influenced by Frank Davey's review of *Twelve Letters to a Small Town* which he reprints in his article: 'James Reaney displays here an extraordinary capacity for capturing and beautifying the naïve and hypersentimental kindergarten teacher's interpretation of the child's world. He stimulates all that is unrealistic and nostalgic within a reader to acclaim his verse as great; it may be only a touch of cynicism that can save a reader from deception, and bring him to want to say, "James Reaney, the world is not so goody-goody." … There is magic indeed in the way Reaney makes the child's world even more than alive, but I am afraid that most people, especially children, would laugh at him. If Reaney is serious in this book, he is sadly out of touch with reality. *Twelve Letters to a Small Town* is strictly for watery-eyed old ladies.'[214] More than just a touch of cynicism in that. A denizen of Blake's world of Experience is trashing Innocence (which is not childishness)? 'The innocence of the adult, where it is achieved, is greater than the innocence of a child, though bought at

Handmade butterfly party favour, 1947.

the cost of much painful awareness.'[215] Well, books read us as we read them. *Twelve Letters* reads me as more 'innocent' or 'receptive' than it does Frank Davey. Which doesn't mean I'm right and he's wrong. That conclusion—that either/or language—is very tempting, but I've read enough Davey to take him seriously as a critic, even when I disagree.

I don't myself see Reaney's butterfly party favour, neutrally presented as the last visual in Tom Gerry's *The Emblems of James Reaney*, as touching his relationship with reality. It was *because* Reaney was viscerally in touch with current reality, with realities he didn't want to accept as fixed, that he worked so hard to offer people images drawn from the whole light-dark gamut of human nature. He wanted to help his audiences understand the culture that enfolds us (*Prisons We Choose to Live Inside* is the title of Doris Lessing's 1985 CBC Massey Lecture), so as to be able to resist the bad in it and, ideally, work for change. Reaney was his own person. He was like no one else I've ever known, but I wouldn't call him naïve. Had he written nothing after *A Suit of Nettles*, his literary sophistication would already have been demonstrated. But he was sophisticated in his own way. A scholar himself, though no standard academic, he felt that engagement with scholarship—research—would have gone quite some way to improving much of the poetry being written in this country. To communicate the essence of complex ideas, his way was to simplify them, often radically, to condense ideas into images so as to make them graspable by a public that he wanted with him in the struggle to improve society. That boiling-down method could never be made to work by one who failed to understand—intimately—the basics of what he was condensing in metaphor. Reaney has said that he was frustrated by the approach to literature as the voice of philosophy or history—the thematic or content approach—but he showed that he knew both in *A Suit of Nettles*. He wanted to help us think by helping us to see.

Certainly there was a nostalgic element to a lot of what he did, how he lived, what he wrote, preference for a simpler time of life on a farm, or a small town like Stratford, and in wilderness back before that, as opposed to pretty well any city like Winnipeg, Toronto or Detroit. But that generalization takes us only so far. To look into the early work, *The Red Heart* and *The Box Social and Other Stories*, is to find rural life not at all idealized. In the stories there is bullying, discrimination, narrowness and bigotry. In some of the early plays there is outright evil. You would never know all that from reading the bucolic *Twelve Letters to a Small Town*, so it's necessary to take the big picture that includes all of Reaney's work, early and late. Doing so discourages easy generalizations about Reaney's view of rural life, and life in Souwesto small towns. He carried the farm boy with him throughout his life—there are not a few photos of him hoeing or

A drawing from *Twelve Letters to a Small Town*.

Ryerson, Toronto, 1962.

otherwise managing a garden outside the ancestral home, and the farm house is depicted on the cover of *Souwesto Home*—but he had an undergraduate degree in English, an M.A. (thesis: 'Novels of Ivy Compton-Burnett') and a Ph.D. (thesis: 'The Influence of Spenser on Yeats'). He was Full Professor at Western University. He was not a standard academic, because he was never standard anything, but to read his work, the nonfiction prose especially, is to see that he was a learned man. Northrop Frye might have the last word on this subject: 'Children live in a protected world which has something, in epitome, of the intelligibility of the state of innocence, and they have an imaginative recklessness which derives from that. The child who cries to have the moon as a plaything, who slaps a table for hurting him when he bumps his head, who can transform the most unpromising toy into a congenial companion, has something which the adult can never wholly abandon without collapsing into mediocrity.'[216]

Serenity

'Instead of driving a car,' Reaney said at one point, 'I have a little magazine.'[217] He finally learned to drive while on sabbatical in Victoria (1968–69), where he also learned to type. He was pleased to be taking his driving lessons from an instructor, Ralph Cossey of the Windsor Driving School, a man who had a neat way with metaphor. 'Take the big picture,' one of Cossey's instructions, became the title of a children's novel that begins in Victoria and follows a rambunctious family back to an Ontario city called Antler River. To *Alphabet* 17, Cossey contributed an article, 'Hot Dogs, Squirters and Red Runners,' about various kinds of bad driver. Being able to drive made it possible for Reaney to pursue his intention to explore every concession road in Souwesto, often stopping to record some scene in watercolours.

But he never liked cars. He often used them as symbols of what was wrong with present-day life in North America. His ideal method of moving from place to place was on foot or bicycle. When he was in high school, he once pedalled all the way from Stratford to Toronto, with friends, to see Walt Disney's *Fantasia*. In his teens he regularly pedalled from the family farm to Stratford and back. Once he rode thirty miles up Yonge Street north of Toronto and discovered David Willson's Sharon Temple. As an adult professor in London, he would take his bike to Toronto on the train.

Performance Poems has a sequence of thirty small poems, 'variations on the theme of the foot and its products—paths, roads, streets, steps in the snow &c.,'[218] called 'Footnotes & Podiatry.' 'Paths & roads,' says poem 30, 'are the stories & odes / of our legs, ankles, soles & toes.'[219] If there are to be roads, says poem 22, let them originate this way:

> Oh Pathmaker cow
> Carolingian cowbells
> You follow the lie of the land

James Reaney, 'Near Fraserburg, Fall 1985.'

Watercolour, 15.24 cm. x 22.86 cm.

Like Gipsy roads though heavier,
Your sentences all cobossed
    Together.[220]

What we have instead—automobiles, highways—is an apotheosis of the wheel. This poem seems to have snuck in among all the others about the foot and walking:

19. You, wheel?
    You, wheel!
    my enemy
        Rubber chisel
    Of freewail
    Of freeroar.[221]

One of the earliest bad Reaney autos appears in the short story called 'The Car.' There, a driverless vehicle is the automotive projection of a small boy, David, whose mother is a whore and woefully neglects him. His tormented mind sends a driverless car out at night to run down innocent, defenceless pedestrians or cyclists. Reaney should have received royalties from Stephen King for the concept of the 1983 novel called *Christine*, later a film, about a 1958 Plymouth Fury with supernatural powers. Reaney's story is supernatural—Souwesto gothic[222]—and both frightening and sad because convincingly told. It's an almost-coming-of-age story. The main character, Bert, is just becoming sexually aware. David's mother offers him 'a piece,' free, which both arouses and scares him. 'It was because he hadn't thought much about that like that before. It seemed part of the car world, not the bicycle world.'[223]

But the innocent bicycle world is about to be lost. Bert's bicycle might even be taking him places he doesn't want to go. 'Had his bicycle been for some time leading him into that country one always suspected of just possibly existing: the Kingdom of Shadows where things disappeared the moment you turned your back upon them and the Republic of Darkness where at the edge of the swamp people came to dump things or make the two-backed beast and at the end of a stubby dead-end lane there waited an empty car, an empty rusted skeleton.'[224] This is the third time that the two-backed beast (out of *Othello*) comes up associated with casual and probably youthful sex in cars. The Republic of Darkness claims the sad, neglected boy. Bert dreams of the boy's end in a junked car and convinces his dad to accompany him to the actual junk yard, where they find what's left of the unfortunate victim of his mother's neglect, behind the wheel of a vehicular skeleton: 'The woman's boy sat steering the wheelless car. His eyes could not see the road that he was driving because the rats had stolen them. But still the steering wheel clutched his hands because the bindweed growing up from underneath the car fastened them there with many a withered convolvular twining. And had fastened them there since early that summer.'[225]

There is also an early poem in *The Red Heart* called 'Klaxon' after the word derived from Greek for an early sort of horn invented by American Miller Reese Hutchison. The cars in this poem are

Murderous cars and manslaughter cars,

Chariots from whose foreheads leapt

Silver women of ardent bosom. [226]

(Certain hood ornaments of the time, since banned for safety reasons, were automotive equivalents of figureheads on a ship.)

The personified cars in this poem, ardently seeking drivers, are doomed to orphanhood:

… no one wished to own them any more,

everyone wished to walk. [227]

Hood ornament on a 1934 Triumph.

Photograph by Martin Garfinkel.

Now there's a wishful fantasy! 'Murderous' is right, of course. 'Since 1899,' writes Nathan Heller in 2019, 'more than 3.6 million people have died in traffic accidents in the United States, and more than eighty million have been injured; pedestrian fatalities have risen in the past few years. The road has emerged as the setting for our most violent illustrations of systemic racism, combustion engines have helped create a climate crisis, and the quest for oil has led our soldiers into war.' [228] As an aid to gauging the veracity of Reaney's apparently whimsical literary inventions, it's often useful to remind oneself of some facts.

In the May eclogue of *A Suit of Nettles*, an argument is made, by 'two strange geese of the scientific variety,' that geese should practice birth control. Too much fertility in the barnyard. With just a couple of goslings, runs the argument, the parental goose unit could afford some of the fine offerings of modern technology:

'You then could buy yourself a kill-yourself-if-you-touch-it
And a watch-everybody-squeeze-up-from-hell-while-you sit;
An electric jelly-fish warmer than a husband to go to bed with you
And a pass-like-a-vulture-shadow and get your sons to do
Two-backed tricks in the back and flatten 5,000,000 frogs too.' [229]

If I were trying to push these technological marvels (and I'm-not-sure-what, a TV, an electric blanket, an automobile), I might have tried to make them sound more attractive. In this particular barnyard, anyway, the geese prefer to walk about, as of old, and they prefer to beget as many youngsters as nature meant them to. For their efforts, the two birth control advocates, despite their best contraceptive efforts, are impregnated by 'two handsome yet/ Sort of grim rakish sly curly young men who looked just like.' This is comeuppance for 'hating being' [230] and going against nature.

The women's loins poured forth a swollen stream
Until the brothers moved them to their granary
Where they were turned into strong & sturdy machinery;

One into a large & squat fanning mill,

The other to a tall conical cylindrical

Iron Maiden used for threshing seeds from ripe sunflowers.

So usefully did end the lives of those insistent life devourers.[231]

Those farming machines are useful; others in Reaney, especially the cars, and everything that automobiles mean in his work, are anything but.

'What I want eventually to do, or have someone do someday,' he writes in *14 Barrels from Sea to Sea*, 'is write a play in which the rats drive us; on freeways, naturally, invisible rats are already corralling us—away from this and into that—hurry!'[232] Reaney's hope for a new theatre was spurred by his desire to wake up the sleepers of his time. '[W]e, in the mass, tend to think in terms of Caliban's wished-for bookless island where, without even a witch to provide some variety, he sits huddled in front of the Cyclops eye of VCR and Cable and Satellite's 150 channels.'[233] It isn't hard to imagine what Reaney would think of so many people nowadays with their eyes locked to the screens of their devices.

In *Wacousta!*, Pontiac—who is endowed with the kind of time-transcending foresight also displayed by the Donnellys—mentions freeways as one of the long-term results of the settler society represented in the play by Fort Detroit. The play makes much of what the automotive centre of Detroit has come to represent in North America and the world, and it isn't pretty. There is a moment in the play when Pontiac refers to Fort Detroit as the one serpent egg among the several egg/forts he could not crush. 'Well,' he says, 'you hatched.' At that point, according to the stage direction, '*Toy friction cars swarm over the stage. In effect, a giant Pontiac stands exactly where the Renaissance Building stands now in Detroit with modern traffic swirling about his feet.*'[234] We are not explicitly invited to ponder the irony that Pontiac has become a brand of General Motors car—blatant appropriation of culture—but it's not lost on me. I learned to drive in my dad's 1956 white-and-turquoise Pontiac, knowing nothing whatever then of the name's origin.

In the essay structured as a dialogue with himself about *Wacousta!*,

Reaney discusses the figure of Wacousta—betrayed in love, he grows to gigantic stature, becomes obsessed with vengeance on his betrayer, and allies himself with Pontiac's people to achieve this goal. Here is Reaney's account of what Wacousta's transformation means to him: 'This white man who's gone over to the Indians and somehow procured a costume for himself that would drive most hippies mad with envy is charismatic enough to invite comparisons with Lord Byron, Satan, Heathcliff, Thoreau, Achilles, Hamlet, a whole nation of souls protesting the way so-called civilization irons out individuality, fantasy and the passions....[235] 'Oh come now,' says straight man Reaney about all this pro-romance musing, provoking a retort that makes it clear where the automobile fits in Reaney's iconography: 'Listen, you idiot questioner, all you believe in is Detroit cars which are all like each other and make us all like each other. I do believe in another world where if he likes Sir Reginald Morton can grow a foot taller as he changes into the renegade Wacousta.'[236] Anyone who takes a more neutral interest in cars may retort that cars are *not* all alike, either in appearance or mechanical operation; Reaney's analogies can be slightly off, even when his point is on, as it is here. The culture of Western 'developed' nations is saturated with pressures to conform.

In the home decorating magazines I sometimes page though while waiting to have my hair cut these days, I find décor after décor that strikes me as antiseptic. Lots and lots of white on white with bits of accent colour tastefully placed here and there. Everything tasteful as hell. Can't object too much to that, really; one person's antiseptic might be another's austere. Maybe we're in a décor/design moment now. Maybe we'll one day look back and see that we were experiencing a 2020 version of William Morris! or Bauhaus! Though I don't suppose we'd be meeting the moment pure in any middle-class magazine: month after month of pretty much the same content, just as other media are obliged to generate content daily. There has to be something on, whether or not there is anything worth being on about. But what I find most discouraging about the décor spreads is that, page after page, mag after mag, all the décor looks very much the same. You might expect one who writes like I do to be partial to a bit of clutter, and you would be right. But it's *my* clutter, mine and Beth's. Our 'clutter.' We didn't go for a *look* by reading some magazine. Most of that here's-how stuff is squandering trees. [237]

Reaney might have found some of his distaste for conformity confirmed by Marshall McLuhan's *The Gutenberg Galaxy*: assembly line repeatability traceable to Gutenberg's invention of movable type. Reaney was a son of Gutenberg himself. Having learned typesetting at Winnipeg Technical Vocational High School while teaching at the University of Manitoba, he hand set the first numbers of *Alphabet* in Baskerville lead type, an already outmoded technology, but he hated further ramifications of technology in general. He regards 'microphones with a great deal of suspicion,' for example. 'Could it be that they are the important part of a giant the rest of whom is invisible? And there is no escape from his banal seed?' [238]

In the introduction to the unpublished *Antler River* may be found perhaps Reaney's most complete rant against technology, contrasted with images of the pastoral world he opposes to it. I reproduce this in caps, as it appears in Reaney's typescript, so that it looks the way it sounds to me, shouted:

AS THE AUDIENCE COMES INTO THEATRE LONDON, THEY SEE ON EITHER SIDE OF THE STAGE TWO MARIONETTES. ON STAGE RIGHT — THE TECHNOGIANT — BLIND, MECHANICAL MONSTER WITH A SATELLITE FOR EYES WHOSE HANDS WE FALL INTO EVERYTIME WE DRIVE A CAR OR WATCH TV. ON STAGE LEFT WE SEE RATTLEBABY — AN ADORABLE KID WIELDING A RATTLE WITH A CURIOUS SWEET SOUND — ALL THE FORCES OF 'PLAY', CREATIVE LAUGHTER, POWER OVER ENVIRONMENT THROUGH ANALOGY RATHER THAN ANALYSIS. THESE QUITE SMALL MARIONETTES CAST SHADOWS. WHEN THE SHADOW OF TECHNOGIANT IS AS HIGH AS THE THEATRE WE SEE ON SLIDE SCREENS: — VIEWS OF INHUMAN CITIES —

HYDRALIKE FREEWAYS SWARMING WITH ANTLIKE CARS, HEARTLESS SKYSCRAPERS, PARKING LOTS, JUNKYARDS. THE WILDERNESS OF THE BRONX AND DOWNTOWN DETROIT ALREADY SPROUT HERE IN SMALL PATCHES. BUT WHEN THE SHADOW OF RATTLEBABY IS BIGGEST WE SEE FOREST CITY FROM CONCESSION SIX, LONDON TOWNSHIP, NEAR HILLS BY ADELAIDE STREET — LITERALLY A CITY HIDDEN BY TREES. WE SEE ALL THE KINDS OF MARVELLOUS TREES IN TOWN HERE, GARDENS, HOUSES, LAWNS, HAPPY-LOOKING STREETS IN ALL SECTIONS OF TOWN. AS THE PLAY BEGINS, THE TECHNOGIANT IS AT HIS BIGGEST AND IN FILE THREE PIECE SUIT EXPERTS TO PRAY FOR ADVICE FROM IT: HIS MOUTH-PIECE IS AN EXECUTIVE KNOWN AS MR EARPHONES WHO HAD LATELY TAKEN PART IN A MULTINATIONAL GRAB OF ALL FOR-EST CITY'S POWER BASES, INSTITUTIONS, SCHOOLS, ETC. THE YEAR IS 1982 AND YOU MAY SAY 'IMPOSSIBLE', BUT SO SAID OTHER SMALL CITIES IN THE PAST WHO NOW SEETHE WITH ANTLIKE ACTIVITY, TECHNOGIANT ACTIVITY, UNCON-TROLLABLE VIOLENCE OR — LIKE GLASGOW OR NEW YORK — HAVE BURNT THEMSELVES OUT AFTER THEIR LOVE AFFAIR WITH THE MULTINATIONAL GIANT.[239]

London, Ontario calls itself 'The Forest City,' and the city does boast a lot of trees. In places, it's very pretty. Then go downtown, where two whole city blocks were razed in order to erect a mall, and a whole block of 'heritage' buildings on Talbot St. was razed to build a stadium. TECHNOGIANT at work. When I was last in London, November 2019, it looked to me as though TECHNOGIANT had got at the university campus, such was the mammoth expansion since I taught there. So yes, the GIANT is loose in the world. The truth of it doesn't necessarily make for good drama. Or good fiction. On their drive home from British Columbia, in *Take the Big Picture*, the Delahay family gets lost and encounters two competing carwashes.

[A]cross the road from the Bigfoot Carwash, was a rival car-cleaning establishment called Mister Automat. Looking, with its plastic and chrome surfaces, ever so much cleaner and efficient, its sign informed you that you could get your car washed automatically by just slipping quarters into a slot, positioning your car over a magnet, and—the machinery took over. Towering above this institution was a figure made of stainless steel, somewhat bigger and taller even than the Bigfoot effigy across the way. It was a cut-out of Mister Automat himself. He looked rather like that trophy they give away in Hollywood every year called the Oscar except that, up above his head, Mister Automat held a huge communications dish. Presumably, this dish received electronic signals from headquarters—in Los Angeles, as Colin later learned—and acted on your car accordingly. [240]

The family that runs the Bigfoot has found a way to sabotage Mister Automat, clearly one of TECHNOGIANT's operatives, so that Bigfoot is the only car-washing option in the neighbourhood. Well, the didactic impulse is driving *Take the Big Picture* throughout, vitiating its effectiveness as fiction.

Back to the bicycle. Just like Jones (in Scene 7: Crosswalk, one of my favourite moments in *Gentle Rain Food Co-op*), Reaney rode his bicycle from 276 Huron Street in London to his classes at Western University. In this scene Jones is

pedalling my bike out of the quieter reaches of the [Western] campus and into some quite heavy crosstown traffic.... As I dismounted my bike and pressed the pedestrian crossing button, (*traffic stops*) I felt, as I always do on such occasions, the tremendous sense of power over brute force it gives a fragile cyclist when he walks his bicycle across in front of two mobs of impatient and powerful, speedy automobiles.

DRIVER: (*muffled by glass of car window*) He's walking as slow as he can. For two cents I'd ...

JONES: But as long as the lights were flashing above me, I was safe.

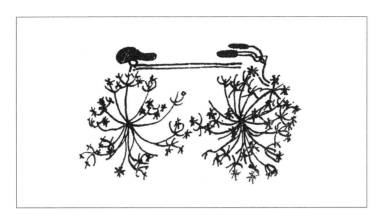

James Reaney, Bicycle with wheels of Queen Anne's Lace,

Twelve Letters to a Small Town.

(*resumption of traffic*) Ah the luxury of saying No! to fifty or so powerful engines throbbing impatiently. [241]

In *Twelve Letters to a Small Town* Reaney does what he can—but only in a drawing of a car, endowed with floral wheels—to make the automobile seem like some figment of the rural imagination. Otherwise,

> Like sharkfish the cars blur by,
>> Filled with the two-backed beast
> One dreams of, yet knows not the word for,
>> The accumulating sexual yeast. [242]

This is in 'Twelfth Letter,' called 'The Bicycle,' where, summing up the spirit of the book, the bicycle stands for the best of everything about small town life. Really, it's about childhood recuperated in adulthood, the very best of that life being ecstatic awareness of the intimate interrelationship of everything in life that Reaney was to lose for a spell during his university days, then later regain—the nub being, as he puts it in the editorial to *Alphabet* 1, his return to the belief that 'metaphor is reality.' [243]

Between the highschool & the farmhouse
    In the country and the town
It was a world of love and of feeling
    Continually floating down

On a soul whose only knowledge
    Was that everything was something,
This was like that, that was like this—
    In short, everything was
The bicycle of which I sing. [244]

A brief abstract analogue of this anagogic bicycle is one of the ideas from William Dale's journals and letters' offered by the Chorus in Reaney's play, *The Dismissal*, then repeated for emphasis: 'The integral versus the fractional life.' [245] Gerald Parker calls this 'the key expression' of the play. [246] Reaney wanted the integral life for himself and for more of his characters than just the heroes of *The Dismissal*. Dale's line will show up more than once below.

Living an integral life, holding on to his integrity and his soul, costs Dale his teaching job at a University of Toronto of 1895 dominated by 'sacred cows and stuffed shirts.' [247] Of the 'St. Mary's music' associated with Dale in the play, an author's footnote says: 'This music is part of the realization of there being a happy, serene Dale world; it first reached the author's ears as snatches of English and Swedish folk tunes coming up through the floor above the girl's gymnasium into the author's geography class at Stratford Collegiate in 1940. The teacher in the room below was Frances Dale, William Dale's daughter.' [248] In an early story, 'Sleigh Without Bells,' a young man from another township who has 'fallen in love with the Donnellys' [249] encounters Mr. and Mrs. Donnelly under duress. 'I saw at a distance Mrs Donnelly helped down from the cutter by a friend. Immediately she was recognizable—towering above all the other people. Both she and her husband were impeded by their being handcuffed, but their dignity and serenity were not in the least affected.' [250]

'World' and 'Kingdom' are frequently repeated Reaney metaphors for the structures people live within, serene or otherwise. Serene worlds are those Reaney sponsors. He recorded support from other sources in the editorial to *Alphabet* 6: 'If Gutenberg's invention produced a society hypnotized by the resultant overuse of the eye, then McLuhan's "unified sensibility" [in *The Gutenberg Galaxy*] provides a way out. Like Frye's vision of an infinitely extended human imagination, McLuhan is defining a goal that our world desperately needs.'[251] In the 'Author's Note' to *Colours in the Dark*, Reaney writes that

Surely one of the things theatre could be about is the relaxed awareness that comes when you simply play.... Life could be an endless procession of stories, an endless coloured comic strip, things to listen to and look at, a bottom-less playbox.

I suppose that in the Age of Dread in which we live this may seem to some foolish. I disagree. At rehearsals … here was such a peaceable kingdom, energetic, joyful and serene—it made the world of dread much easier to face afterwards.[252]

The peaceable kingdom allusion here is to the American Quaker minister Edward Hicks, whose sixty-two painted versions of Isaiah 11:6 date from the 1830s. In perhaps the most famous of his pictures, wild and domestic animals consort with each other and with three young women. It's another of these pictures that Northrop Frye picks to help him sum up 'emblematically' the argument of his 'Conclusion to a *Literary History of Canada*': In the background of this Hicks picture

is a treaty between the Indians and the Quaker settlers under Penn. In the foreground is a group of animals, lions, tigers, bears, oxen, illustrating the prophecy of Isaiah about the recovery of innocence in nature. Like the animals of the Douanier Rousseau, they stare past us with a serenity that transcends consciousness. It is a pictorial emblem of … the reconciliation of man with man and of man with nature: the mood of Thoreau's Walden retreat, of Emily

Dickinson's garden, of Huckleberry Finn's raft, of the elegies of Whitman. This mood is closer to the haunting vision of serenity that is both human and natural which we have been struggling to identify in the Canadian tradition. If we had to characterize a distinctive emphasis in that tradition, we might call it a quest for the peaceable kingdom.[253]

It's telling that Frye cites not only an American painting but also so much American literature before basically saying that what the Americans have is what Canadians are searching for. Not that it matters in the present context. Reaney was certainly looking for the peaceable kingdom (a worldly version of Eden and the New Jerusalem), doing his own best to establish it (and occasionally finding something of it in the native tradition—though David Willson, one of his exemplars, came to Canada from the United States in the era when many Canadians could be defined as Americans who rejected the revolution. *Taptoo!* is populated by such American-Canadians.)

Serene worlds are like the Bicycle world of 'love and feeling,' symbolic worlds anagogically containing 'everything.' Images for these worlds show up again and again in Reaney's writing. Near the end of Act One of *Night Blooming Cereus*, for example, the characters in Mrs. Brown's house '*stand tableau still as if time had quietly and suddenly stopped while in the gray sky above the village appears a vision of the night-blooming cereus opening in slow beach crashing swarming splendour and glory, a blossom larger than airplanes or zeppelins, four times really the size of the village, three times the size of Toronto, twice the size of Bethlehem and once the size of Eden.*'[254] The symbolism of this vision, quite clear in the words, would be difficult to show on the stage.

These anagogic worlds show up in some of the poetry of others that has been of special importance to Reaney: Isabella Valancy Crawford's poem, 'Malcolm's Katie,' for instance, and Jay Macpherson's poem, 'The Anagogic Man,' among them. The reprint of Crawford's *Collected Poems* comes with an Introduction by James Reaney; the passage in question is also quoted in his cross-Canada play, *Canada Dash, Canada Dot.*[255]

('She had a mind that was no doubt daily thinking about an iconic backbone of Eden, Beulah, Fallen World, Hell....')[256] 'The Anagogic Man' is a poem in Macpherson's book, *The Boatman*. Macpherson contributed a Preface to Reaney's play, *Listen to the Wind*. She was also a contributor to *Alphabet*, where the 'emblem drawings' she made to illustrate *The Boatman* appeared for the first time.[257] Here are two serene, inclusive passages side by side, which is how I believe they were companioned in Reaney's mind, along with instances of anagogy in his own works. Crawford:

> For love, once set within a lover's breast,
> Has its own sun, its own peculiar sky,
> All one great daffodil, on which do lie
> The sun, the moon, the stars, all seen at once
> And never setting, but all shining straight
> Into the faces of the trinity—
> The one beloved, the lover, and sweet love.[258]

Macpherson:

> *Noah walks with head bent down;*
> *For between his nape and crown*
> *He carries, balancing with care,*
> *A golden bubble round and rare.*
>
> *Its gently shimmering sides surround*
> *All us and our worlds, and bound*
> *Art and life, and wit and sense,*
> *Innocence and experience.*
>
> *Forbear to startle him, lest some*
> *Poor soul to its destruction come,*
> *Slipped out of mind and past recall*
> *As if it never was at all.*

O you that pass, if still he seems
One absent-minded or in dreams,
Consider that your senses keep
A death far deeper than his sleep.

Angel, declare: what sways when Noah nods?
The sun the stars, the figures of the gods.[259]

Those poetic expressions of wholeness, of everything gathered into one global, encyclopedic symbol show up again and again in especially intense key moments in Reaney's writing. They are expressions of anagogic sensibility.

The need to work toward a recovery of that integrative capacity might be illustrated by 'Winnipeg Seen as a Body of Time & Space,' Part II of a suite of poems called 'A Message to Winnipeg.' The poem records an historical decline from anagogic existence to severely limited existence trapped in the quotidian and enveloped by technology. The metaphorical technique is the blazon, or catalogue of body parts.

Before human occupation, Winnipeg had hair of grass, arms of burr oaks. Its backbone 'was a crooked silver muddy river,' and so on. At the end of the first stanza, 'your blood was a people/ Who did what the stars did and the sun.'[260] The local and the universal are—they were—one.

The second stanza brings in the settlers, identified later as French Métis. This first stage of development is seen as more or less neutral, not objectionable or harmful, because the minds of those occupying the land are still attuned to something beyond themselves: 'your people/ Had a blood that did what a star did and a Son.'[261]

The third stanza brings us right up to date by detailing a rape of the land and its accommodating occupants by TECHNOGIANT. Unsurprisingly, car parts figure in the body of this villain:

Then on top of you fell

A boneyard wrecked auto gent, his hair
Made of rusted car door handles, his fingernails
Of red Snowflake Pastry signs, his belly
Of buildings downtown; his arms of sewers,
His nerves electric wires, his mouth a telephone,
His backbone—a cracked cement street. His heart
An orange pendulum bus crawling with the human fleas
Of a so-so civilization—half gadget, half flesh—
    I don't know what I would have instead—
    And they did what they did more or less.[262]

I think I know what the speaker and the poet would have instead, sup-posing it were possible: a reversal of this decline: retreat from so-so, ho-hum, drifting, day-to-day, plain old existence back towards Eden or ahead to the New Jerusalem and anagogy. In many different works and ways, Reaney can be seen moving forward by moving back—to a time of 'unified sensibility,' to 'the integral rather than the fractional,' up and out—and recommending that all others do the same. The 'Invocation to the Muse of Satire' (another blazon poem) opens *A Suit of Nettles* this way: 'With Punch's stick (he holds it in his hand)/ Beat fertility into a sterile land....'[263] Meanwhile, in 1954, Reaney was obliged to look through the so-so civilization to see that 'beneath its *mask* of disorder and disconnection there lay somewhere a poetic city, a possible New Jerusalem, sometimes breaking through to whatever part of one's mind catches such messages.'[264]

Reaney is not with those poets who 'side with T.E. Hulme in regard-ing man as a limited bucket,' but rather with those who 'think that man is a limitless giant in power who may be asleep but is slowly rousing him-self...,'[265] those like himself, in other words, who follow the something-outside-themselves once called a muse: 'You don't challenge yourself very much when you just use your own personal experience, whereas the kind of muse that Yeats and Blake and Milton had is a genuine otherness that you have to tackle, you have to work at. It's not easy. Or [else] it's just confessing things.'[266] It may be a bit of a leap, but I seem to hear those writers who limit themselves to writing up 'personal experience' being associated with 'human fleas/ Of a so-so civilization.'

In reflections on a draft of this book, Sean Kane offers a timely reminder of pitfalls in following Blake on anagogy, one of them being to simplify what Blake does not. Conflating serene Beulah-like worlds and The New Jerusalem, as Reaney seems to do, is one of them. 'Beulah,' says Kane, 'is "a soft Moony Universe feminine" (Four Zoas). It is the desire for talking animals, motherly security, divine providence, peaceful order, the people "married' (*beulah*) to the land in Isaiah 62:4, literature, medicare, bicycles, pastoral self-satisfaction, harmony. But a state of perfect social harmony must mean the end of the life of the imagination. Blake is careful to separate "soft Beulah's night" from Eternity, which is the Voice in the whirlwind, fiery creativity, adventure, tricksterism, discovery, exuberance, wild beauty, wonder.'[267] '[I]t's difficult to write about anagogy,' he goes on, 'without having it distorted by the prejudices of time, space, and causality of the material world in which that writing is done—reducing the New Jerusalem to present-day reality rather than struggling to envision that reality transformed. Why Blake doesn't picture Eternity so well as epic struggles in the soul in getting there.'[268] Perhaps why The New Jerusalem in Reaney tends to count at the level of concept, compelling to him, but falling short of embodying what Kane elsewhere calls 'the majesty of the conception.'[269] Of course it's common enough for a writer to write *about* something, attempting to animate an idea and so offering much that is interesting but well short of the visionary. It's Reaney's *The Donnellys*, on the page and especially on the stage, that lifts off into the timeless, the universal.

Lighting Its Own Way

Reaney was a cyclist and a health food devotee. In these ways and many others, personal and literary, he opted out of life under the technologies that have us in thrall. But perhaps his most creative stand against technology was his do-it-yourself dramaturgy. In *Alphabet* 4, arguing for the importance of a 'native drama,' he says 'There should be a club that does nothing but seasons of plays by Canadians. It should do them in a bare, long room up above a store, probably infested by Odd Fellows or orangemen on easily avoidable nights. Nobody should have any truck with that grand Bugaboo—Lighting. Five two hundred Mazda watters always turned on will do for any play that lights its own way, as a play should.... What is most of all needed is not money, but a simple, austere idea.'[270] Of *Names & Nicknames*, he says 'This play takes place in the southwestern Ontario hamlet of Brocksden around 1900. The play was written with a bare stage in mind; all the stage setting can be accomplished with words, pantomime, the human body, music from rhythm band instruments, the audience themselves.... Dress the stage with a stepladder; when Thorntree climbs up on the roof to listen down the chimney this stepladder is all that is needed.'[271]

In various places, Reaney has acknowledged attending a performance of the Peking Opera as an influence on his plays, but it may be that the seed for open-concept drama was planted very early. '[O]ddly enough,' he says in an interview, 'I remember a lot of the old Samuel French catalogues for play equipment that my mother had. There was a Chinese play in one of them and the instructions for staging it said that you didn't have to have scenery for this and the stage-hands could be visible, moving things around and handing out the props. I read that in 1934, and it stayed with me for all those years. *Our Town* by Thornton Wilder is a North American example of that kind of play.'[272]

Here is how Jay Macpherson describes Reaney's dramaturgical

austerity in a production of *Listen to the Wind* that she took in: 'The music, composed or put together by the excellent teenage musicians we see on stage ['In homage to the Peking Opera whose visit to Canada changed my life, I always have music in my plays with the musicians in plain sight.'[273]], and the sound effects contributed by the chorus, provide half the life and atmosphere of the play. The chorus mime, recite, sing, thump, clap and play instruments from recorder to pop-bottle; waving antlers they are a forest, surging and whooshing they are the sea, holding flowers and twittering sweetly they are a dewy English garden. When needed, they mingle on stage as party guests or a pack of starving dogs. A letter sent to London in the inner play is passed from hand to hand through the chorus to its recipient standing far right: in such ways they are not there just to comment, like most choruses, but actively push the action on.'[274] Half the life and atmosphere of the play, that is, is created out of next to nothing. Macpherson goes on about the 'child's-play simplicity of the means by which [the] effects are created.... [W]hat is astonishing in Reaney's production is the sense of play, of freedom, of creation before one's eyes. Far from being instant or impromptu theatre, every action has been carefully planned; but the whole company has contributed to its planning, particularly in the highly inventive work of the chorus.'[275]

Each play makes different demands. Earlier I mentioned the lists Reaney compiled to begin forming *Wacousta!* Here is how he describes workshopping those lists: 'As I recall now, we took words and phrases from the novel and used them in choral chants which, with such musical instruments as eighty elastic bands, a drum (Laurie Bradley), piano and harpsichord (Dennis Kucherawy), fiddle (Jean McKay) and elmbark rattles I bought years ago at an Oshweken Arts Fair, shaped the sounds till the ear-picture was three dimensional and textured.'[276] 'Why the elastic bands?' he asks elsewhere. 'Their thrumming can be a most ominous sound suggestive of bowstrings, minds snapping, terror.... Our corner grocery gave me a whole bag of elastic bands for nothing, by the way, and hours can be spent just modulating this sound according to the varying lengths and thicknesses.'[277] Properly manipulated, in other words, plain old rubber bands may create aural metaphors. Who sees the metaphorical potential in such household items? A man of synaesthetic, 'innocent' imagination.

I mentioned above that the Prop List for the Donnelly Trilogy took up a whole page in *14 Barrels from Sea to Sea*. I won't list all the props here, just those for *Sticks & Stones*, the least prop-heavy play of the trilogy, and the list of general supplies for all three plays, every item notable for its ordinariness:

Sticks & Stones:
breaking fiddle, 2 thorn branches, handspike, surveyor's peg, bamboo cane, slingshot, I sawing block, 7 medium stones, 1 house window, cats cradle string, turnip sword, 5 water cloths, Mr. D silver glasses, rope handcuffs, 1 petition, 2 Union Jacks, census book, deed, mouth horseshoe, [278] pregnancy pillow &c.

SUPPLIES
fiddle sticks—15 pair
maple keys—48 handfuls, 3 handfuls a performance
ice block—1 does for 3 performances but
altar candles—6 pair
briquettes—85, 5 per performance
snow paper—just keep making it
milkweed—32 handfuls—30 pods enough
black veils—17
straw—33 handfuls for *St. Nick's* & *Handcuffs* 1 handfull &c.
barrels—13 medium, 1 huge. [279]

Craig Stewart Walker has a useful summary of what the props are used for in *Sticks & Stones*:

In the first play there are the eponymous sticks and stones. The obvious reference is to the child's defensive taunt, but Reaney makes it clear that name-calling *does* do a great deal of damage, a theme he treated earlier in *Names & Nicknames*. The sticks and stones introduce the theme of the dualities, the array of various opposing forces that are united in their efforts to crush the Donnellys. These images are given a physical presence in the ladders (sticks) and barrels (stones) of the play's set and props as well as in the conceptualized staging, which has the chorus continually breaking into 'sticks' and 'stones' factions—sometimes as armed Protestants and Catholics, sometimes as a simple gauntlet of enemies. The actors deliberately, relentlessly define the theatrical space; they dance in a reel that turns into a gauntlet; ladders are used to map out Biddulph ... and to pin a negro settler to the ground while his house is burnt ...; barrels filled with thorns and nails, in which social dissenters are rolled, come precariously close to steam-rolling members of the Donnelly family ...; rope is used to create an enormous cat's cradle—a plastic expression of the complex tensions between opposing ideological forces. Gradually, systematically, we see and hear the Donnellys threatened and hemmed in by, alternately, their neighbours' opinion and their own property boundaries. [280]

What is difficult to convey in words is the concurrent manyness of the theatrical experience of *The Donnellys*. It must have been extraordinarily difficult for the actors to be responsible for following so many more cues than those involved in blocking and speaking their lines. They were also tasked with miming non-human creatures, creating sound effects with voices as well as props, knowing when to sing or dance. All actors, on stage at all times, were an audience within the play, but they were almost never idle. This whirlwind of sight and sound became more organic as the run went on, but workshopping had made sure that the through-line of the story always caught up the audience and carried it along.

To Grumble

I want to pick up from where I left off in the section before the one just above. It would be easy to get one's back up at an image of ordinary human life ('human fleas/ Of a so-so civilization') conceived of as so very small and parasitical. *My* back goes up at times. It wants to object that art can be and has been made out of personal experience, that there are more roads to art than are dreamt of in your philosophy, Jamie. I hope that's not just my prairie boy's inbred resistance to being told what to do. (My mother understood perfectly well that seat belts in a car improve passenger safety, but she still resented government for telling her she *had* to buckle up.) Anyway, once in a while, Reaney's prescriptive tone makes me feel like grumbling. I think it's only honest to register this occasional flare-up of resistance. After all, I approach Reaney as a particular person with 'personal experience,' as a critic who has not burned off all his individual peccadilloes so as to represent himself as some paragon of objectivity. That critic says I'll go my own way on the path we share, Jamie. I'll wander off it as often as I like and in as many directions as I wish. There are a lot of writers likewise wandering. A good many of them have changed my life. All that prefab scaffolding erected by others on which to hang their symbols—I want to build my own containers from the ground up. Start that way, at least. Improvise. Not without company: 'random is a kingdom too   its fiefdoms confederated by collage'[281] (Phil Hall).

Also, and I've addressed this elsewhere at greater length,[282] I'm interested in what lies outside the 'verbal universe' and suspicious of the naming that aims to haul it all inside. It's not that Reaney is all for words; he has a deep respect for humble things, but there is still in his work the sense of primacy accorded the humanist world of words. 'Let the forest be in you, Frederick, not always Frederick in the forest,' says Oucanasta to Frederick de Haldimar in Reaney's play, *Wacousta!*[283] That's a lovely sentence, built on the criss-cross rhetorical scheme called chiasmus, and it's worth thinking on. It may have come from a book on Eskimo masks by D.J. Baker referred to in 'A Letter from James Reaney': 'Through the mask this society joined subject and object and implemented the very poetic belief ... that Baker sums up in: "Not me in the world, but the world in me."'[284] A less pleasing formulation of the same idea occurs in Reaney's essay, 'Vision in Canada?' 'In reading [David] Willson I used to get the feeling that he was turning you inside out and that you contain the world rather than the usual London, Ontario notion that the world contains you.'[285] On first reading Oucanasta's advice to Frederick de Haldimar, I thought, that makes sense: decentre the human, embrace the identity of the other. That is actually how it's meant to be taken. Oucanasta and Le Subtil, indigenous inhabitants of that forest, represent unspoiled wilderness and the open, loving mindset associated, for Reaney, with simpler times and undeveloped places, while the 'boneyard wrecked auto gent' of Detroit represents the opposite of all that in the play.

Still: the forest in Frederick. When I hear *Reaney* saying those words, rather than Oucanasta—and Reaney wrote them—they land a little differently. The forest goes within to join everything else in the 'inner world' of the verbal universe. Part of me says no, leave it be. There is a compromise position, of course: value the objective being of the 'outer world' for itself, *and* understand language to be a tool, often glorious, worthy of reverence, but not all-in-all. If one believes that there are important things, crucial experience, that cannot be put into words, that there is a kind of integrative thinking that is non-verbal (more on this later), and also knows of non-human networks of communication (more on this too), then one has to understand the limitations of the 'verbal universe.' Something of everything lies outside it.

As much as Reaney idealizes open space, forest, wilderness, there is a contradicting sense, perhaps reinforced by Frye, that nature is monstrous and hostile and must be conquered with words. Here is 'the basic state of man,' according to Reaney in an essay called 'Search for an Undiscovered Alphabet': 'man in the centre of an imprisoning universe, an island of joy washed by seas of dread.'[286] 'The surface story,' Reaney says of Henry

James's novel, *The Sacred Fount*, 'is a brilliant example of what Northrop Frye calls "displacement." Glorious archetypes swing by and so do noble terms with which thought has wrung a design from the ignorant chaos about us….'[287] That word 'ignorant' will jump out at any reader of contemporary books, like Peter Wohlleben's *The Hidden Life of Trees*, Diana Beresford-Kroeger's *To Speak for the Trees*, and Anna Lowenhaupt Tsing's *The Mushroom at the End of the World*. They show that even vegetation is smarter than we used to think.

> The brain of a tree argues
> more slowly [than ours]. It is busy
> remembering, calculating
> the complications of water,
> the needs of a neighbour,
> the translations of chlorophyll.
> It doesn't care to convince us.[288]

And the word 'evil' will scream out of this: 'Both Canadian and American literary symbolists have always been fighting to free New World man from the spiritual death that results if he succumbs to an unredeemed and secretly evil environment so frequently miscalled "natural."'[289] As Jesper Hoffmeyer says about the 'schism between nature and humanity … it is, of course, Descartes' dualism that is at work here, the idea of things intellectual as being independent and superior to things material.'[290]

'[W]hen you *really* get scared in our world,' Reaney says later in the article just quoted from, 'myth-making and the kind of image that humanizes our environment are an almost inevitable answer.'[291] I'm scared now, scared on behalf of the biosphere. I don't want to scuttle mythmaking, but I do want anthropocentric humanism mitigated by other contemporary approaches to theory and politics. 'Feminist concerns with matter take place in the context of a much broader intellectual shift that has emerged in the wake of humanism, structuralism, and poststructuralism,' writes Victoria Pitts-Taylor.[292] 'Most broadly,' she goes on, 'new materialism aims to rethink the terms of social theory, such that the social is seen as a part of, rather than distinct from, the natural, an undertaking that requires a rethinking of the natural too. New materialists are interested in exposing the movement, vitality, morphogenesis, and *becoming* of the material world, its dynamic processes, as opposed to discovery of immutable truths. New materialism sees a physical and biological world operating not according to fixed laws and blueprints, but rather one teeming with dynamism, flexibility, and novelty. Such a world is not determined; rather it is constantly in the processes of its making.'[293] 'Human lives' are always 'enmeshed in more-than-human worlds,'[294] says Stephanie Clare.

Now let me offer a poet's foray into this intersectional thought. Don McKay is himself one of the 'nature poets' he alludes to in his essay, '[ ] or Iconostalgia.' In disarmingly casual style, McKay loads a paragraph with information drawn from the science wing of New Materialist thinking.

Strains of thinking like New Materialism and Biosemiotics can provide inspirational support for the nature poet, blursed [blessed and cursed, McKay's neologism] as she (he, they) is with the task of addressing the natural world with symbolic language. Becoming aware that iconic and indexical signals are ubiquitous and effective certainly puts a crimp in human exceptionalism, but it also confirms our suspicion that more is going on than meets the analytic intelligence—a suspicion that has often been implicit in metaphor. Didn't it sometimes seem as though the trees in the forest were 'thinking'? Well, guess what. Do the Russula mushrooms have a thing going on with the Birch they're always hanging around? Yup. Did it seem that the shrews who abandoned their holes for higher ground sensed the hurricane's arrival a few hours later? Uh huh. And how about the signal sent from a corn species when under attack by caterpillars that you read about in one of Jesper Hoffmeyer's books? The corn emits a volatile compound called a terpenoid, that is carried on the wind and picked up by parasitic wasps, who are alerted to the presence of their caterpillar hosts on the corn plants, and (you guessed it) follow the terpenoid trail back to the imperiled corn, where they lay their eggs inside the invading caterpillars. (There are more things in heaven and earth, Horatio

….) A friend who is nursing tells me that if her baby gets sick, the presence of the virus alerts her body to produce antibodies, which are relayed back to the baby in the milk. Also that if her baby is very thirsty, a more watery milk of greater volume is delivered. (Horatio, make that more things in heaven, earth, and us.) [295]

The tone is light, but the ecological content, well outside the humanist box, is serious.

'To modern science,' says Jesper Hoffmeyer, '[Cartesian] dualism still holds good as a way of dividing the world into two kingdoms, those of mind and of matter, the cultural and the natural spheres. Non-intervention is still the easiest compromise and one which ensures that both the humanities and the natural sciences can get on with their work undisturbed. And it is this boundary that biosemiotics [life seen as a net-work of sign processes] seeks to cross in hopes of establishing a link between the two alienated sides of our existence—to give humanity its place in nature.' [296] As we'll see, Reaney came down hard on the humani-ties side of the 'two cultures.' He parted company from pretty well any kind of science quite early on. Humanism was under critique even in his own time, of course, and it looks even less viable now that poets and scien-tists are reaching across the divide to learn from each other. It's no reproach that Reaney wasn't up on thinking that really began to flow together after he was gone, though it was already present in writers like poet and scientist Loren Eiseley, but it's always cautionary to find gaps in the work of an expansive thinker.

There is obviously, palpably, something material that is outside our-selves. It's called the biosphere. Once closely and respectfully examined, it can't be viewed as a mere stage for humans to act on and otherwise take for granted, let alone as something foreign. It has order—well, *orders*: multiple, dynamic systems. It has 'wisdom,' and it certainly is inspiring. Reaney's humanism did not position him to appreciate all that in its full significance, even though, in some ways, he was right on the edge of it. The farm boy never forgot the cycle of planting, growing, harvesting. For years, he maintained a garden at the ancestral home outside of Stratford and planted evergreens there to replace trees that had been cut down. He'd be out there gardening on weekends. There were two flower garden plots back of the London house, one Jamie's and one Colleen's. Colleen also had a vegetable plot.

Reaney sometimes taught Ontario Literature and Culture, a graduate course focused on 'one of the most unpopular and misunderstood Canadian provinces' that he hoped students would come to see as 'a big poem rather than an elusive mystery or an exercise in materialism.'[297] '[I]f the course were just Ontario literature,' he says, 'you would be missing a big echo chamber'[298] of 'extradisciplinary layers'[299] composed of Indigenous materials, history, 'thinkers' like William Maurice Bucke, Harold Innis and David Willson, painters like David Milne, and geographers (Chapman and Putnam's *Physiography of Southern Ontario* was a text). Fred Urquhart's *The Ontario Leaf Album*, a sort of botanical manual/workbook, was also on the course. I liked the idea of such a book and bought a copy for myself. Reaney wanted his students foraging outside literature, into related disciplines and especially into nature. 'Men who love wisdom,' Heraclitus wrote, 'must be good enquirers into many things indeed' for 'Nature loves to hide.'[300]

'In a way,' says Reaney, 'killdeer [bird], tree and weed identification is what my course is all about. I happen to believe that if you don't know the weed that grows at your doorstep—knotweed—or the grass that grows in cemeteries—orchard or poverty grass—or the name of the tree outside your window, then you're not rooted in your environment.'[301] *The Ontario Leaf Album* was to encourage students to venture out into The Forest City or the country, identify a member of each species and gather a leaf to press into the book. The field trips were 'to enable students to take time to look around themselves at leaves and bark; there's a great deal of mooning about forested landscapes but precise knowledge shows real love and breeds the same quality.'[302]

We are clearly not looking at a standard English course. Trees are not texts, at least they were not for other members of Western's English department, and tree-readers would still be scarce in English departments elsewhere in the world. Not that Reaney was going for a biologist's approach to trees. 'You may ask,' Reaney writes, 'what difference does this really make?'[303] and he goes on to make something interesting of a brief passage in Alice Munro's story 'Wild Swans' ('As the train crossed the Niagara Escarpment above Dundas, as they looked down at the preglacial valley, the silver-wooded rubble of little hills, as they came sliding down to the shores of Lake Ontario....'[304]) I'm reminded of Reaney's description of the *Alphabet* procedure: 'What every issue of *Alphabet* involves, then, is the placing of a definite geometric shape near some face cards.' Clearly, physiography text and leaf book and all the rest were to be the geometric shapes placed beside poetry and fiction on the course, and clearly that strategy works. At least it does for me. I had never given any attention to that Munro passage; seeing it highlighted was an eye-opener. New eyes to see with: a gift.

Something else: I once met Reaney in the hall of University College, Western's arts building, holding a mushroom delicately between thumb and forefinger. I didn't say anything, I just smiled and passed by. I hope now he didn't think the smile was satirical. A fungus-toting prof might occasionally be encountered in the biology building, but arts? I'd like to have the moment back so I could ask Jamie where he got that mushroom, what kind it was, what he meant to do with it.

Trees and mushrooms take us back to those thinking trees and mushrooms hanging around with birch in what Don McKay says above. Because it turns out that trees *are* texts, and so are mushrooms. Reading them, as Suzanne Simard figured out how to do, shows that they communicate with each other. As a kid, Simard loved the British Columbia rainforest where she grew up. Anyone who has visited that forest will remember it as magical and, like Simard, will probably lament clear-cutting. As an adult biologist, she got to studying those forests and discovered that when the unprofitable birch and aspen were removed from clear-cuts, reseeded Douglas fir did poorly. To figure out why was to help unsettle a central tenet of Darwinian thinking—competition—that had become fixed, and to complicate the picture with the fact of species cooperation, or symbiosis. ('Translated literally from the Greek, symbiosis means the state of living together, and in biology it denotes a very close and enduring association between two species.'[305]) 'It seems that every big idea, however revolutionary its origin,' says Don McKay about competition, 'has the potential to become both rigid and imperial.'[306] (I remind myself and my reader that it's in people that those big ideas get stuck. We get stuck in smaller ideas too, and the ruts often go deep.)

Simard began to wonder what was going on under the soil that might shed light on the relationship of birch, aspen and fir. She discovered that they were in fact cooperating members of a cross-species family. They were communicating through mycorrhizal networks. Simard calls them 'inter-linking fungal highways.' 'Mycorrhiza,' she says, 'literally means "fungus root." You see their reproductive organs when you walk through the forest. They're the mushrooms. The mushrooms, though, are just the tip of the iceberg, because coming out of those stems are fungal threads [hyphae] that form a mycelium, and that mycelium infects and colonizes the roots of all the trees and plants. And where the fungal cells interact with the root cells, there's a trade of carbon for nutrients, and that fungus gets those nutrients by growing through the soil and coating every soil particle. The web is so dense that there can be hundreds of kilometers of mycelium under a single footstep. And not only that, that mycelium connects different individuals in the forest, individuals not only of the same species but between species, like birch and fir, and it works kind of like the Internet.'[307]

The experimental method was to inject radioactive carbon isotopes into the trees to plot where they might turn up. They turned up in the vascular systems of trees far from the injection site. Further tests showed that the fir were receiving more carbon from the fungal system than they were transmitting. That's why they declined when birch were removed. Reforestation good, monoculture bad. On the cover of *Nature*, where Simard's findings were published in 1977, were these words: 'the wood-wide web.' The forest, Simard demonstrated, was a 'cooperative system' producing 'forest wisdom.' She calls this 'a kind of intelligence.'

In a Ted Talk, and two talks at Ted Summit, 2016, which summarize her findings for a general audience, Simard makes it clear that *everything* in the forest is interlinked. Bears feed on salmon, for example, then leave the bones to rot useful nitrogen into the soil which is picked up and passed along by those mycorrhizal networks. In one talk she compares the support group of friends and family helping her through breast cancer to the interactive systems of nature. Her final point is that humans are not aloof from all that. We are a part of it, it *is* us, and our own survival depends on whether or not we can turn around and become custodians of a whole multifaceted complex that is eloquently nonverbal.

As I've suggested, there was a large part of Reaney that headed out: away from the academy and books, back to the farm or into the woods, a part that embraced culture *and* nature and regularly denounced the deleterious effects of unchecked technology on both. But there was a block to advanced thinking along those lines: the humanist verbal universe that was supposed, in what is now often called 'the linguistic turn,' to subsume everything. It valorizes human language over every other communicative system; it makes humans paramount, disastrously superior to and detached from the biosphere. '*Protagoras*/ says Socrates, says Plato,' writes Robert Bringhurst,

> *spends a lot*
> *of time indoors.* How else would anyone
> imagine *Homo sapiens* the measure
> of all things?[308]

Frye was much more the indoorsman than Reaney, but Reaney, despite his love of nature, also remained a humanist. Consider one of my favourite late Reaney poems, 'The Wild Flora of Elgin County.' It was quoted in full, above, but I'd like another look at the concluding lines:

> So all these plant families are people,
> People you should know,

And become more serene & thoughtful

In doing so

He loved those flowers, but he personified them. Or should that be *and* he personified them? There are two ways to look at this and I mean to keep both: 1) to make flowers into people is to efface their biological identity, 2) to make flowers into people is to acknowledge that they are family. When I first read this poem, I flat-out loved it; now there's a *but*. *But* the personification anthropomorphizes. Yes, let's get to know these families, let's by all means become more thoughtful, *but* let's also try to get to know these flowers on their own terms. Reaney was all about revolution, on *his* terms. With much assistance from fascinating research outside Reaney's range, I now see that he was conservative in some ways, *but* I have no intention of letting go of most of what he was and stood for (same goes for Frye). I don't want all that flung out with the bathwater. Here is one reason why:

Act one of *The St. Nicholas Hotel*, second play of the Donnelly trilogy, begins with a race between the (Protestant) Finnegan Stage and the (Catholic) Opposition Stage run by Will and Michael Donnelly. This is well *before* the feud has reached its climax. But the scene is intercut with another that takes place long *after* the massacre, when Will Donnelly and his wife Norah are running the hotel in Appin, Ontario. In the present, Will and Norah have a guest, a Presbyterian minister who was in and out of Biddulph during the bad times, but never involved in the feud. 'It's seldom anyone comes down this road from the past, from up there,'[309] Will says, so he inveigles the minister into staying an extra night, partly to save him from 'driving seven miles on through a blizzard,'[310] and at night, but mainly to have an opportunity to reminisce. This night is not just any night. Will has lit a candle to remember his brother Michael, who was killed on this night, December 9, 1879, first Donnelly to succumb to the vendetta. Time and place, voices and perspectives, are layered in pretty well every scene in this and the other two plays. One reason I think of this subtly designed scene now is to say that the whole trilogy is structured very like one of those complex, interlinked underground systems identified by Suzanne Simard. Another reason is the word 'competition' that appears in it.

Right here, two times and places are woven together. Also, fourth wall and dialogue suddenly and seamlessly give way to narration addressed to the audience, which is again 'interrupted' by an exchange of dialogue from over twenty years earlier:

DONALDSON Now, sir, I've met you somewhere before. The name of the hotel you are running is the St. Nicholas Hotel, proprietor is—

WILL My name is William Donnelly. *pause*
Perhaps you'll want to hitch up your cutter again.

DONALDSON Now why would you say that, Mr Donnelly?

WILL Aren't you afraid of me?

DONALDSON No. Quite the contrary. I remember you and your brother when you ran the stage between London and Lucan, excuse me **one** of the stages. The Opposition stage.

NORAH That must be a good many years ago, sir. Twenty years?

DONALDSON More than that. I started visiting the Presbyterian Church in Lucan on appointments which I would receive, oh let me see now—the fall of 1875. I preferred your stage although people at the church warned me not to patronize your line. *to us* Once I happened to come down to Lucan from Parkhill by train—hence to Irishtown by your rival's stage—The Finnegan Line. I asked the driver how the new railway had affected the stage route between London and Lucan. What has become of the Donnellys?

STAGE DRIVER *belching* Ugh, the Donnellys've been run off the line at last.

DONALDSON   And what do they do now then?

STAGEDRIVER   Yes, what don't they do, sir. They're a bad lot and we're bound to get rid of them.

DONALDSON   Yes, Mr. Donnelly. A small glass of wine would not go amiss. Thank you. Then I said *to him* It's strange that young men so good looking and polite as I've always found the Donnelly boys to be, should be so much run down and set on by all parties, Romanists, Protestants and Secretists, when they are so very polite and strive so hard to live down all this opposition, by attention to business, and kind treatment of all who favour them. He replied:

STAGE DRIVER   You do not know them, sir. They just put on appearances to deceive strangers. I once thrashed Mike and I will thrash him again.

DONALDSON   *pause*   Which son is Mike?

STAGE DRIVER   The second youngest. No sir, the people are bound to get rid of that family some way or another and that too before too long.

DONALDSON   We had reached the railway station and I told him what I thought as a teacher of the Gospel. I said: 'You surely do not mean what you say, or you would not speak so to a stranger: there's room enough for the Donnellys and their opponents also in the world. Why, man, competition is the life of trade; we are all the better of the opposition lines.'

STAGE DRIVER   *laughing*   You're too good yourself, sir, to understand what this family is like. **We** are bound to snuff out that family and we shall do it, so that it shall never be known how it was done.

DONALDSON   He turned on his heel and left. So, yes, I was never afraid of the Donnellys. William Donnelly. Mike Donnelly.

WILL   About when would that conversation be?

DONALDSON   In January of 1879. As early as that

WILL   As early as that then we were marked out for slaughter.[311]

Donaldson was outside the feud, as I've said. He never understood the
hatred that drove it, never saw what more was going on in those stage races
than mere commercial rivalry. Reaney was no fan of capitalism—money
'seems like an uncontrollable demon in our society'[312]—but he properly
lets his character espouse it. Reverend Donaldson's endorsement of
competition came to me as I was thinking of the symbiotic cooperation of
plants. In one of her Ted Talks, Suzanne Simard doesn't venture far into
politics or economics, except to push for mitigation of industrial clear-
cutting to slow climate change, but she was on the way to a critique of capitalism. It's to books like Anna Lowenhaupt Tsing's *The Mushroom at the
End of the World: On the Possibility of Life in Capitalist Ruins* that we may
wish to turn for that.

  'First nature,' for Tsing, is the ecology of relations including both
nature and humans. 'Second nature' brings in capitalist inroads: 'all that
taming and mastering has made such a mess that it is unclear whether life
on earth can continue.'[313] 'My book then,' she goes on, 'offers "third
nature," that is, what manages to live despite capitalism.'[314] Partly
informing the explorations she goes on to make, and recalling Reaney's
focus on STORIES, are 'fabulists, including non-Western and non-civiliza-
tional storytellers, [who] remind us of the lively activities of all beings,
human and not human.'[315] The stories Tsing tells are like those: 'such stories might be simultaneously true and fabulous. How else can we account
for the fact that anything is alive in the mess we have made.'[316] The main
'character' in the stories she tells is the matsutake mushroom ('wild mushrooms that live in human-disturbed forests'[317]) with its supporting cast:
the forests in which matsutake thrive, the matsutake foragers, and the
economies they improvise. 'To even notice third nature, we must evade

assumptions that the future is that singular direction ahead. Like virtual particles in a quantum field, multiple futures pop in and out of possibility; third nature emerges within such temporal polyphony. Yet progress stories have blinded us. To know the world without them, this book sketches open-ended assemblages of entangled ways of life, as these coalesce in coordination across many kinds of temporal rhythms.'[318] This again recalls Reaney: 'Maybe if we get used to seeing our society as being based on a story, we'll wake up and realize we can get a better story....'[319] Jesper Hoffmeyer wants a better story, one in which 'our individual life stories' are not 'divorced from our genetic history. Or, to put it another way: *Not one but two stories are being enacted in the human body and consciousness.'*[320]

Those mushrooms and all that they mean are so fascinating that I could keep going on about them, but I have a little more (affectionate) grumbling to do. I need to push a little harder at some of the grounds for my resistance. I actually echo Reaney's faith in some ways, though I'm not a Christian. The figure of Jesus suffuses Reaney's work; it scarcely enters mine. I have never had any overwhelming revelation. No angel has visited—except maybe once, in a wordless dream so vivid that I often think of it with wonder. It has never been for me as it was for Margaret Avison:

Early on the morning of January 4, 1963, dressed for work as usual, I read on [in the book of John] 'You believe in God, believe also in Me' (John 14:1). I did believe in God. Whoever had spoken, the 'Me'—it was not visual, but not a mere feeling—that Person was impingingly present, before me. Not even questioning this strange visitation, I spoke: 'If I believe in You, You will take over. I'll believe, but oh, don't take the poetry. It's all I've got left.' An ancient poet describes the confrontation: 'Put me in remembrance; let us contend together. State your case' (Isaiah 43: 26). It infuriated me to feel that my 'case' was weakened and about to crumble. Finally I hurled the Bible across the room and said, 'Okay, take the poetry too!'

I think I expected to lose my identity then. But what happened was odd. On the cleared desktop, what looked like iron filings appeared, all joggled about, until they began to arrange themselves in a design—angles, arcs, curving lines. After a few moments the desk was its plain, old surface again, cluttered with papers.[321]

Take that remarkable passage out of context, as I've just done by cutting it out of Avison's autobiography, and it may seem as though conversion came out of the blue. It didn't. Put it back in the context of Avison's upbringing in the loving family of a minister father, her period of apostasy during university days and thereafter, an annoying encounter with a true believer, and, two years after that, an impulsive decision to enter Knox Presbyterian Church in Toronto for a Sunday service, the same church she used to pass, with a bottle, on the way to university parties. She sits in a pew on Sundays for months, with her bible but without faith, though respecting the sermons of the minister, Dr. William Fitch. 'Finally, leaving the service one time, I stopped a woman outside and said: "I keep hearing about faith in there. You people have it. I don't. What am I supposed to do?" She suggested I make an appointment through his secretary and ask the minister. In due course I did.'[322] It was Dr. Fitch who suggested that she 'go home and read and reread the Gospel of John—daily.'[323]

All that preamble leads up to the conversion but doesn't explain it. Not even Avison's intellectual curiosity and the primacy of poetry in her life, her capacity to bring on 'a slight dissociation of sight and hearing, so that undirected receptors allow the world around to flow uncensored into consciousness'[324]—in other words, to subvert the reasoning faculty— not even all that will explain it. In fact I don't want to explain it. I just want to respect it and try to say something about why I'm bringing it in here. I've been thinking that some version of a preamble, like Avison's preparation for her vision, might be shared by many people never decisively impinged upon by any Person. I wonder if the thousands of aha! moments (aha!: eureka effect, mild form of epiphany) that accrue in a life dedicated to finding things out might build to something—perpetually pre- conversion, but nevertheless preparation for belief that conversion does happen, that some people really do have visions. Half the way there?

Three quarters? I like what Iain McGilchrist says about belief held in the right hemisphere of the brain, as distinct from the left, where certainties become fixed. 'The disposition of the right hemisphere, the nature of its attention to the world,' he writes, 'is one of care, rather than [left hemisphere] control. Its will relates to a desire or *longing* towards something, something that lies beyond itself, towards the Other.'[325] 'The right hemisphere does not "know" anything, in the sense of certain knowledge. For it, belief is a matter of care: it describes a *relationship*, where there is a calling and an answering, the root concept of "responsibility".'[326] One thing is plain to me: some of the most important things cannot be explained. If words could ever be definitive, the works of a writer like Shakespeare would not have excited whole libraries of commentary. The mystery keeps us going. It must be respected. Truly respected, it might make some of us think differently.

'I don't know whether you've ever had the … the experience of having your life changed by a quite trivial incident. You know, nothing dramatic like the death of a parent, or the birth of a child. Something *so* trivial you almost can't see *why* it had the effect it had.'[327] This is psychiatrist William Rivers talking to his colleague, Henry Head. They are people who actually lived, fictionalized in Pat Barker's novel, *Regeneration*. Before he was a psychiatrist, Rivers was an anthropologist. The incident happened on a mission boat, the Southern Cross, while Rivers was on a research trip to the Solomon Islands. Meeting a group of islanders on the boat, Rivers decides to go through his 'usual routine' and ask them questions, the first being what would they do if they found a guinea. Would they share it? If so, with whom? The questions are intended to 'uncover all kinds of things about kinship structure and economic arrangements, and so on.' Rivers asks his questions, then the islanders decide to turn things round and ask him the same ones.

Starting with: What would *I* do with a guinea? Who would I share it with? I explained I was unmarried and that I wouldn't necessarily feel obliged to share it with anybody. They were *incredulous*. How could anybody live *like that*?

And so it went on, question after question. And it was one of those situations, you know, where one person starts laughing and everybody joins in and in the end the laughter just feeds off itself. They were rolling round the deck by the time I'd finished. And suddenly I realized that *anything* I told them would have got the same response. I could have talked about sex, repression, guilt, fear—the whole sorry caboodle—and it would've got exactly the same response. They wouldn't've felt a twinge of disgust or disapproval or … sympathy or anything, because it would all have been *too bizarre*. And I suddenly saw that their reactions to my society were neither more nor less valid than mine to theirs. And do you know that was a moment of the most *amazing* freedom. I lay back and I closed my eyes and I felt as if a ton weight had been lifted.'

… It was … the *Great White God* de-throned, I suppose. Because we did, we quite unselfconsciously *assumed* we were the measure of all things. That was how we approached them. And suddenly I saw not only that we weren't the measure of all things, but *there was no measure*.[328]

One more thing, a story out of personal experience that may have some bearing on this matter. A fellow grows up in the 1940s, 1950s and 1960s. He's reasonably smart, big reader, graduates from high school and university, gets a good teaching job. How could such a with-it fellow also be a simpleton? Easy: he has no clue that he's blindly and blithely living inside the patriarchal system. It formed him; he can't see it. So he gets married, expects the wife to do the shopping and the cooking. He's not a total twit; he'll do the washing up, take out the garbage. Bully for him. He and his wife have kids. Who does most of the child rearing? You're getting the picture. So how to wake this guy up? Fracture the marriage, transform him into a single parent. Now who's doing all the shopping and cooking and child rearing as well as the teaching? Struggling to keep it all together? That's right. He is enlightened and chastened. 'I was blind but now can see,' goes the spiritual, and so it goes for him. But it's only one new thing he sees now—one big thing that was recently, appallingly, invisible. How can he trust his personal vision now? He can't. He is estranged from himself. Good thing.

Enough of the third person. I do think of myself as a faltering believer. I have had my own sort of religious experience. During a transcendent evening at the Stratford Festival in 1972, William Hutt as King Lear made me forget I was in a theatre. That was one of the times when I felt in my bones what it is I'm living and working for. I was again transported into that bone-deep, reverent affirmation by viewing each of the Donnelly plays one by one, then by *living* the trilogy all on one day.

One strand of *The Stonemason*, a play by Cormac McCarthy, is the standard dramatic interaction between members of the Telfair family; the other is a series of monologues by Ben Telfair, who loves working at masonry with his grandfather. In the monologues, he outlines his deep consciousness of what they are both engaged in. 'I don't know where the spirit resides,' he says. 'I think in all things rather than none. My experience is very limited. But it is because of him [his grandfather] that I am no longer reduced by these mysteries but rather am one more among them.'[329]

[T]rue masonry is not held together by cement but by gravity. That is to say, by the warp of the world. By the stuff of creation itself. The keystone that locks the arch is pressed in place by the thumb of God.... He talks to me about stone in a different way from my father. Always a thing of consequence. As if the mason were a custodian of sorts. He speaks of sap in the stone. And fire. Of course he's right. You can smell it in the broken rock. He always watched my eyes to see if I understood. Or to see if I cared. I cared very much. I do now. According to the gospel of the true mason God has laid the stones in the earth for men to use and he has laid them in their bedding planes to show the mason how his own work must go. A wall is made the same way the world is made. A house, a temple. This gospel must accommodate every inquiry.[330]

The stonemason's gospel is anthropocentric in this version, but I like the reverence. Some such gospel should attend every sort of making.

'[O]nce you are in touch with the tradition,' Reaney says, 'there's not much you are missing, in a way.'[331] Well, I am in touch with my tradition and also with my miracle of a planet. I owe each of them a debt that cannot be settled. Like any debt that must be carried, these obligations are sometimes heavy, but never mind that. For those with some intellectual capacity and/or artistic inclination, it's a responsibility to keep growing, keep on seeking better ways to shape whatever is given us to make, because whatever we make is not for ourselves alone.

But I have no grid. I'm constitutionally eclectic. I improvise away. It makes me happy. That's who I am, so I have to make the best of it—even if it shows me to be a fool, and therefore insignificant, because 'fools are of no importance in any age.'[332] 'The wise man,' says Northrop Frye, 'has a pattern or image of reality in his mind into which everything he knows fits, and into which everything he does not know could fit, and therefore his approach to knowledge is something that the dung-beetles of unorganized learning cannot even grasp.'[333] I *can* grasp and even respect what the 'wise' ones do with their portmanteau patterns—if not, I wouldn't be writing this—but I don't have any such pattern myself, neither do I want one, not to start out with. Moil around in the ordure, I guess, see what I can figure out from there.

Actually, that might not be a bad idea. Look at the crap and learn from it. That's what Jane Bennett has done. One of the new materialists mentioned above, she had her own sort of vision while looking at a pile of garbage in Baltimore, Maryland:

Glove, pollen, rat, cap, stick. As I encountered these items, they shimmied back and forth between debris and thing—between stuff to ignore, except insofar as it betokened human activity (the workman's efforts, the litterer's toss, the rat-poisoner's success), and, on the other hand, stuff that commanded attention in its own right, as existents in excess of their association with human meanings, habits, or projects. In the second moment, stuff exhibited its thing-power: it issued a call, even if I did not quite understand what it was saying. At the very least, it provoked affects in me: I was repelled by the dead (or was it merely sleeping?) rat and dismayed by the litter, but I also felt something else: a nameless awareness of the impossible singularity of *that* rat, *that* configuration of pollen, *that* otherwise utterly banal, mass-produced plastic water-bottle cap.[334]

'Why advocate the vitality of matter?' Bennett asks in her book, *Vibrant Matter*, as she moves into her capacious study of 'thing-power,' embracing philosophy, the sciences and the arts: a confluence of sophisticated thinking that bears on ecology, and is meant to influence political theory and practice. 'Because,' she answers, 'my hunch is that the image of dead or thoroughly instrumentalized matter feeds human hubris and our earth-destroying fantasies of conquest and consumption.'[335] 'We need to cultivate a bit of anthropomorphism—the idea that human agency has some echoes in nonhuman nature—to counter the narcissism of humans in charge of the world.'[336] Why? Because what Don McKay, updating Christopher Smart, says of trilobites must be said of so much more of the non-human: 'for they mean but do not speak or write.'[337]

I think of Jane Bennett and William Rivers as kin of poet and scientist Loren Eiseley. His writing predates that of Bennett and the new materialism, but Eiseley was also a reader of garbage.

No one, I suppose, would believe that an archaeologist is a man who knows where last year's lace valentines have gone, or that from the surface of rubbish heaps the thin and ghostly essence of things human keeps rising through the centuries until the plaintive murmur of dead men and woman may take precedence at times over the living voice. A man who has once looked with the archaeological eye will never see quite normally. He will be wounded by what other men call trifles. It is possible to refine the sense of time until an old shoe in the bunch grass or a pile of nineteenth-century beer bottles in an abandoned mining town tolls in one's head like a hall clock. This is the price one pays for learning to read time from surfaces other than an illuminated dial. It is the melancholy secret of the artifact, the humanly touched thing.[338]

Another thinker who had his eyes opened. All Eiseley learned brought him to a melancholy, awed humility before the mystery of life. It brought him to this 'dictum':

in the world there is nothing to explain the world. Nothing to explain the necessity of life, nothing to explain the hunger of the elements to become life, nothing to explain why the stolid realm of rock and soil and mineral should diversify itself into beauty, terror, and uncertainty. To bring organic novelty into existence, to create pain, injustice, joy, demands more than we can discern in the nature that we analyze so completely. Worship, then, like the Maya, the unknown zero, the procession of the time-bearing gods. The equation that can explain why a mere Sphex wasp contains in its minute head the ganglionic centers of its prey has still to be written. In the world there is nothing below a certain depth that is truly explanatory. It is as if matter dreamed and muttered in its sleep. But why, and for what reason it dreams, there is no evidence.[339]

There are mountains of evidence for *how* matter behaves, all of it amassed in pursuit of the infinitely regressive *why*.

Eiseley was a teacher who urged students to maintain a measure of freedom from teachers, 'Freshmen, sophomores, with the gift of youth upon you,' he once said, addressing students as recipient of an honorary degree, 'do not be prematurely withered up by us. Are you uncertain about your destiny? Take heart, in middle age I am still seeking my true calling. I was born a stranger. Perhaps some of you are strangers too.'[340] Was I born a stranger? I don't think so. I think I had to become one. In any case, well past middle age, I am a perpetual stranger, still writing my way home.

I have no grid, yes, but I am working hard, in my own way, to learn more. I'd like to be ready for a flash visit by some spirit like the practical joker in Reaney's poem, 'The Ghost.' The ghost is an ex-human whose 'knowledge was chopped from my power,' meaning he died and must now do without a body. He thinks it's a hoot all suddenly to reveal himself to one of the intellectually unready among the living and overload his mental circuits.

The awkward doltish low I.Q. farmboy shambles down the steps,
The empty pitcher echoing in his hand:
I am!
Ha ha! And his hair stands straight up like brambles.

Everything—Egyptian hieroglyphs and crystallography,
Diary of shadows,
Vast God and the interiors of tree trunks, snowflakes
All spin like a fiery corkscrew into his psychology.

For I know everything now having passed into source,
Even
Through me he knows himself—a kidnapped prince.
It is too much for him—he falls down—hoarse
As they shriek and lift him up—I am not. [341]

'An influx of divine intelligence / can be disorienting,' [342] says poet Joseph Donahue, severely understating the case.

There. *That's* why I push to keep on learning, packing as much as I can into my noggin like a cut-rate (anagogic) Noah wannabe: to survive overload from any such sudden overwhelming infusion of source. I would hope to have a better chance than the poor, deprived farmboy (though I do wonder how much could be expected of such a low IQ fellow—him or, say, George, 'A chop-the-harp and fish-with-the-strings sort of oaf' [343] in *A Suit of Nettles*. Richard Maurice Bucke would fare better. Perhaps he *was* so visited—with the 'intellectual illumination' that left 'an aftertaste of heaven' [344]—and was found prepared.

I do wonder about something the poem does not invite me to consider: would *anyone* who passes into source, whether low IQ farmboy or polymath, automatically know everything? I'm putting that question on hold. The poem doesn't address it, should not be expected to. Still, there is a halo of possible implications here and one seems worth a mention—some wise people already take a lot with them when they go, supposing they are allowed to keep it, and those ones must have a head start on the rest of us dung-beetles and dolts. Jay Macpherson was thinking of Frye, her mentor and colleague, when she wrote 'The Anagogic Man.' 'You could sometimes see him wafting from one mysterious point to another,' around Victoria College, University of Toronto, says Margaret Atwood, 'surrounded by a nimbus of eminence.'[345] Reaney calls him 'a man who is himself a walking repository of all the ways stories and metaphors fit into each other, parallel each other on various levels, and eventually provide us with a string through the labyrinth.'[346] If ever there was a man who could almost be said to know almost everything, while living, at least about world literature and the other arts, Frye was that person. And Reaney was no slouch. 'James Reaney,' a poem by George Bowering, avowed postmodernist yet admirer of Reaney's writing, begins with an image of Reaney 'walking over the wooden bridge on/ the street in his home town,' and ends this way:

> If your head
> is between the stars of unwavering light it is
> a large head, large enough & round enough
> to contain the dark & the whiteness con-
> tending, large enough to let it be & to feel
> the tug that produces colours for the earth
> you see when you step off the end of the bridge.[347]

Frye and Reaney: organized, ready for Everything! Me, I'm ardently scrounging interesting bits and pieces from here and there and working them up into my own kind of crazy quilt.

From 'The Ghost' (one of my favourite Reaney poems) it seems natural to step along to Halloween, the yearly festival which lends its name to Reaney's series of theatrical newsletters:

I am calling the whole series *Halloween* because that festival is the one theatrical event put on in this country which doesn't seem to need directors brought in from foreign lands; it is put on by thousands who are really into their parts and are not just worrying as the actors do at the St Lawrence Centre in Toronto about the dread possibility that the director might let the rehearsal go on past the time for a coffee break; the audience for Halloween numbers in the millions, understands the script thoroughly even when it involves the most esoteric and ancient matter of Light's yearly fight with Darkness; no character or situation is beyond the technical range of the participants—I have seen them dressed up as everything from TV sets to tramps to demons to Adolf Hitler and all without Canada Council support, yet fed so well that the participants can sometimes barely struggle home with the take. So everything that Halloween stands for—direct, sentimental, sensational primitive theatre is one thing this series of letters is going to be about.[348]

It's typical of Reaney (and informative) to stress the archetypal Light-Dark combat in the October 31 event that has become commonplace in this country. I doubt that most participants and audiences, either in 1976 when Reaney was writing or in 2020–21, when I am, *are* aware of the pagan, archetypal origins of Halloween. It's also typical of Reaney to have things as he would like them to be, eliding what they really are when it suits him. One of the reasons his essays are so entertaining is that he's willing to let fly—sometimes in the face of logic or hard fact. To point that out may be to make prose of his poetic exuberance, but the intention is not to refute. It's just to observe the lively play of his dramatizing rhetoric, to stand far enough away from it to notice what's going on—including the also typical digs at those who behave in ways of which Reaney disapproves. I'm flagging the hyperbole but taking it seriously, with a smidgen of reservation, as one of his listeners failed to do during the Vancouver stop of the national *Donnelly* tour: 'Had an argument in the car with someone about rock music;' Reaney writes, '... I said that thunderstorms had been the first amplified rock music and he kept saying N O , T H U N - D E R S T O R M S W E R E N O T T H E F I R S T R O C K B A N D S , S T O P S A Y I N G T H A T !' [349] Who to go with on this one? Not Someone, because where's his sense of humour. Not Reaney—besides the anthropomorphizing, you can no more dance to a thunderstorm than to *The Well-Tempered Clavier*— though I have to admire how cleverly he got Someone's goat.

Above, I quoted Reaney endorsing the reader who 'rouses his faculties.' The roused reader, the loving reader, shows up in a Reaney article on

Henry James's *The Sacred Fount*, love being a key Reaney word and a value at the heart of his work: 'Since some of the critics love James they get far more out of him than do those who retreat, angrily huffing and puffing, from this book, which is James at his most exuberant and essential.'[350] '[T]he basic relationship between a work of literary art and its reader,' he goes on, 'cannot be one in which the reader sits passively absorbing. No, the reader has to act in front of this mysterious fiction. It will be as clear and sane as he is clear and sane. The more he is able to accept the more he will get. It is with such roused and athletic readers in mind that the late style was formed, a style that enforces attention since it gives nothing otherwise.'[351] He goes on to figure out the 'delightful literary puzzle'[352] of the ending of *The Sacred Fount*.

Reaney especially wants the reader to be open and responsive to romances he has known and loved. '… *I discovered that if you're generous to Richardson,*' he says, meaning Major John Richardson's gothic novels *Wacousta* and *The Canadian Brothers*, out of which Reaney made plays, '*he'll be generous to you.*'[353] '*Give in to the story,*' he adds, '*and see what you get.*'[354] One of the novels behind Reaney's *Listen to the Wind* is 'Rider Haggard's *Dawn*. It's a melodrama, but it still affects me very powerfully because the patterns in it are not only sensational but deadly accurate. This is a world. Give in to its rules a bit and you'll find that it guides you out of the abyss we live in a bit more quickly than some dramas I could name….'[355]

It's right to defer the critical take so as to receive a text on its own terms. Seen that way, Reaney's advice is good, but it won't work across the board, at least not for me. I've found it difficult to follow with respect to some of the stories, Richardson's *Wacousta* included, that Reaney found haunting and wished to make canonical. I have less difficulty with Reaney's own plays, particularly the early ones, than others have had, at least while reading them. These plays were more conventional than the later plays, but not altogether so. In them, characters do things and say things that occasionally burst the bounds of plausibility, sometimes in strange and interesting ways. Once in a while the minds of certain characters seem fascinatingly transparent, turned inside out, lacking any filter between what they think and what they say.

Reaney says the early plays were 'constructed like rivers in voyageur journals. You go smoothly along in an apparent realistic way, and then there is this big leap—which director, actors and audience have got to take, or is it just bad dramaturgy? and are they going to take it? Let me give an example. At the end of *Easter Egg* one night some one came up to me and said, "But no one ever feels he has to get married just because he killed a bat."'[356] Even though he moved on to writing plays that he says are 'all rapids'[357] (some of them based on lists), you can tell he still wants audiences to be able to go with those early plays. He was using the metaphor of rapids in 1969; in 1972 he was still winningly making the case for the leap required by *The Easter Egg*: 'I'd be the first to complain if the rules of logic were completely suspended, but it helps the play enormously if audiences can be cajoled into just "listening" to the story. I know perfectly well that in real life no one marries somebody because she got him to kill a bat; but here, in this story, they **do**, you see.'[358] I like the sound of that. It cajoles. Of course, the question does remain: isn't the play itself obliged to do the cajoling? Else how could it be said to work with an audience?

This interesting question might be pursued further. It has two forks: 1) Reaney will declare that some of his work is intentionally left open as a way of inviting others in, of offering us cocreator status. He likes *The Sacred Fount* because in it Henry James works 'indirectly and economically as if to show how much can be done through inviting the reader to imagine, rather than through complex presentation.'[359] 2) Some works he has 'finished' are not completely realized. Expenditure of readerly generosity will not redeem them, not even by a Reaney partisan like myself.

Let me expand. 1) 'Not all of the poems are finished,' he says, introducing *Performance Poems*, 'but challenge you to expand their patterns into larger works with your own local reference.'[360] An intriguing stance: you don't get all the good out of these works unless you make something out of them yourself. In this he will be either ignoring or departing from Northrop Frye, his mentor, who says that 'All vagueness and obscurity in art, all uncompleted and roughly sketched statements, come from "leaving something to the imagination," and artists who think of imagination as a residue of vision are not to be trusted.'[361] Well, wherever Reaney went, he was always trying to induce people to engage their imaginations. Workshops for his plays were meant to be community-building activities. In fact, drama always involves collaboration between playwright, director, actors and all the others involved in figuring out how to stage a play.

Mostly, Reaney's process seems admirable, even when it looks chaotic. It was admirable to Patricia Ludwick, the actor who so memorably played Mrs. Donnelly and other Reaney characters. 'Reaney's passionate belief in the stories that grow out of his own particular patch of earth has infected us all,' she writes, meaning those who've worked with him. 'There are stories everywhere; look around you, see it fresh, and make it communicable with the simplest possible means. Oh, say the children's faces, you mean I know something worth sharing?'[362] Not that everyone bought in. 'I am tired of defending Reaney,' she goes on. 'The usual charges are "pretentious or childish, too busy, unedited, a shying away from violence." But the man is dealing with light; he focuses on good and evil, has a vision of life lived in an awareness of God, man, and nature. I believe that, at its best, the visual imagery has the power to evoke primal responses, that the use of unmasked theatricality can awaken an audience's own imagination, that the material of our own stories transformed by a poet's insight can make us see ourselves new, see with our hearts as well as minds.'[363] I am reminded of Tom Smart's account of what his experience with the NDWT company meant to him: 'The world Reaney ushered me into was complete, a holistic model of a profession—a life—absorbed in an environment entirely defined by art, artistic expression, the imagination and the power of metaphor to elevate experience to a mystical plane.'[364]

Patricia Ludwick makes a passionate defence of Reaney. And yet she is the only Reaney collaborator to register reservations about his expectations, at least the only one I know of who does so in print—unless we count Keith Turnbull on Reaney's workshop process: 'I think finally after *Antler River* we made very clear, we're not having any more to do with those god damn community god damn workshops. They're wonderful training, actually, for a director, they're superb training. From that point of view, I never regret them. But creatively, it's just – uhhh.'[365] Ludwick's issues came to a head over the post-workshop script for *Wacousta!*. With the play now in rehearsal and Reaney sending rewrites to the cast by bus, his actor-collaborators are trying to whip the script into shape. 'Reaney arrives and is appalled with our changes, misinterprets our efforts as anti-Reaney sentiment. But, I argue, this is a period piece, high melodrama, it's already stretching the audience's ability to suspend disbelief. Give them a break here, let them in. Reaney is adamant. And suddenly I realize that for Reaney we will never be fellow artists. He must follow his vision solo, even in this collective endeavour. He sees us as means to his end, taking poetic flashes from our persons, as he does with the children and amateur actors in his workshops.... Reaney's imagination is all-consuming; this is his genius, and our dilemma. Since an actor's job is to make choices that focus the audience's understanding, how do we encompass all the rough edges and loose ends that divert their attention and send them reeling back in confusion?'[366] Ludwick wasn't going behind Reaney's back with her essay. She sent it to him. His only direct comment is 'She's right.'[367] I find *Wacousta!* far more interesting to read than I did to watch it, as staged in Western's Talbot Theatre. Just reading the play requires more suspension of belief than may be warranted, but even when I find myself unconvinced by the plot—this is true of other Reaney works as well—I always find something of real interest in the concept and the writing.

2) In a retrospective essay called 'Ten Years at Play,' Reaney calls *Listen to the Wind* a play 'which broke with reality completely, used shorthand for everything, forced the audience to provide lighting and production and sets and even ending....'[368] '[M]y own marionettes for *Apple Butter*,' he says elsewhere, 'are roughly made because I'm no Junior League seamstress, can't carve wood but also because I'm quite content with the resultant primitive effect which all the money in the world couldn't buy so far

as forcing the viewer to complete my work for me is concerned....'[369] Forcing. There is an occasional note of impatience in Reaney's essays. It's proper to expect a lot of audiences—as long as you've put in your own work. Quite often the bare-bones list factor works very well for Reaney, when augmented by mime and sound effects. He can make a very little go a very long way. But there are instances of his not fully imagining works, so that they fall short of the art they might have been.

The two most obvious artistic disappointments, among the published books, are the children's novels, *The Boy with an Я in His Hand* and *Take the Big Picture*. As is always the case with Reaney, there are interesting bits in these stories, but the plots are filled with unlikely coincidence and some of the content, particularly in *Take the Big Picture*, is patently implausible. These books were written by a man who was fine with romance (as, in general, am I), but seemingly too impatient to do the detailed work necessary to form a novel into a literary world. In *Anatomy of Criticism*, Frye speculates on what a reader might say had most impressed him about James Joyce's *Ulysses*. 'First,' he says, 'the clarity with which the sights and sounds and smells of Dublin come to life, the rotundity of the character-drawing and the naturalness of the dialogue.' These are only the most down-to-earth characteristics, the most novelistic elements, of a book which combines the forms of novel, romance, confession and anatomy, making it 'a complete prose epic with all four forms employed in it, all of practically equal importance, and all essential to one another, so that the book is a unity and not an aggregate.'[370] That comes pretty close to describing the integrative nature of *The Donnellys*, an epic to whose total effect naturalistic detail is crucial. Even Blake will defend detail:

All broad & general principles belong to benevolence
Who protects minute particulars, every one in their own identity.[371]

Since verbal texture is merely waved at in a novel like *The Boy with an Я in His Hand*, I skim along on the surface of that book. It doesn't grab me, as other so-called children's or young adult books have very often done:

Anne of Green Gables, The Sword in the Stone, Watership Down, A Wizard of Earthsea. Those books are fully imagined. Because they draw me in, have done so over and over as I've read them, silently many times, and taught them, and read them aloud to my children and my wife, I have drawn them into me. Permanently.

'[T]here is a didactic impulse behind [*The Boy with an Я in His Hand*]' Reaney says in an interview with Catherine Ross '—to teach kids about the problems of society and the unfairness of things under certain systems.'[372] (There are lessons in *Take the Big Picture* too: big technology, vivisection and additives in foods are bad; the unorthodox life is good.) That is one source of the problem with both books: too much stress on the lessons, too little effort made to embed them. 'I had the terriblest time with the editors [of *The Boy*],' Reaney goes on. 'There is a sequence at the beginning in which one of the kids falls into the lake from the boat and then he falls in again at the end. And they said, "Why do you have *that*?" I said, "Well it's a design; it's a story; you repeat; kids like that." They said, "But it's not very *real*. It's coincidental." I realized that there was something the matter with the children's department at that publishing house.'[373] Another possible source of the problem: bare design trumps texture. These editors may have been idiots, as Reaney suggests; I have no way of knowing. I do know that the relationship between editor and author is meant to be collaborative. It works only if each party is willing to listen to the other. Reaney was unlikely to hear any appeal to the requirements of verisimilitude. And he felt justified by responses to the work. 'The book is still in print,' he says in the same interview. 'It has been reprinted several times and is quite popular. I get a lot of letters about it.'[374] One of the last things he says in the interview is, 'What depresses me about the children's literature racket—and it is a racket—is that adults write down to kids.'[375] He's right about that; children are too often offered much less than they can handle. He himself may not have written down, but neither has he written up. In my opinion, he missed the chance to make his children's novels appeal to readers of all ages.

It's interesting that Reaney proved in the stories of *The Box Social and Other Stories* that he *could* do the basic work with fiction. When I encounter the supernatural 'rapids' in these stories I am prepared, because attention has been paid to 'real world' detail. Also, narrative voice is unobtrusive but palpable, occasionally ironic. Witty and humorous at need, distinctive voice textures and so graces these fictions. Narrative voice in the two children's novels is serviceable but generic. That is also the case with dialogue in several of the plays. In them characters mostly speak like each other. They are differentiated by what they say, not by how they say it. It's in *The Donnellys* that all the levels are deeply and thoroughly considered. It took Reaney many years to get the trilogy right. It's possible that his deep desire to change things ('It's a fight for people's souls'[376]), together with an imagination that overflowed with more ideas than he had time or patience to flesh out, sometimes led him to require more of audiences than they should feel obliged to grant.

While working on this book, at the unrelated insistence of my daughter, I read Terry Pratchett's novel, *The Truth*. I had never paid any attention to Pratchett before, and here he is, or was, before his death in 2015, according to the first sentence inside the book, 'Britain's bestselling living author.' 'Bestselling' wouldn't have enticed me, but I enjoyed the book so much that I've been wondering why I've been oblivious to Pratchett. Well, I tend not to notice cheap mass market paperbacks. This book *looks* like it could have been written by anyone. Also, it's a so-called genre book, the genre being fantasy romance. I haven't been keeping up with romances, though some of my favourite novels do fall into that category. But when the vampire showed up on page 134, I decided it was time to write the book in here. Up to that point there had been only wizards, alchemists, dwarves, werewolves, gnomes, zombies, a scruffy talking dog and a mix of humans, all of them living and interacting in a Discworld city called Ankh-Morpork. You may not be expecting me to declare such a fictional hodge-podge a fine book, but it is: absorbing and hilarious and founded on serious matters. It's a satire on the fraught relationship of print (and people) with truth. It probes the modern world of capitalism, politics, class structure, racism, etcetera. It has sprightly narrative, convincing dialogue and a well-managed plot, which is coincidentally (given that I've been writing about *The Boy with an Я in His Hand*) about the first use of typesetting and printing to establish a newspaper. I give it one paragraph to point out that a veritable onslaught of the implausible, even the impossible, can be rounded up and whipped into artistic shape by a smart novelist committed to forming all the levels of his or her narrative.

One paragraph for that, and three more to counter any thought that Reaney would be too serious in his own work to go for any novel so irreverent as *The Truth*. Always a teacher, he was not always didactic. In *Alphabet* 2, he printed parodies of T.S. Eliot—satires of academic life, by R.K. Webb—and introduced them this way in his editorial: 'One is aware of how beautiful Eliot's technique and form are when one sees them containing an entirely different content, poured in, of course, with great skill by Mr Webb. Humour is something I have also fought a great many battles over. Some people seem to regard it as frivolous. But that is another issue and these parodies are but the first barrage in that battle.'[377]

The battle is joined in *Alphabet* 5: '1. The one thing a humorous writer cannot understand is someone who says that he is not being serious since laughter is harder to produce than so-called ideas, 2. a teacher of mine once pointed out that it was simply a fashion that thinkers spent so much time analysing the state of dread. It might just as well be the state of joy, 3. & why in this country have we no colouring book for our Prime Minister? But as reviewers used to say in our learned quarterlies, "Here is God's plenty."[378] What follows immediately is a series of parodies presented as drawn from 'the very best of Toronto's morning papers—THE GLOW-WORM & MALE [which] 'has back issues going back maybe three thousand years.' Reprints from this organ and of 'drama reviews from two other Toronto papers—THE DAILY CATARRH and THE TWILIGHT JELLYGRAM,'[379] though attributed to various others (Join Krakling, Angels Fang, Wan de Backmitz, Rosalinda, and Nasal Cone)—look to have been written by Reaney himself. At least they follow directly on from what are clearly editorial remarks.

Reaney's work usually has a serious enough purpose, even when it's funny. That claim is harder to make for a weird outlier to his work: his appearance as James Weeny in *The Bicameral Review*, a photocopied and collaged magazine published by 'The Bicameral Society for the Stimulation of Brainwaves While You're In, Above or Near the Water.' This very odd zine has several distorted versions of the same photograph of Reaney on the front cover, with two captions: 'Wow! Weenyworks' and 'Will the REAL James Weeny please SIT STILL.' Inside are sixteen pages under

'Rural Dandy,' James Reaney self-portrait.

the title of 'James Weeny Retrospective: Undercover story,'[380] with words and images by Reaney. Some Reaney poems are reprinted as they appear in his books, there are photographs of Reaney at the University of Toronto, 1944, of himself and Colleen Thibaudeau, himself and his two boys (the younger, John Andrew, died of meningitis in 1966), his mother, the family home, his grandmother and great grandparents in Perth County, scenes from South Easthope, and several fantastic Reaney drawings, including a couple of male nudes. Much but not all of the mag is given over to Reaney; there is at least one other graphic hand at work in it. The other content, all satirical, has nothing in particular to do with him. In *Alphabet 5*, Reaney refers to a magazine called *Gambit* as 'probably the cleverest piece of insanity on the scene.'[381] *Gambit* is the 'mother publication'[382] of *The Bicameral Review*, according to 'Brain Waves,' the introduction. My copy of *The Bicameral Review* is addressed to me in Reaney's hand, but I don't believe he ever said anything to me about it, so I'm obliged to Tom Smart for the information that 'ultra-contrarian'[383] John Richmond was the editor of both *Gambit* and *The Bicameral Review*, that he published Weeny in both magazines, and to Susan Reaney for telling me that her father sent Richmond the material and then Richmond did the collaging. The Weeny pseudonym may have also have been Richmond's idea, but Reaney was happy enough to go along with it, so he was party to a certain amount of Richmond's 'insanity.' It must have tickled what Brian Bartlett has called Reaney's 'madcap intelligence.'[384]

'Laughter is harder to produce than so-called "ideas."' Presumably Reaney means weak ideas, since he was always advancing the propulsive thoughts behind his own writing. But he was serious about the seriousness of humour. He could be very funny in a play that is no comedy, *The Killdeer* for example. Here is the latter part of what, early in the play, Harry Gardner tells his mother about a party he has attended at the house of his employer, Mr. Coons, with hostess Mrs. Coons, who has 'such a lovely English accent,' their daughter Vernelle and other guests. Pre-dinner drinks have been served, and Harry, unaccustomed to the effects of alcohol, has knocked over a big bowl of peonies which scared the family cat up one of the curtains. There she remains for most of the meal. At dinner Harry is seated beside Mr. Coons's 'horrible old sister':

> So there's this roar of talkersation. Roar!
> Do you know what I hear my boss, Mr. Coons, saying?
> That all schools and colleges, conservatories
> Should be closed because they breed – communists!
> Well, I just said – 'Sir, how can this be so when …'
> And, 'On the other hand only an idiot would say …'
> And 'That's really not so, is it, sir? Is it?'
> I smashed his arguments. I was stunning.
> Dark outside. It's *me* talk. Me talk now –
> A funny feeling on my left upper leg.
> My God! This old hag beside me is putting
> Another silver spoon in my pocket! I turn –
> Catch a crystal goblet which goes flying –
> Crash! Whoosh! The cat gives a howl!
> Leaps down from the curtain onto Mrs. Coons' head
> Where it proceeds to tear up the clover.
> Screams! Mrs. Coons wears a wig and she swears
> In pure Canadian. 'Get this goddamn cat off me, Bert!
> Get it off!' Blur – a card drops in front of me,
> It says, 'Come to garden and talk to me.'[385]

Harry's *me* talk has just cost him his job at the bank, but out in the garden he gains an offer of marriage from Vernelle Coons. He's in love with another, but feels obliged to marry Vernelle to advance his career. That doesn't end well. There are few laughs from here on in in the play, though most things do come right in the end.

In the tragedy of *The Donnellys* the humour is more organic. In fact it's an important seam in the whole trilogy. What is important about being funny in a tragedy? It demonstrates that life as a whole is never merely grim; even when savage machinations are afoot, life is still potentially layered with all sorts of different tinctures and textures. Real life, life whole, is mixed. Let's consider just one scene in *The St. Nicholas Hotel*, the middle play of the trilogy. A bit of background: as mentioned above, the play opens in competition between two rival stage lines, one run by John and Pat Finnegan, the other by Will and Michael Donnelly. Competition for passengers is fierce. Sometimes it becomes a race. One race ends in collision. And once, just before the scene in question, the Finnegan stage crashes because it has lost a wheel. Given the rivalry, and given the deteriorating reputation of the Donnellys, Finnegans naturally assume that Donnellys have somehow got at their wheel.

Cut to the home of Dr. Maguire, protestant minister, and Mercilla, his spinster daughter. Maggie, their domestic servant and cousin to Patrick Finnegan, delayed by the recent accident, is late for her evening duties. Just after she appears, so does George Stub, 'foremost merchant of Main Street,'[386] and a firm enemy of the Donnellys. He has proposed marriage to Mercilla, 'a **decisive** lady at the top of her youth.'[387] Mercilla shows herself to be much Stub's superior in intelligence and wit, but she has a mercenary streak and will entertain his proposal of marriage, even though her father has no use for the man, on condition that he become a Somebody. One source of the humour in this scene is the mismatch between Mercilla's verbal dexterity and Stub's dullness:

GEORGE Mercilla.

MISS MAGUIRE Who are you anyway?

GEORGE I've been a self made man. You know what a great thing I've made of the store, and I'm—

MISS MAGUIRE One of the rules I might make tonight is that I expect the man I marry to be somebody, really somebody, like a member of parliament. What about that George?

GEORGE It'll never come to pass. I'm far better behind the scenes. I get too excited in public.

MISS MAGUIRE Didn't I hear you say once that you'd been promised a senatorship if you could get a Conservative candidate in in this riding?

GEORGE Yes.

MISS MAGUIRE Then that's the rules. It's some day to be Senator Stub, or else. I have depths of meanness, George. Don't ruffle them.

GEORGE If I promise to obey the rules, I want things to be clearer.

MISS MAGUIRE You mean when? I'll think it over tonight after you'll be gone.

GEORGE I'd like something on – all this.

MISS MAGUIRE Something on account. Here take my hand.

GEORGE No.

MISS MAGUIRE Oh, my mouth. Here, stop me from talking so much. *Her father enters.*

MISS MAGUIRE Remember sir, I am no widow. You may be a hot blooded widower, but my father has kept me in his parsonage, a chaste spinster, for many more years than Jacob served Laban for both Leah and Rachel. And I haven't minded that a bit.[388]

Stub is already an enemy of the Donnellys, as I've said, and Donnellys will be seeing to it that a Conservative candidate is *not* elected in the rid-ing—this transpires in the final play of the trilogy—turning Stub's enmity to hatred. So the action we're looking at now, with fallout in the following play, is a piece of the overall design of the trilogy—which is really one play in three parts.

Now Mercilla has agreed to have Stub's Masonic banner mended. For the purpose, she will need silk thread from Maggie's sewing basket.

Maggie, now rushing out to vespers, having forgotten what else she has in her basket, says just help yourself. 'What are these strange lumps of metal, George,' Mercilla asks.[389] 'These are the nuts off the axles of a wagon,' George says, 'her father must have given her a list of things to bring him home on the farm out there.'[390] No, George, Maggie has sabotaged her cousin's stage in hopes of riding with the Donnellys. The other thing Mercilla finds in the basket is a locket containing a portrait of Will Donnelly, to whom Maggie is secretly engaged. The scene looks ahead to the personal love tragedy resulting from the standoff between religions: Maggie is Protestant, Will is Catholic. They will not be allowed to marry. They are not the only local couple to be thus severed by religious intolerance. In *Handcuffs*, Dr. Jerome O'Halloran and Katie Johnson's union is denied by O'Halloran's priest. No marriage for them, but a suicide pact.

But it's humour, not tragedy, I'm on about here, and one of my favourite scenes in the trilogy features a surprising appearance of Ezekiel's chariot. (Elsewhere, of course, Reaney and Blake are quite serious about the wheel within a wheel.) Dr. Maguire mentions that he has officiated at the wedding of Will's brother Patrick.

GEORGE You would have met the whole monstrous family then.

DR MAGUIRE Monstrous, not at all. They were a very handsome, unusual family with a – as if there was something they weren't telling you. I disagree with you totally, Mr Stub and here's the text for my sermon. Four wheels! *picking up the nuts.* Now as I behold the living creatures, behold one wheel upon the earth by the living creatures, with his four faces. The appearance of the wheels and their work was like unto the colour of a beryl....

GEORGE Mercilla, I must leave. Please show me down.

MISS MAGUIRE Follow me, Mr Stub. Father, George Stub is leaving, oh it is no use when he starts quoting scripture, no use at all. *They leave. As he goes on quoting from scripture (Ezekiel 1) he juggles the four nuts:*

DR MAGUIRE And they four had one likeness; and their appearance & their work was as it were upon a wheel in the middle of a wheel. When they went, they went upon their four sides; and they turned not when they went.

Maggie enters with a cup of tea. She collects the nuts, the locket, and begins to work at the banner with the coloured thread.

MAGGIE Miss Maguire suggests, sir, that you take a drink of this camomile tea to calm your nerves. I have lit the lamp in your bedroom and changed your pillow case.

DR MAGUIRE Ah, I have frightened him away. The Bible is a great help in getting me rid of people I don't like.[391]

Yes, I'm stressing humour just now, not the tragic, but the light and the dark are intimately threaded together in the trilogy. This whole scene has its lighthearted moments, but one sort of dark undertone is there for anyone who remembers Tom Cassleigh, another Donnelly enemy, confessing to James Donnelly, in *Sticks & Stones*, that 'Already your sons are blamed for things they [Protestants] do to us. And when we [Catholics] do things to them we're spreading the word it's you.'[392] The Donnellys really don't need bad things done on their behalf by people on their own side, like Maggie. Even friends will eventually be turned against them, the result of a conspiracy to which well-meaning, 'innocent' acts like the removal of those nuts will have contributed. And since there is never any doubt about what is going to happen to the Donnellys, no incidence of light-hearted normality like humour is ever unshadowed by the darkness of multiple murders to come. Even comic 'relief' may leave a sad ache in a viewer's mind.

Anagogic

A few grumbles and reservations having been noted (though later on I'll come at Reaney's undervaluing of realism from another angle) here I go again, respectfully keeping on, looking first at the several placements and functions of Reaney's poem, 'Granny Crack,' dated 1959 in *Poems*, though Granny Crack makes her first appearance in the 1949 poem, 'Winter's Tales.' The poem finds a place just before 'The Ghost' in *One Man Masque* (1960), then, with adjustments, appears in *Twelve Letters to a Small Town* (1962) and *Colours in the Dark* (1969). The frequency of the poem's appearance suggests its importance to Reaney. So does the symbolic content of the final stanza.

Before we get to the words of the poem, it's time to say something about the meaning of anagogy. It goes back to the Middle Ages, when, as Northrop Frye says, 'a precise scheme of literal, allegorical, moral, and anagogic meanings was taken over from theology and applied to literature.'[393] The scheme is caught by Dante in *Il Convivio* (*The Banquet*) about four senses in which a text may be interpreted, a system that Frye still finds useful, with adjustments, for 'tracing the different phases of literary symbolism....'[394] The simplest sense, or level, is the literal: means what it says. The second, the allegorical, refers to the Church and its teachings and is plain enough in this usage: something beyond the literal is going on. The third sense is the moral: right behaviour. The fourth, the anagogic, is properly slipperier. It has to do with spiritual or universal meaning. 'The fourth sense is called anagogical, that is, transcending the senses: this is brought out when a work is expounded with regard to its spiritual meaning; even though the work is true in a literal sense, what is said there speaks also of things beyond our knowledge relating to eternal glory.'[395]

This fourteenth century gesture to the prophetic or visionary seems to be imported into the twentieth century via eighteenth century anagogic poet William Blake. The sense I take from usage in modern mythopoeic poets and their critics is of a containing figure, a vast verbal node, a symbolic person or thing so large as, by implication, to embody everything, or almost everything: an all-embracing symbol like the grain of sand/universe, but with character and story attached, sometimes by allusion. 'Nature,' says Frye, 'is now inside the mind of an infinite man who builds his cities out of the Milky Way. This is not reality, but it is the conceivable or imaginative limit of desire, which is infinite, eternal, and hence apocalyptic.'[396] Jay Macpherson's Noah is the postdiluvian patriarch, epitome of the human: everything we are was potential in him, or, in Reaney's version, him and his sons, Shem, Ham and Japhet (Japheth in Genesis). These are archetypal personages. '[O]f them was the whole earth overspread.' (Genesis 9: 19) Some of Reaney's own character creations are also meaning writ thus large. Granny Crack, for example. Who is she, ultimately? This is how she tells it:

> I was the mother of your sun
> I was the sister of your moon
> My veins are your paths and roads
> On my head I bear steeples and turrets
> I am the darling of your god.[397]

Under another name, Granny Crack may have been an actual person of Reaney's rural experience. This is suggested by the way he introduces the poem in 'Seventh Letter: Prose for the Past,' of *Twelve Letters to a Small Town*: 'There was an old woman called Granny Crack who every child has heard about who wore seven dresses all at once and walked the length and breadth of the country begging for a living, trading and begging.'[398] The poem's distinctive structure, borrowed from the conjugation of a verb (first-person singular, second-person singular, and so on), affords a multiple perspective. Granny Crack introduces herself, first-person, as beggar lady in the first stanza, then doesn't speak again until the last stanza, just quoted. The intermediate stanzas, opening with 'You,' 'She,' 'We,' 'You,' and 'They,' are views of Granny Crack as she is seen by others. They stress her earthiness, her salty language, her sexuality, her vulnerability—and also something else important to Reaney and never to be forgotten in all his thrust towards the transcendent. In the penultimate stanza she is

> The spirit of neglected fence corners,
>   Of the curious wisdom of brambles
> And weeds, of ruts, of stumps and of things despised.[399]

In Reaney's work, the symbolic transcendent seems at times to diminish the significance of mundane, low-grade 'personal experience' (I've said something about this already and will come back to it again), but look again and see, again and again in his work, those 'neglected,' 'despised' particulars. They are precisely the kind of thing that might have grounded his children's novels; odd that he never saw fit to mobilize them there. Here are a couple of examples: first, poem (a) from 'Brush Strokes Decorating a Fan,' a whole alphabet of poems in *Souwesto Home*:

> Chair, table, cupboard,
> Dishes, books, my outside boots,
> Dear good things
> That wait
> Patient-
> Ly
> All night
> For me & the morning.
> Still there
> When I get up
> And come down
> To you.[400]

These 'dear good things' may take us back to an early poem (1953) in which personified kitchen implements clamour to be recognized for their own parts in valuable household functions:

The whole kitchen filled with unseen, half-seen

Boastings, jumping up and downs of kettles, ovens,

Of lids, jars, ladles, pans, sieves and graters,

Basins, dippers, sifters, pots, dampers, lifters, pokers,

All the utensils in that darkening kitchen who

Considered their goodness, their civilization,

Their speechless, silent holding together of people,

Eating and drinking around a table. [401]

So Reaney's wish is not somehow to abandon this earth and the ordinary, common things of it, but rather to gather together the kinds of interesting humble things Granny Crack represents, human and non-human, and then suddenly raise the stakes with what else she is, when her past tense ('I was') turns to present ('I am'). Then the human Granny Crack takes on another identity: archetype of everything, flesh *and* spirit, anagogic.

In *One Man Masque*, the Granny Crack poem appears intact, just as in its first appearance, but it's now one link of a string of other poems and prose and props in what Reaney has called a poetry reading built on an armature of 'the conflicting gyres of life and death,'[402] the progress or cycle of the soul from birth to death and on into rebirth. Then in *Twelve Letters to a Small Town* the poem annexes an extra stanza to fold in a whole other complementary dimension of human life, the masculine. This is all represented by the high school janitor, another often ignored 'nobody' figure who fascinated Reaney. '[W]hat and where did I learn most from,'[403] asks the speaker of 'Sixth Letter, the Cloakroom of the High School.' The answer is off the curriculum:

The insoluble mystery of the cloakroom

And the curious question of the janitor

In some way so centre and core

January man and cloakroom

From which the moon each month unlocks

upon the wave

A white bird. [404]

The masculine complements Granny Crack's feminine, as winter balances summer in a new stanza appended to the Granny Crack poem. Here opposites meet and meld:

> The old woman of the country, Summer Wanderer,
> The old man of the town, Winter Janitor,
>   Old woman, Granny Crack
>   Old man, old woman
>   Revolving back to back
>   Looking down
>   Granny Janitor Angel
>   On my town. [405]

Unisex Angel. I'll just highlight this image for now. There will be more to say about angels later. But I don't know how many times I've read those lines about the white bird released by the moon upon the wave without thinking what might be said about them—well, really without thinking there *was* anything to say. Now it occurs to me that my silence to myself will have been, and is, because I am looking at a mystery insoluble. No janitor or cloakroom I've ever known has harboured any kind of bird. And what wave? Maybe the bird anticipates the angel. Maybe there is a hint of Noah releasing the dove. Anyway, so smoothly and quietly that it took me forty years to pick up on it, an enharmonic change in the poem introduces and releases a winged symbol of the spirit. 'If you remain within arbitrary and artificially created boundaries,' says Jung, 'you will walk as between two high walls: you do not see the immensity of the world. But if you break down the walls that confine your view, and if the immensity and its endless uncertainty inspire you with fear, then the ancient sleeper awakens in you, whose messenger is the white bird.' [406]

In scene 6 of *Colours in the Dark*, Granny Crack is now a character, one of the identities of Gram, '*an old beggar woman who used to wander the roads of Perth County. Far back in time she remembers when our world was underneath a glacier. Then it melted and coniferous trees were the first to come back. Then came the deciduous hardwoods and they're still pushing the fir trees farther and farther north.'* [407] That's in Granny's first scene, where she offers her memories to the Son who will be growing up throughout the play. In scene 16, she reappears, *'walking down a road. She sings "Beulah Land,"'* while *Gramp, 'dressed as an old tramp … now goes by in the opposite direction singing [a secular song] "The Big Rock Candy Mountain."'* [408] Gramp takes the place of janitor in the version of the Granny Crack poem now introduced. Here, the different perspectives, once indicated by pronouns only, are voiced by characters who may have been all but there in Reaney's mind—conjugation as protodramatic form—when he was first writing the poem. Gram gets stanzas one and four as well as her final, anagogic stanza, which appears at the end of the scene.

Containing anagogic figures like Granny Crack appear over and over in Reaney's work. Possibly the strangest and most interesting of these is the New Jerusalem alphabet of the poem called 'The Alphabet,' but before I reach that one, which in a way is also to reach back to Bucke's fire vision, let me introduce some of the containing images in the opera, *Night Blooming Cereus.* I've already mentioned the immense image of the blossoming cereus itself. In the stage direction to scene two, which takes place in the crowded interior of Mrs. Brown's house, 'The things in Mrs. Brown's house look so familiar and have been where they are so long that they seem to be part of a card game for children.' [409]

As Reaney lays out the various cards, a reader may be reminded that a pack of cards is itself a symbol of visual and numerical containment. On the most capacious of these household cards *'there is an harmonium which is a sort of stove; that is, if the stove contains a forest of trees jumping back into light and sun, the harmonium contains the forest sighing into the darkness of the demon summer midnight storm, blowing pipe twigs, bugle branches and trumpet boughs.'* [410] Directions like this, and the one about the blooming cereus, impossible to realize on the stage, are for reader, not viewer, though a clever stage manager might find a way to image the spirit of these metaphors. Further along in the opera, other cards appear bearing more poetic directions, things sliding together, metaphors piling up: *'This is a card with a cupboard on it which has a clock made in Connecticut on top of it that is another sort of stove and harmonium since it burns time with a slow golden winking pendulum fire....'* As the moment of blooming approaches, the clock strikes *'twelve o'clock midnight.'* Then, outside, can be heard *'the card of the night train that has always passed thunderously close to Mrs. Brown's—like a huge front door lock on wheels roaring and crying: Cease your dreams. I am (unless stopped for a train strike) that which is. Your plant with its angel flower can't change me.'* [411] If this reality monster had not been a train, it might have been an automobile, *'mere reproductive machines,'* both of them, *'slaves of the whirring clock.'* [412] Clock and train and automobile are cousins on the dark side of the mechanical continuum of technology that Reaney despises. In answer, however, and to be expected in Reaney's kingdom, is *'a huge book, Mrs. Brown's Bible. It too was a sort of stove, a harmonium, a clock and a thunderous train and in it the whole world burned and did not, spoke and did not.'* [413] The opening of the flower is like a promise made by this same Bible. All those assembled in Mrs. Brown's room respond thus:

> When I behold
> All this glory
> Then I am bold
> To cross Jordan.
>   Open, flower. [414]

This is a greeting and a prayer. The opera ends with everyone on their knees.

Across Jordan into the New Jerusalem established in the unusual poem which might be said to hold it all—all the anagogic images so far presented. This is 'The Alphabet,' a poem of 1960, perhaps written with *Alphabet* magazine in mind, since it first appears in *Alphabet* 1. I think the reader needs have this whole poem available, since it won't be so easy to picture on the basis of anything I say about it, but before I get to that, I'll slide into type and visual symbol.

Part of the middle section of a case of what appears to be
12 point Baskerville, at one time resident in the basement
of the Reaney-Thibaudeau house on Huron Street
in London.

The word 'alphabet' may be the noun of most frequent appearance in this book. For Reaney, alphabet is a metaphor for the iconography of the imagination, but there is a simpler and more evocative way of saying what it means to him. He has William Lyon Mackenzie say it in *The Boy with an Я in His Hand*. Young Alec in this young adult novel is an apprentice in Mackenzie's printing office. He is learning how to set type for, among other things, Mackenzie's newspaper, *The Colonial Advocate*. In the chapter which describes the print shop, Alec finds himself looking at some

type that was set up, tied together with string so it wouldn't fly apart.... He loved the look of it. Mr. Mackenzie came up, put one hand on Alec's shoulder and one on the set-up type.

'There's freedom and liberty, lad. There's the mind of man. All his thoughts that thousands of people will read and find helpful—all these in thousands of wee bits of lead stuck together.' [415]

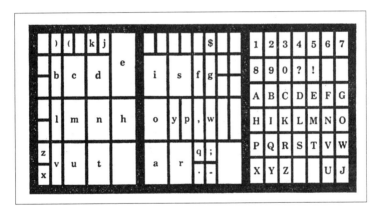

Type case from James Reaney, *The Boy With an Я in His Hand*

The mind of man is in the letters and numbers contained in a box of type.

I think it's important to say that the alphabet is not abstract to anyone who has set a text in lead type and printed it on any of the basic printing presses that go directly back to Gutenberg. The basement of University College, Western University, when I was there, had a large room on the door of which was a plaque that read 'The Belial Press.' Belial may have been suggested by the fact that printing apprentices, like Alec, were called 'printer's devils.' The press was established and looked after by Jim Devereux, who used to take his history of the book students down there to set some type and put themselves in the mindset (and fingers) of others who had done so, time out of mind. By this time, Reaney's run of *Alphabet* was done. So was his own typesetting, which he had in any case farmed out to younger colleagues for the later issues. But his Baskerville type had found a home, along with cabinets and cases of other fonts, at The Belial Press. I used it to set the type for *Ten Letters*, Colleen Thibaudeau's chapbook, though I wasn't press-handy enough to print the book myself.

THE COMPLETE WORKS

```
± @ # $ % ¢ & * ( )    +
 1 2 3 4 5 6 7 8 9 0 - =

Q W E R T Y U I O P ¼
 q w e r t y u i o p ½

A S D F G H J K L : "
 a s d f g h j k l ; '

Z X C V B N M , . ?
 z x c v b n m , . /


*any possible permutation
 of all listed elements
```

bpNichol, 'The Complete Works,' from *An H in the Heart*,
McClelland & Stewart, 1994.

Applegarth Follies did that. To pick every letter out of a type case and place it in a composing stick, backwards, because pages come off in mirror image—that is time-consuming. I also found the process meditative, as perhaps Reaney did not, since he would have been working to a deadline. Each letter, each space, horizontal or vertical, has weight. A tray of type is heavy, and that seems right to me. Working with 'the mind of man' is a heavy business, in the 1960s counterculture sense of 'Heavy, man.'

There is the mind of man in the box of type from the illustration in *The Boy with an Я in His Hand*. There it is again in bpNichol's concrete poem, 'The Complete Works.' That title usually appears on a gathering of everything an author has produced, but, as it describes the keyboard of a typewriter, it's a pun. Word processors have many more characters and

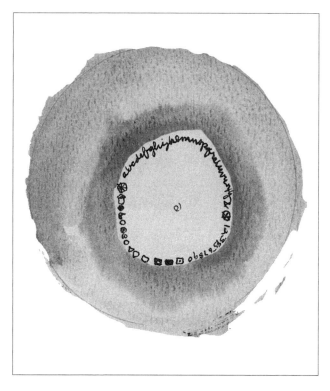

James Reaney, from 'Animated Film,' 1983. Cover, James Reaney issue,
Essays on Canadian Writing 24–25 (Winter-Spring 1982–83).

fonts available, but numbers and letters still render the mind of man. In the Reaney picture chosen for the cover of a number of *Essays on Canadian Writing* that I edited, the alphabet is represented as a long string of letters joined in Reaney's cursive. It looks like one long word. Letters and numbers are here again, as in the type box and on the typewriter keys; other signs in the centre of the vortex/circle are visual symbols Reaney worked into the emblem poems explored in Thomas Gerry's *The Emblems of James Reaney*. Reaney's three symbols for a man, for instance: a heart (heart, the emotions), a circle (belly, the body), a spiral (mind, the intellect). The small spiral in the middle of the composition suggests that the whole concatenation of circles, painted and written, is in motion, revolving. In fact the single image was intended to be part of an animated film that was never completed.

Separating the alphabet from the numbers and symbols are two asterisks within circles. I'd say the circles are meant to emphasize and contain the asterisks, which represent stars (the derivation, something Reaney surely knew, is late Middle English via late Latin from Greek asteriskos 'small star,' diminutive of aster). The star is a flower. The star is a personal symbol of Reaney's. He always added a star to his signature. I'd say that star was a compact visual way of joining himself to the heavens, the beyond, the world of the spirit. In Rhoda Kellogg's *Analysing Children's Art*, a book Reaney admired, there are three fascinating tables of what she calls 'Combines' formed when two 'Diagrams are put together.'[416] One of these Combines is a 'Radial,'[417] a Greek cross (+) plus a diagonal cross (x), the two forming an asterisk the way Reaney makes his.

Some of the other symbols, so tiny that they are difficult to make out, are certainly connected with what Reaney called his 'Search for an Undiscovered Alphabet.' The extent to which he wished to try thinking in visual terms is recorded in a curious, speculative article published in *Canadian Art*. 'What if one were to look directly at diagrams,' Reaney writes, 'instead of looking at them through words or music or photography. Is there a possible key to the way they can directly express reality?' 'What we want,' he goes on, 'is an alphabet of diagrams; "alphabet" suggests that we discover the first letter and the most important letter if we can.'[418] So he tries rendering various texts both verbally and diagrammatically, most of them in terms of variations they play on the circle shape: 'N. Frye's Ptolemaic teaching diagram', 'Plato's *Timaeus*,' 'Spenser's Castle of Alma—a ground plan,' 'Yeats' Vision,' 'Whitman's "Song of Myself"', 'Dickinson's "& hemispheres reversed themselves",' 'Melville's island in the sea,' and others.

Citing a Northrop Frye 'article on David Milne, one of Canada's most brilliant painters,' Reaney contrasts 'western painting with its emphasis on perspective and the separation of objects from the observer; and oriental painting which plays down perspective and blurs this sense of separation.'[419] Rather than saying anything directly about Canadian paintings, Reaney lets two of them speak for themselves in reproduction: Homer Watson's 'On The Grand River at Doon,' c.1880, and David Milne's 'Waterfall and Easel,' 1921. Watson's pleasant landscape is perspectival; Milne's is not. In the analogy being developed, the latter would be 'oriental,' but it also makes me think of the Italian painter Mantegna in Margaret Avison's poem, 'Perspective.'

We stand beholding the one plain
And in your face I see the chastening
Of its small tapering design
That brings up *punkt*.

...

Your fear has me infected, and my eyes
That were my sport so long, will soon be apt
Like yours to press out dwindling vistas from
The massive flux massive Mantegna knew
And all its sturdy everlasting foregrounds.[420]

The poem is about different ways of seeing, one timid and limited, the other bold and expansive. It takes a while to come out in Reaney's article, but since his discussion is leading up to the eye, it too is about seeing.

All we set out to do here was to find the first letter in our alphabet of spatial diagrams and that is demonstrably the circle with a dot in the centre of it since this represents the basic state of man: man in the centre of an imprisoning universe, an island of joy washed by seas of dread. Also this first circle is like that organ without which visual spatial diagrams would be impossible—namely the eye [auge in German].

I did not see how this was so until I read what Jacob Boehme says about the eye in his *Treatise of the Incarnation.* 'Thus we find,' he says in William Law's translation, 'that all Substances are shut up in an Eye, AVge, and that is as a Looking Glass, wherein the Will beholdesth itself what it is.' His 'AVge' is cabalistically interpreted: the A stands for the alchemical symbol for fire—an upright triangle and the old fashioned U in its V shape stands for the upside-

James Reaney, 'Boehme's diagram of the first six days of creation.'

down triangle that represents water. All substances can be said to be shut up in fire and water because these two substances represent the uppermost and lowermost bounds of creation respectively.[421]

Reaney calls another diagram, also from Boehme, 'a cabalistic interpretation of the eye image or diagram.' 'What could be more basic or essential' he goes on, referring mainly to the previous image, 'than a circle with a dot in the centre of it? Why it is the pupil of a human eye! In the perceived world our eye is literally the *first* thing and what an eye sees when it gazes at man's situation is also itself.'[422]

One might wonder whether an alphabet of very basic shapes would have any practical application for new art, rather than just as a template for rather arid reduction of complex works to simplified shapes that might be said to structure them. Perhaps there is a germ of something larger, though. It might take one to a book like Rudolf Arnheim's *Visual Thinking*: 'What we need to acknowledge is that perceptual and pictorial shapes are not only translations of thought products but the very flesh and blood of thinking itself.'[423] Reaney doesn't go there, or anywhere, really. The article makes no connection between the shapes and his own work, but Gerald Parker does. He goes on to discuss the 'complex series of design images [of *The Donnellys*] that, like those of *Colours in the Dark* especially, manifest improvisational playing as well as symbolic patterning.'[424] Parker shows how various metamorphosing configurations of lines, squares, circles and crosses are also eloquent scenic design elements of other plays: *Listen to the Wind* and *Wacousta!* and, to a lesser extent, *The Dismissal* and *King Whistle!*. He also acknowledges director Keith Turnbull's contribution to conceiving scenic patterns for *The Donnellys*.

In the magazine cover referred to above, there are more shapes than circles. Some of these are too small to read easily. There may be a triangle. There does seem to be a sequence of four square shapes. The content of one is white or blank, one is all black, one is black except for a white dot in the middle, one is white with a black dot in the middle. Perhaps Reaney discovered more than the first letter of his alphabet of shapes. The four squares are evocative, but I don't know whether they meant anything in particular to Reaney, at least in general, though squares were there in his early formulation of what was to become *Colours in the Dark*: 'At the very beginning,' he writes, 'John Hirsch asked me to do what I liked—something free form, personal and using as much material already written as possible. I took out my diaries and notebooks and started not writing but drawing. Paul Klee's *Magic Squares*, each square either a slight variation on or contrast to its neighbouring square, is really the design behind the play.'[425] (Magic Square was the theme of *Alphabet* 9, without reference to Klee, and the only square material in the issue is quite arbitrarily linked: *'JUXTAPOSITION: Myth & Documentary. Ralph Cunningham's poem and note on the Magic Square of the Temple at Sharon faces Greg Curnoe's diary of what he saw in the Magic Square of the mirror on a Coke truck.'*[426])

As you look at the shapes on the magazine cover, and compare them with this illustration in Kellogg's *Analysing Children's Art*, you may be as struck, as I was, by some of the similarities. These are what Kellogg calls

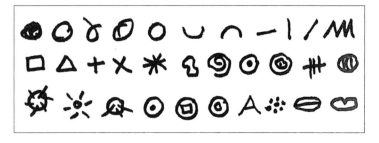

Gestalts, from Rhoda Kellogg, *Analysing Children's Art*. The symbols used as finials at the end of each chapter are also from Kellogg's book.

gestalts'[427] commonly used for eyes in drawings of humans by children aged four to seven years. I don't know if Reaney had read this book, but he did call Kellogg's earlier *The Psychology of Children's Art* 'a really influential book.'[428]

'Man has need of the word,' says C.G. Jung, 'but number is a much more important thing. In essence, number is sacred. Lots of important things might be said about it. The quaternity, above all, is an essential archetype. The square, the cross. The squaring of the circle by the alchemists. The cross in the circle, or, for Christians, Christ in "glory." '[429] I have been stressing letter and word here, because Reaney does also, but when the numerical in his work is considered—threes and fours (the quaternity) and twelves among his grids, for example, or six days of creation—it's clear that numbers deserve their almost equal place in his circular symbol of the whole. It's also tempting to see that circle as the globe, whirling in the surround of chaos, or coming to be out of chaos, as in Genesis. And that reminds me, first, of the Allan Fleming cover design for *Alphabet*, and, next, of an ad for *Alphabet* I once saw in another magazine—which magazine I don't now remember:

> Life is B M Q I B C F U
> Art is A L P H A B E T

The first line makes no sense without the code-breaker second. With it, an order is seen to be implicit in the seeming chaos of the first. There could hardly be a more concise way of representing what Reaney's magazine was about: document (life) clarified by myth (*Alphabet*).

There is at least one other way to look at the circular arrangement I've been describing. To see it as a mandala is to remember something Reaney says about Kellogg's *The Psychology of Children's Art*: '[S]he says that what children draw with their fingers in sand, their toes in mud, and crayons when they can get them are—not stick figures, but mandalas; these mandalas grow into suns, and these suns eventually become portraits of mother and father. Come time to go to school [here Reaney departs from Kellogg], we teach them how to print and mandalas disappear to be replaced by much smaller drawings of railway tracks in perspective, or other such objects from the documentary world rather than the mythical one.'[430] Mandalas aren't the first things children draw, according to Kellogg in *Analysing Children's Art*, her later, more complex, book. First, in her terminology, come Scribbles, Diagrams, Combines, and Aggregates.

Mandalas appear in Chapter 8. Reaney's main point stands, though. '"Mandala" is the Sanskrit word for circle,' says Kellogg. 'The word is applied in Eastern religion to various line formations, chiefly geometric shapes in a concentric organization. The same sort of line formations occur spontaneously in the art of children. Mandalas made by children are often Combines, formed of a circle or a square divided into quarters by a Greek cross or a diagonal cross, or Aggregates, formed of a circle or a square divided into eighths by the two crosses together. Concentric circles or squares also are Mandalas.' 'Mandalas have an enclosing perimeter,'[431] Kellogg goes on. Are the Radial/stars encircled on the book cover mandalas within a mandala?

Making mandalas, adorning his signature with a radial star—and maybe this goes for those shapes on the magazine cover as well—Reaney's childhood is active in his adult life. Children drawing mandalas belong not only in the company of eastern ancients, but also of C.G. Jung, another adult in touch with his childhood self. During a period of psychic turmoil after his split with Freud, and with other things, like war, on his mind, Jung found himself in a phase of self-experimentation. He was inducing fantasies, then analysing what he found in them to bring aspects of his unconscious to the surface. During one period in 1916, he drew a mandala every day. In word and picture, these mandalas and other material were gathered into what became *The Red Book*. Jung reflected on the process of discovering what the mandalas were about in his autobiography, *Memories, Dreams, Reflections*: 'My mandalas were cryptograms concerning the state of the self which were presented to me anew each day. In them I saw the self—that is, my whole being—actively at work.... The self, I thought, was like the monad which I am, and which is my world. The mandala represents this monad, and corresponds to the microcosmic nature of the psyche. ... When I began drawing the mandalas ... I saw that everything, all the paths I had been following, all the steps I had taken, were leading back to a single point—namely, to the mid-point. It became increasingly plain to me that the mandala is the center. It is the exponent of all paths. It is the path to the center, to individuation.'[432] 'Now according to [David] Willson's thinking,' Reaney writes in his biographical sketch of one of his great exemplars, 'as revealed in a long list of publications, manuscripts, hundreds of hymns, and even in the symbolism of the buildings he designed, "God is peace" and lies at the "centre" of the divine-human soul or mind; "the mind hath as many parts in it as there are in the creation, and the centre of it we wish to find."' [433]

Jung was a much more sophisticated visual artist than Reaney. His mandalas are complex, often gorgeous (his calligraphy in *The Red Book* is also beautiful). And his approach to myth is less polemical than Reaney's. 'I have no system,' he said once, 'no doctrine, nothing of that kind. I am an empiricist, with no metaphysical views at all. I have only hypotheses. From them I have gained some basic principles.' [434] In the interview from which that quotation comes, he goes on to mention a few of those principles: the self, the archetypes, the collective unconscious, aspects of the 'psychological and theological cosmology' [435] he developed. Jung *did* have a system, at least a method, based on the understanding that we are 'all the carriers of the entire history of mankind,' [436] but the system, in its application, had give. To benefit individuals under one's care, it had to be flexibly, intuitively, responsibly brought to bear. Dream analysis, he says, 'is not so much a technique that can be learned and applied according to the rules as it is a dialectical exchange between two personalities.' [437] Reaney certainly read some Jung. Had he read more, even more Kellogg—she acknowledges Jung in *Analysing Children's Art*—he would have found himself in the company of a kindred spirit, a man who lived even more exhaustively than he did with and for the archetypal.

It takes someone like Tim Inkster, printer and publisher, to appreciate the labour involved in producing *Alphabet* by hand, and to couch his account of that in lingo appropriate to the discipline:

[T]he most impressive bit of bibliography revealed on the masthead [of *Alphabet* 1] (for me) is that the entire 86-page issue, of which more than half is justified prose set 36 lines to a page 28 picas wide, was typeset by hand in 12pt

Baskerville from monotype arranged in California job cases by Reaney himself. That is something like 2,200 little bits of lead type that would need to be assembled, one at a time, by hand, per page. And Reaney had no casting machine. And he did not have deep pockets, so the quantity of monotype sorts in his cabinets would have been constricted by the shallow depth of his pocketbook and the demands of his young family. Which meant that the monotype composition for each page would necessarily have to have been 'un'composed a letter at a time and the sorts replaced in their slots in the California job case, which would have required individually handling each of the

Tim Inkster photo of a Nolan proof press, once in the basement
of the house at 276 Huron Street in London, Ontario.

2,200 pieces of lead a second time, to allow for the composition of the next page. This task would have demanded a near inconceivable commitment of time from a young English professor just starting an academic career at the University of Western Ontario who was also the father of three young children. I suspect the support of Colleen Thibaudeau, which is largely undocumented, MUST have been critical, essential and indispensable.[438]

The first *Alphabet* was actually typeset when Reaney was in Manitoba. In a 1966 letter to the Ontario Arts Council, requesting funds for linotype production of the magazine by the University of Toronto Press, he translates all the moves Inkster details into temporal terms: 'A page takes three and one half hours and the issues that are handset represent a dedication to Canadian literature that just takes too much out of me.'[439] He had set all of *Alphabet* 1 to 6, and was responsible for parts of others thereafter. And it's not clear if that three and a half hours includes the activity of printing: two facing pages printed at a time on a single sheet of paper inserted into the press and withdrawn from it forty-three times (for an issue of eighty-six pages), then turned over and reinserted to print the back of those pages, times the number of copies being produced. No wonder it all got to be too much for a man who had plenty of other things to do.

But what does the fact that he did it *at all* tell you about the man and about the antiquated technology he was employing. Recall that 'play in which the rats drive us; on freeways, naturally, invisible rats are already corralling us—away from this and into that—hurry!'[440] Writing and hurry don't belong in the same sentence. Though there came a time when Reaney could not afford the time to handset his magazine, he was always resisting the technologically driven headlong rush of modern life—this in the days before personal computers and the internet have exponentially sped everything up!—and setting type by hand was resistance. I know what it's like to set type. I feel nostalgia for the day when I could find the time required for it. But I'm also grateful for my word processor. Paradoxically, it allows me to be more painstaking than I was when pounding the keys of a typewriter and revising less because changes were so much more laborious to make. Take the time; put in the work required to get the sense as right as possible, weigh and pattern each sound. In that way, I'm still slow. In that way, I'm still honouring the Reaney who wanted to slow things down.

The Alphabet

Where are the fields of dew?
I cannot keep them.
They quip and pun
The rising sun
Who plucks them out of view:
But lay down fire-veined jasper!

For out of my cloudy head
Come Ay Ee I Oh and U,
Five thunders shouted;
Drive in sardonyx!

And Ull Mm Nn Rr and hisSsings
Proclaim huge wings;
Pour in sea blue sapphires!

Through my bristling hair
Blows Wuh and Yuh
Puh, Buh, Phuh and Vuh
The humorous air:
Lift up skies of chalcedony!

Huh, Cuh, Guh and Chuh
Grunt like pigs in my acorn mind:
Arrange these emeralds in a meadow!

Come down Tuh, Duh and Thuh!
Consonantly rain
On the windowpane
Of the shrunken house of the heart;
Lift up blood red sardius!

Lift up golden chrysolite!
Juh, Quuh, Zuh and X
Scribble heavens with light,
Steeples take fright.

In my mouth like bread
Stands the shape of this glory;
Consonants and vowels
Repeat the story:
And sea-green beryl is carried up!

The candle tongue in my dark mouth
Is anguished with its sloth
And stung with self-scoff
As my eyes behold this treasure.
Let them bring up topaz now!

Dazzling chrysoprase!
Dewdrops tempt dark wick to sparkle.
Growl Spark! You whelp and cur,
Leap out of tongue kennel
And candle sepulchre.

I faint in the hyacinchine quarries!
My words pursue
Through the forest of time
The fading antlers of this dew.

A B C D E F G H I J K L M

Take captive the sun

Slay the dew quarry

Adam's Eve is morning rib

Bride and bridegroom marry

Still coffin is rocking crib

Tower and well are one

The stone is the wind, the wind is the stone

New Jerusalem

N O P Q R S T U V W X Y Z![441]

There is nothing about 'ordinary experience' in this unorthodox composition, symbolic all through, though I dimly recall a time when students
were taught how to pronounce the letters of the alphabet; they are sounds,
after all, or can be. To speak this poem aloud is to make breath militant; it's
a kind of sound poem. Physicalizing the alphabet, pulling it out of the
merely conceptual, reminds one of the role of the body in making sounds.
Each sound, spelled with a capital letter, also reads like a proper name. The
vowels have their own stanza; the consonants are spread out over five.
Vowels and consonants come together in stanza eight, and in the final
stanza, now in the usual A to Z arrangement, with two ranks of thirteen
letters framing and containing the final words of the poem.

So the alphabet is letter, sound and word. Also wall, the identity
between letter/sound/name and those precious stones of New Jerusalem's
wall having been proclaimed.

Letter by letter, stone by stone, the walls of the holy city are being
built *in* the poem. They are called into being, it seems, by a speaker who
for most of the poem is lost or in doubt ('acorn mind,' 'shrunken house of
the heart,' 'anguished,' 'self-scoff'), but who rouses himself ('mouth,'
'tongue') to speak the city into being—at least assuming that those itali-
cised commands are his—and the imperative does continue into the
roman words. He has a physical body ('head,' 'hair,' 'mouth'), as well as
'mind' and 'tongue,' the latter being both what shapes the sounds he

— 182 —

makes and the language those letters allow him to speak. It's almost as though his person is, body part by body part, being incorporated into the New Jerusalem (which is both house and meadow and marries the opposites of Adam and Eve, bride and bridegroom, coffin and crib, tower and well, stone and wind, plus fire, water, earth and air) along with the letters and the stones. A lot is coming together to make this 'glory,' this 'treasure.' The process is also a hunt for a quarry, a deer ('antlers') made of dew.

The poem is derived from chapter 21 of the book of Revelation. In the Bible, the New Jerusalem descends 'out of heaven from God,' intact. All those jewels, already in it—we've met them before in *A Suit of Nettles*— are listed in the order in which they appear in the poem, but the biblical city also has particular dimensions plus twelve gates of pearl and a street of gold. Those images recall the gospel songs they have inspired.

And somewhere behind this poem is also one of William Blake's prophetic texts, part of his preface to 'Milton: A Poem in 2 Books,' that became an English anthem when set to music by Hubert Parry. The final stanza:

> I will not cease from Mental Fight,
> Nor shall my Sword sleep in my hand:
> Till we have built Jerusalem,
> In Englands green & pleasant Land. [442]

I taught English 138 on my own as a summer course one year. I asked Reaney to come in and read to the class. After his concluding dynamic performance of 'Doomsday,' from *One Man Masque*, one student told me that he'd had to revise his first impression of the man: mild-mannered to powerhouse. I would have liked to hear Reaney perform 'The Alphabet.' Maybe he'd have lifted that poem up off the page. On the page is where it tends to lie for me: the composition intricate, the concept orchestrated, but not a poem one loves because it sings and goes in deep.

For the latter part of what his friend Richard Stingle calls a 'strenuous life' [443] in London, Ontario, in Souwesto, Reaney was building his version of New Jerusalem with great vigour—through he was still in Winnipeg when he wrote 'The Alphabet,' learned to set type, and hand-set the first number of a magazine devoted to creating that symbolic edifice. Blake says it's 'we' who are building; Reaney would like that. He always wanted readers and listeners to join him in the making. He was pushing for native art in a country that had little art of world significance when he was starting out, and for a long time afterwards. 'Always this feeling of circumference for the native artist,' he says in the editorial to *Alphabet* 4, 'centre for everybody else!' [444] He wanted the centre.

For his short story, 'Memento Mori,' Reaney may have borrowed from what Stephen Dedalus writes ('himself, his name and where he was' [445]) on the flyleaf of his geography book. Young Loyal O'Hanley also writes down his address, but he inscribes it 'on the flyleaf of every book in his small but largely curious library.' [446] Like young Stephen Dedalus, he is linking his personal locale with everywhere else in the outer world:

Loyal O'Hanley

Lot 39

Concession XII

West Williams

Middlesex Country

Ontario

Canada

The New World

The British Empire

The Earth

The Milky Way

The Stars [447]

(Illustrating another story, 'The Ditch: Second Reading,' is a map of Souwesto, with inset centred on Easthope, the community near Stratford where Reaney was brought up: his literary territory par excellence.)

Loyal is not really much concerned with the global and cosmic

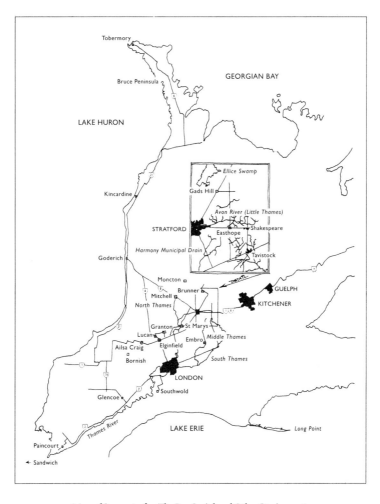

Map of Souwesto for *The Box Social and Other Stories*, 1996,
drawn by Tim Inkster at the request of James Reaney,
who wanted Stratford, Ontario placed in the middle.

context into which he sets himself, though 'to the stars and beyond them if at all possible became his quest.'[448] He seems to be an early mask of his author, then obsessed with the dark side. Loyal's reading runs to the gothic, and his 'mind began to take on unusual capacity for seeing odd angles and dark corners. Incidentally, his parents did not know about *Maria Monk* which was hidden under a loose floorboard in their son's bedroom. It was a long time before its occasional reader puzzled out just what the "criminal connections" actually meant in real life. Real life! What was that? No, the real life for Loyal was not in the world of things, although he, with book in hand or pocket, managed to help his father on the farm quite well enough; no, the real life was in the kingdom of shadows in the small, much thumbed library, and in the mushroom-and-Indian pipes mental landscape that found its nourishment in the chlorophyll of writers, most of them long since dead.'[449]

The reference is to a Canadian book, *Awful Disclosures of Maria Monk, or, The Hidden Secrets of a Nun's Life in a Convent Exposed* (1836), which claimed to expose systematic sexual abuse of nuns, and infanticide of the resulting children by Catholic priests in Maria Monk's convent in Montreal. I was once appalled to hear people of my acquaintance—these were not readers, but knee-jerk anti-Catholics—casually mention the killing and burial of children, born to nuns, by priests. Did Maria Monk's exposé somehow flood the banks of the book and make its way by mouth to Alberta? Well, that book and the others Loyal has read, including *Wuthering Heights* and *Daniel and the Book of Revelation*, draws him deep into the dark side of the supernatural, and obsession claims his life at the age of nineteen. His experience and his fate would slide nicely into a tale by Edgar Allan Poe. The address written out as his story begins is the epitaph on his tombstone at the end. His author made out better: lived until he was eighty-two, maintained a productive fascination with gothic romance for his whole life.

Angels

Let me now recapitulate the appearance of angels so far in this essay: 'Granny Janitor Angel' (*Twelve Letters*); 'the passage of the angel of time ensures that what once seemed so banal and commonplace will quickly become that magic thing; the past remembered and organized by the humblest of formulas—the patient daily record' (*Performance Poems*); 'All of Jesse's stem and the various ranks of angels' (*A Suit of Nettles*); 'the bright angel feet/ Of Elwy Yost' (*Imprecations*); '*Your plant with its angel flower can't change me*' (*Night Blooming Cereus*);

> *Angel, declare: what sways when Noah nods?*
> *The sun, the stars, the figures of the gods.* ('The Anagogic Man')

Many angels. And the list of angels in Reaney's work could be much longer. Here's just one more instance, for now, from *Souwesto Home*:

> How many things seek their voice in us?
> Unsuspected demons & angels
> Wait for the arrangement we provide
> Of gut, enzyme, funny bone, nervous system, mind. [450]

Yes, demons too, but we're looking at angels just now. What is an angel? From what you've just read, the answer varies: an innocence, an aurora, an audience, an intermediary, a source.

Why trace angels through Reaney's work? I thought to do so after finding angels mentioned just once in a very different work, Jan Zwicky's *The Experience of Meaning*: 'Western European languages don't have a term for entities that are *like* ideas yet exist independently of any mind. "Angel" may be the closest they get. But to claim forms are like angels is, these days, to ask for trouble rather than to solve it.' [451] Of Aziraphale, angel protagonist in Terry Pratchett and Neil Gaiman's novel, *Good Omens*, it is said that 'Technically Aziraphale was a Principality, but people made jokes about that these days.'[452] With roots deep in Romanticism, especially in Blake, Reaney never shies away from the term angel. The word is so naturally part of his lexicon that he can even use it, rather oddly, for the passage of time. He is a different sort of poet than Jan Zwicky, who is also a philosopher. It may be the poet in Zwicky who is tempted by the word angel, but it's as philosopher, anxious to redirect the dominant course of Western thinking, that she veers away, and I'll return to this.

Angels typically act as messengers, intermediaries between God and humans. The most famous annunciation, for those brought up in the Christian tradition, is in the first chapter of The Gospel According to St. Luke, where the Angel Gabriel appears to Mary the virgin:

And the angel said unto her, Fear not, Mary: for thou hast found favour with God.

And, behold, thou shalt conceive in thy womb, and bring forth a son, and shalt call his name JESUS.

He shall be great, and shall be called the Son of the Highest: and the Lord God shall give unto him the throne of his father David:

And he shall reign over the house of Jacob for ever; and of his kingdom there shall be no end.

Then said Mary unto the angel, How shall this be, seeing I know not a man?

And the angel answered and said unto her, The Holy Ghost shall come upon thee, and the power of the Highest shall overshadow thee: therefore also that holy thing which shall be born of thee shall be called the Son of God. [453]

I've seen no evidence that Reaney read Northrop Frye's *The Great Code: The Bible and Literature*, though it would be surprising if he had not. The book contains a succinct summary of the appearance and significance of angels in the Bible:

'Above' the human world is a world of spiritual beings or angels, metaphorically associated with the sky.… Two kinds of angels are mentioned especially in the Old Testament: seraphim (Isaiah 6 and elsewhere) and cherubim (Ezekiel 1 and elsewhere). Later theology developed a more elaborate structure of nine orders of angels, but retained these two as spirits of love and contemplation respectively, and medieval painters colored them respectively red and blue.… All this implies a special connection between angelic messengers and verbal communication: in Galatians 3:19 and elsewhere angels are said to be the agents of the giving of Scripture. [454]

In *Il Convivio*, Dante calls angels 'Intelligences.' [455] His angels have knowledge beyond anything vouchsafed humans—or ex-humans like Reaney's ghost. That should be easy for a human to grasp, there being so much, even in ordinary life, that none of us, not even the smartest and hardest-working, can take in. But, accepting what 'the spouse and confidant [of the Saviour], Holy Church, states, believes and preaches,' Dante also lists the whole nine orders of angels, almost as if he himself was familiar with them: 'The first is that of the Angels, the second that of the Archangels, and the third that of the Thrones; these three orders comprise the first hierarchy—not first in respect either of nobility or of creation, for the others are certainly more noble than they and all were created together, but first in respect of our movement upwards toward their level of being. Then come the Dominations, followed in turn by the Virtues and the Principalities; these comprise the second hierarchy. Above these come the Powers and the Cherubim, and highest of all, the Seraphim; these comprise the third hierarchy.' [456] A modern may be comfortable enough with the idea of Intelligences and boggled by the crowd in that hierarchy. Questions might arise: are some kinds of angel smoother dancers on the head of a pin? The modern might also wonder how humans came to know some kinds of things about angels. Jacob Boehme, for example: '[A]n angel hath no guts, neither flesh nor bones, but is constituted or composed by the divine power in the shape, *form* and manner of a man, and hath all members like man, except the members of generation, and the fundament or *going out of the draff*, neither hath an angel need of them.'[457]

Well, irony is a necessary 'bullshit detector;'[458] it may highlight amusing aspects of matters one actually takes seriously, but it doesn't take us far with angels. Better to go with the likes of C.G. Jung and accept them as symbols. 'Why, when Pope Pius XII in one of his last discourses deplored that the world was no longer conscious enough of the presence of angels, he was saying to his faithful Catholics in Christian terms exactly what I am trying to say in terms of psychology to those who stand more chance of understanding this language than any other.'[459]

The ranks of angels appear in Reaney's 'A Trip to the Globe Theatre' (*Performance Poems*), listed in a section of that workshop script/collage called 'The Sphere of the Earth as Memory System,' where they are joined by other symbols. The numbers below follow from a listing (1 to 14) of 'The Theatres of London, 1576–1642':

15	Seraphim	8	Saturn
16	Cherubim	7	Jupiter
17	Thrones	6	Mars
18	Dominations	5	The Sun
19	Principalities	4	Venus
20	Powers	3	Mercury
21	Virtues	2	Moon
22	Archangels	1	Fire
23	Angels		Air
24	Crystalline		Water
25	Primum Mobile		Earth—The Globe[460]
9	The Stars		

'[T]his play focuses a group for discussion of how we might produce symbolic art and architecture once more.'[461] Reaney is presenting items on his list, even the hierarchy of angels, as legitimate material for art. Even in the twentieth century. He doesn't list the parallel hierarchy of demons, though in *Take the Big Picture* he shows that he knows them. The triplets in his children's novel go nuts and become monsters when their diet is not confined to organic foods. Their given names are Jeremiah, Habakkuk and Ezekiel but, when they act like demons under the influence of additives, other biblical names are thought to be more appropriate: 'Asmodeus, Beelzebub, Satan!'[462] (In Reaney's play, *Gentle Rain Food Co-op*, the good guys buy and eat locally grown, organic foods; the bad guys' diet has 'the stimulating additives that keep other people mean and suspicious.'[463] The Reaney-Thibaudeau family were members of the London Food Co-op founded by Greg Curnoe, as was I for a while.[464]

For the Globe Theatre collage Reaney chooses passages from Shakespeare plays to cover the whole symbolic universe, top to bottom: 'The above scenes from *The Tempest, King John, Hamlet*—show the complete range of The Globe Theatre, from the white magic of Prospero that attains Seraphimhood to the dark world that kills Prince Arthur as he tries to escape his wicked uncle, to the elemental under-earth where a vicious demon ghost lures Hamlet to kill eight people instead of one, a great many of them innocent.'[465]

Angels. Even in the twentieth Century. How about the twenty-first? Aren't angels obsolete in this secular age? January 27, 2020. After having written the above, I closed my computer, opened *Niagara & Government*, a book of poems by Phil Hall, and soon found an angel where I would not have expected to:

Acting crazy
   we were stopped
             by a stand-up bass
  on its side in the pasture

  morning   no one else around

   the angel who grew inside it   like a snail

has abandoned it   & gravity

cello   viola   lute
each housed a different breed of angel

Don't say   angel   that's stupid. [466]

In one voice Phil Hall giveth; in another he taketh away. He has it both ways, as I'm also inclined to do. His angels are not Reaneyesque, but their presence in *Niagara & Government* shows that angels still call to writers very different than Reaney. (Phil Hall is an admirer of Reaney, though, and has made a homage drawing for *Twelve Letters to a Small Town*, 'Reaney & I go for a ride in his carriage pulled by my white porcupines.' [467])

Phil Hall's porcupines (top) are based on Reaney's chickens (bottom).

It seems worth giving some space to angels I have met in the modern arts, by way of gathering some company for Reaney's angels. For anyone who keeps company with angels, as I do not, not as a rule, what follows in this chapter may seem obvious, even redundant. Feel free to skip it. I make no apology for the next few pages, though. It's not every day that a gate in the mind swings open—Phil Hall's poem: click—on a new path too tempting to ignore.

In the present secular age, angels may not be ubiquitous, but any casual survey of the subject will show that the figure is anything but played out. Pratchett and Gaiman's exuberant novel *Good Omens* (another recommendation of my daughter) is a comic recasting of the end times. Among the dramatis personae, are Aziraphale, 'An angel, and part-time rare-book dealer' and Crowley, 'An angel who did not so much Fall as Saunter Vaguely Downwards.'[468] Over the centuries of their assignment in it, the pair have become accustomed to 'the pleasures of the world.'[469] '[T]he world was an amazing interesting place which they both wanted to enjoy for as long as possible,'[470] so of course they are not looking forward to the Apocalypse. Damiel, the Bruno Ganz angel in Wim Wenders' 1987 elegiac film *Wings of Desire* (Peter Handke, writer) is one of the invisible guardian angels in the film, immortal spirits who tenderly watch over troubled humans in Berlin. He falls in love with Marion, a lonely trapeze artist, played by Solveig Dommartin, and chooses to become mortal so as to experience the life of the senses.

In the 1996 film, *Michael*, John Travolta plays an archangel nearing the end of his time on earth. Whether or not he has his member of generation—the movie doesn't go there—he exudes manly charisma in the dancing sequence (ironically to Aretha Franklin's 'Chain of Fools') that draws to him every last woman in a rural bar. It's lucky that Michael loves battle, because he is then obliged to take on every jealous man in that same bar. The film is very funny, but, for its human characters, if not for the audience (I knew right away that Michael really was an angel), it raises serious questions of belief. Can an unlikely looking angel with bedraggled wings make a believer out of a cynical journalist like the one played by

William Hurt? Belief, in this case, involves the capacity to love. As Michael's human sojourn comes to an end, he laments the terrible loss he is about to suffer. Unlike his human companions on the road trip intended to make him into a tabloid story, he knows what a gift his temporary human existence has been and has had the good sense to live it up.

Wings of Desire and *Michael* are very different movies, and thematically opposite in one way: Damiel becomes human, Michael shuffles off his human frame, after which it seems as though he enters the guardian role as spirit. But both know the glory of earthly life in a human body. For this very same reason, bright and dark angels in *Good Omens*, having 'gone native,' connive together to ensure that their story has a different end than the one scripted in the Book of Revelation. Addressing Odysseus in the underworld, Achilles might have been speaking for both Damiel and Michael. 'No man in the past or hereafter is more blessed than you,' says Odysseus, man of many wiles.

'When you were alive before, the Argives honored you
Equal to the gods. Now you greatly rule over the dead,
Being here as you are. So do not grieve now you are dead, Achilles.'
Thus I spoke, and he at once addressed me in answer:
'Noble Odysseus, do not commend death to me.
I would rather serve on the land of another man
Who had no portion and not a great livelihood
Than to rule over all the shades of those who are dead.'[471]

In Jeanette Winterson's story, 'The Lion, the Unicorn and Me,' Me is the donkey who narrates the story. She or he and the other two beasts have been shortlisted in a competition, judged by an angel, for the privilege of carrying Mary and Jesus to Bethlehem. Donkey is chosen for best tiebreaker line: 'if He is to bear the burdens of the world, He had better be carried by me.'[472]

Jane Siberry's lovely song, 'Calling All Angels,' opens with a spoken invocation of saints:

Santa Maria, Santa Teresa, Santa Anna, Santa Susannah
Santa Cecilia, Santa Copelia, Santa Domenica, Mary Angelica
Frater Achad, Frater Pietro, Julianus, Petronilla
Santa, Santos, Miroslaw, Vladimir and all the rest

The song calls on angels for help in keeping on with a bewildering life in which 'pain and suffering' coexist with 'the beauty of the light upon this earth.'[473] Will angels still respond to such heartfelt pleas for spiritual assistance? The answer, not in the lyrics but in ethereal melody, in vocal and instrumental harmony, is yes.

Here are the last verse and chorus of one of my favourite gospel songs:

I've almost reached my heav'nly home:
My spirit strongly sings.
The Holy Ones, behold, they come.
I hear the noise of wings.

> Oh come, angel band,
> Come and around me stand;
> Oh, bear me away on your snowy wings
> To my eternal home.
> Oh, bear me away on your snow-white wings
> To my eternal home.

'Angel Band' was written by Americans Jefferson Hascall (words) and William Batchelder Bradbury (music) in 1862, but, like any good song, it's very much alive in, say, the high old lonesome bluegrass harmonies of the Stanley Brothers. And in many other current versions.

It's interesting that, in some views, the joys of this life are such that angels desperately want to be here, on earth, while in so many gospel songs wayfaring strangers like us want to be there, on the far side of Jordan, in the company of the angels and loved ones gone on before. In

Gerald Squires, 'St. Francis Receiving the Stigmata,' 1988.

Acrylic on canvas, 152.4 cm. x 213.36 cm.

those songs, this life is a vale of tears and death is a release. Joys and tears: a pretty good summation of human experience.

Gerald Squires is a Newfoundland visual artist whose early religious background was protestant, Salvation Army to be exact, but, after coming into his mastery, he was often commissioned to make art for Catholic institutions. In Mary Queen of the World Parish Church, Mount Pearl, Newfoundland, may be found his *Crucifixion and Resurrection*, his *Last Supper* and *Stations of the Cross*. For Alverno Church Monastery in Orangeville, Ontario, in 1988, he painted his own version of an ancient subject, *St. Francis Receiving the Stigmata* (the five wounds of Christ). That transfer will be happening sometime after the moment recorded in the picture, because the angel is caught right at the moment of landing. Even though he has just appeared from another dimension—out of the light behind him—he can be seen to have actually flown. His legs are flexed, his wings sweep forward in braking motion. To make his visitation, this heavenly messenger has assumed the forms of both man and bird, a bird with fully functional wings.

Squires' religious pictures embody his own spirituality. He gave his own face to both the crucified Christ and the man who drives in the nails. There is a source photograph of Squires in the pose he wanted for St. Francis. His faith was often assailed by doubt, but it would be fair to say that, like the saint in the painting, his arms remained open to the angel.

For many readers of my generation, particularly those brought up on the Canadian prairies, Margaret Laurence's *The Stone Angel* is an important book. The angel of her title, introduced on the opening pages of the novel, could hardly be less like the kinetic presence in Squires' painting. No wonder the narrator, Hagar Shipley, views her ironically:

Above the town, on the hill brow, the stone angel used to stand. I wonder if she stands there yet, in memory of her who relinquished her feeble ghost as I gained my stubborn one, my mother's angel that my father bought in pride to mark her bones and proclaim her dynasty, as he fancied, forever and a day.

Summer and winter she viewed the town with sightless eyes. She was doubly blind, not only stone but unendowed with even a pretense of sight. Whoever carved her had left the eyeballs blank. It seemed strange to me that she should stand above the town, harking us all to heaven without knowing who we were at all. But I was too young then to know her purpose, although my father often told me she had been brought from Italy at a terrible expense and was pure white marble. I think now she must have been carved in that distant sun by stone masons who were the cynical descendants of Bernini, gouging out her like by the score, gauging with admirable accuracy the needs of fledgling pharaohs in an uncouth land.

Her wings in winter were pitted by the snow and in summer by the blown grit. She was not the only angel in the Manawaka cemetery, but she was the first, the largest, and certainly the costliest. The others, as I recall, were a lesser breed entirely, petty angels, cherubim with pouting stone mouths, one holding aloft a stone heart, another strumming in eternal silence upon a small stone stringless harp, and yet another pointing with ecstatic leer to an inscription.[474]

Anything, no matter how sacred its origin or nature, may be cheapened: mass-produced cemetery angels are a case in point. Hagar's ironic view of the statue is itself ironic, since, as the novel proceeds, many details make it clear that she has been all but describing herself. She is sitting 'Rigid as marble'[475] at one point; again and again she is associated with stone. Her character is stubbornly stony. She has a rich inner life, but it's locked away, shared only with the reader.

Later in the novel, on a visit to the cemetery with her son John, Hagar finds the angel toppled. Reluctantly, John agrees to try to set it upright, and here, in a book soaked in Biblical tradition (Hagar's name is from Genesis and Galatians), is another angel: 'I wish he could have looked like Jacob then, wrestling with the angel and besting it, wringing a blessing from it with his might. But no.'[476] Hagar has another son, Marvin, the one who calls his mother a 'holy terror' when she's on her deathbed, and the one who now reaches out to her with a love she has always found difficult to return: 'Now it seems to me he is truly Jacob, gripping with all his strength, and bargaining. *I will not let thee go, except thou bless me.* And I see I am thus strangely cast, and perhaps have been so from the beginning, and can only release myself by releasing him.'[477] A memory of the stone angel appears again, not long after this, near the end of the book, so it's a framing device, but this contending angel—Hagar now—has the capacity to bless. So much emotion is held so tightly in, throughout the novel, that every slip of affection feels momentous. A sudden, dramatic, final shift in Hagar's character and behaviour would betray the book. Less being more, the small release into love that Hagar manages is huge.

For Jungian psychotherapist Donald E. Kalsched, 'archetypal powers, sometimes appearing in our dreams as *angels* or *demons*, represent primitive forces from deep within the psyche/soma.' They are 'elemental emotional powers' he has discovered 'in my work with a particular subgroup of patients—namely those who have suffered from catastrophic early childhood trauma.'[478] This subgroup would once have included fellow psychotherapist Robin van Löben Sels. In the story of her own early trauma and eventual recovery, she records an angel dream, that filled her 'with awe and then with an extraordinary sensation of opening to feeling and a bodily sense of myself,' this after she had been shut down for about three years. After a very long wait in a bare landscape, *'Suddenly in the distant sky I see what looks like a moving light, bright red-orange and yellow. I see that it is an enormous being of light, entirely made of flame. A fiery angel alights on the hill beside me, feathers of flame falling from it, scattering over the dark ground, and I am filled with awe. The flaming angel is hermaphroditic, an enormous woman with great flaming wings and flaring garments, yet with a penis. The angel wraps me in its arms, folding us in together with its wings, and its penis penetrates me. Finally, I am warm again, all the way through, inside and out, and I talk and talk, telling the angel everything.'* [479] What a gift to meet such a confidant(e) (*with* member of generation), and to experience such warming of spirit and body, such release. It was the beginning of a transformation for the dreamer.

It should be no surprise to my readers, given the importance to Reaney of William Blake's symbolic system, that Kalsched illustrates his argument with Blake's picture, 'The Good and Evil Angels Struggling for Possession of a Child.' [480]

I think Reaney would find the power of his own symbolic universe validated by the reality of his symbols for Jung and for Jungians like Kalsched and van Löben Sels. Working to uncover buried archetypes, they are healers, helping to release tormented psyches from bondage. In Kalsched's case, that means assisting his clients to re-establish contact with their pre-trauma 'soul-child,' [481] a first step toward re-establishing psychic wholeness. For van Löben Sels, exploring the world of the archaic shaman is the route to identifying a 'shamanic complex' that is still workable today. A 'shamanic therapist,' she says, 'helps us know more fully what it is that we are experiencing, what it is that we live … not so that we become more self-centered, but so that we become more self-connected—more inwardly related, more humanly related to our own potential wholeness, which includes our fellow human beings and the wholeness of the world.' [482]

'Things you've lost are inside things you don't like.' [483] I find myself

William Blake, 'Good and Evil Angels Struggling

for Possession of a Child,' c. 1793–94.

Pen and ink and watercolour on paper, 43.8 cm. x 58.5 cm.

wondering whether that line in *Colours in the Dark*, the line out of all the others in the play that has taken on a life of its own for me, might compactly suggest why psychic excavations by therapists like Kalshed and van Löben Sels are so necessary. The line occurs in scene 16, 'The Fable of the Babysitter and the Baby.' The sitter is a university student who has been inveigled into sitting not an actual baby, but rather an armless, leg-less 'monstrosity' in need of loving attention. At first the student is repulsed, but eventually he finds within himself the care-giving love that is needed. [484] One might expect the line in question to be the moral or key to the fable, but it doesn't quite attach there. It doesn't directly attach to anything else in the play either, but given that its story backbone is the growth of an individual, through layer upon layer of complex psychic experience, from infancy to adulthood, the line resonates—within the play and outside it: 'A psychological equation decrees that if we can't make an inner situation conscious,' says van Löben Sels, 'it will constellate outside of us as fate.' [485]

As I have said, Reaney knew some Jung. Referring to the period when he was working on *Night Blooming Cereus*, a time when he says his 'poetic affairs were in a very muddled state,'[486] he found Jung helpful: 'There is a rule in literature which says that to any tea party, or gathering of any sort, the Four Living Creatures of Ezekiel's vision attend. Actually, at this time one of the few sentences of literary symbolism that had sunk through to me was Carl Jung's division of the human soul into four parts represented by an old woman, an old man, a young man and a young girl. The old woman is shadowy and terrifying, the old man is wise and helpful; the young man seeks the young woman but cannot find her until he has come to terms with the older pair.'[487] The cosmology within which van Löben Sels works is a nexus of two dimensions: 'Symbolically speaking, a horizontal dimension refers to collectivization and secularization, while a vertical dimension refers to individuation and sacralization.'[488] Here is Reaney in equivalent symbolic territory: '[P]rophecy pushes both Life and Literature away from the horizontal to the vertical—Heaven up there, Hell down here, with the sceptics and the nay-sayers.'[489] Well, this is not a neutral description. Hell is usually lower than 'here'; Reaney is having a go at his usual bugbears, the antimetaphor, anti-anagogy gang. At any rate, his cosmology, whether illustrated by the range of Shakespeare plays, from seraphic white magic to the demonic, or 'the four-fold Christian cosmos'[490] (divine order, visionary world, natural world and demonic world) is always in Jungian territory

The inquiring mind may leap aside to a different sort of horizontal/vertical scheme: Reaney's backbone for *Canada Dash, Canada Dot*, an east-west/north-south nexus laid flat on the Canadian landscape to structure Reaney's celebration of Canada's 1967 centenary. F and M are female and male voices.

F1:   Draw a line across Canada, east to west
       From here to here to here to here ... to there,
       here.
       The Line Across.

Draw a line up and down crossing the first
line.
This second line is of time.
We drew it north, north into the past.
Now and now and now and now from now to
now to now to now to then, then, then,
then now, now now.
The Line Up and Down.

M1:   Now: Where the two lines cross is a dot
that is neither here nor now, neither there nor
then—but is timeless, spaceless. Listener,
these are dots—objects of love—things that
are always present in my mind. Things my
country gave me the chance to love. [491]

It's important to remember that we're looking at libretto. 'Since the lib-
rettist is supposed to write something which the music completes and
extends, the lines have to be cleaned and scraped until there is nothing to
stop the music flowing around them.' [492] Some Canadians may find the
main 'vertical' line heading north on Yonge Street out of Toronto (to fetch
up at Sharon Temple in East Gwillimbury) is a little too Ontario-centric, so
I'll return to something said earlier about centre and circumference. This
time it's Northrop Frye on the poetry of William Blake: 'Our fallen senses
hollow out a tiny grotto in a boundless stretch of mystery, and this grotto is
our home. But the center of the real universe is wherever we happen to be,
and its circumference the limit of the radius of our experience. In the
perspective of the awakened mind, the radius of our experience *is* the universe, and art reveals to the senses of distant contact, eyesight and hearing,
a universal home, or Paradise which is ready for us to inhabit.' [493]

    Those dot/images are created at many horizontal/vertical intersec-
tions as the vertical axis of *Canada Dash, Canada Dot* slides across the
whole country. We're *all* at the centre, Canadians. Create your own
vertical. May your circumference touch the stars.

Back to the angels. In his article, 'Wrestling with our Angels: Inner and Outer Democracy in America Under the Shadow of Donald Trump,' Donald Kalsched turns his analysis to the 'polarizing us-them narrative [which] has taken over much of our common culture.' The 'national psyche' of America is in trouble. Whether they are bright or dark, angels in Kalsched's work are problematic. 'I am working for inner tolerance and for a democracy of the psyche, with all parts of the self allowed to exist in a central governance that we call the ego. This means wrestling with the absolutist powers—the "angels" of the dissociative system—in order to transform them—just like the Biblical Jacob did at the River Jabbok in the Old Testament (Genesis 32:22–32).'[494]

As a high school student, Reaney was excited to read in a physics text that the atom was structured like the solar system, so I'm pretty sure that, like me, he would also applaud Kalsched's diagnostic metaphor: individual inner conflict mirrors an outer public conflict dire in political effect. Here is a thoughtful, responsible citizen struggling to formulate the strongest possible version of democracy: 'Inner and outer democracies are always breaking down fundamentalistic, totalistic, and absolutist categories into relativistic, provisional, and contingent ones—always transforming 880 volts into usable electricity—always generating conflict and then resolving it. Democracies, in this sense, are to the collective polity what healthy families are for bringing up civilized, emotionally literate children. They are transformational containers. They are projection-eating machines. They take in evil, digest it, and give it back as hate and finally as civil disagreement. This struggle increases consciousness.'[495] Here's to radically increased consciousness and emotional literacy in the future of the United States of America. The word America brings back Tony Kushner's play, *Angels in America*, and the movie made from it, but that's enough. Angels are all around us yet.

But many of those angels just discussed aren't Reaney's sort, so we've come a long way around from him. Or have we? Yes and no. Yes, angels in cellos ('that's stupid'), show-off cemetery statues, comic angels doubling as booksellers, even angels come down to earth to be human and mortal—they're a far cry from anagogic. No, because remember Reaney saying 'all "isms" come out of or go back into myths or STORIES, so why not present the concrete version of your favourite "ism" rather than try to jam existentialism or Maoism or naturalism down your audience's throats.'[496] Jacob and the angel is a story. Pleas for help from angels ('Calling all angels'), summoning angels ('O come, angel band') originate in story. Angels still exercise much of their power of old for psychiatrists who draw inspiration from reading the ancient stories, not only Biblical, that still live within us. 'Angels are stories some of us tell, if pressed, I think,' says Robin van Löben Sels, 'while others dream them.'[497] So again, no: almost every angel in this section owes its origin to the Bible, Reaney's own primary source. He might look askance at a few of them, but for the most part I think he would enjoy the company. And it surprised me to discover, by setting out to write about angels, how ubiquitous and usable they still are. Here is 'This Elastic Moment,' by Colleen Thibaudeau:

Yes we are that too: we are everything who feel it.
Everything that has meaning has the same meaning as angels, these
hoverers and whirrers: occupied with us.
Men may be in the parkgrass sleeping: or be he who sits in his
shirtsleeves every blessed Sunday: rasping away at his child who
is catching some sunshine: from the sticky cloud hanging over the
Laura Secord factory: and teetering on the pales of the green
iron fence: higher up than the briary bushes.
I pass and make no sound: but the silver and whirr of my bicycle
going round: but must see them who don't see: get their fit, man
and child: let this elastic moment stretch out in me: till that
point where they are inside and invisible.
It is not to afterward eat a candy: picket that factory: nor to
go by again and see that rickety child on the fence.
When the band of the moment breaks there will come angelic
recurrence.[498]

The Integral

For Reaney, writing about Jay Macpherson's *The Boatman*, a long poem with a population of angels, angels are 'the structure of the Bible,' and 'Miss Macpherson knows her Bible.' '[W]hat the poet means by an angel,' he goes on, 'is anything or anybody or any being seen in its Eternal aspect, that is, at its most glorious and most real, its most expanded.'[499] That might be, at bottom, what angels mean to Reaney too, but he enjoys quite a bit of latitude in his metaphorical use of the term. In an article entitled '"Your Plays Are Like Movies—Cinemascope Ones,"' about his later plays that are 'ribbon collages of metaphors both visual, tactile and auditory,'[500] he explains the flexible inclusiveness he's going for: '[E]ven in the dullest movie the moment the camera starts floating, pursuing and watching, the possible effect on the viewer is that he is outside his body and flying about. Using the Chinese name for movies—electric shadows—I should then like to capsulize my film theory as being that of the Electric Shadows Angel. Yes, the effect of seeing films is to give you the sensation of immense powers over time and space; e.g., with a dime in my pocket I once walked three miles into town, met my cousin, bought tickets at the Classic Theatre in Stratford for *David Copperfield*, went in and sat down, and from the moment the credits came on we became Electric Shadows Angels.'[501]

'Immense powers over time and space.' That agrees well enough with 'anything or anybody or any being' 'at its glorious and most real, its most expanded.' Messengers of the ineffable that they are, angels must always be hovering over messages, over visions, that they do not deliver in person. '[I]n 1600, Boehme experienced his first great revelation. Exactly what comprised the revelation is not known, but von Franckenberg's explanation of the experience as resulting from the reflection to him of his soul in a pewter dish is suggestive in that the image of an eye reflecting back upon itself from its mirrored likeness is one that Boehme used at a number of points in his later writing.'[502] The revelation is alluded to in a Reaney poem, 'Pigeon's Necks,' about fascination with colours and their names. The title 'refers to the brilliant mixture of metallic colours the male pigeon sports. One look, and I am transported past the Beulah mating world he is in, and beyond, to some other state.'[503] (Also transporting: the iridescent emerald green in a male mallard's neck and the shimmering blue-green shine in a polished piece of labradorite.)

Damn you, philosopher,
For saying I am frivoleer.
Did not the mystic cobbler,
Jacob Behmen,
Make a complete religion
Out of a coloured flash from a sunbeam
Smacking a pewter kettle upon
Its accidentally dented brim?

In all this greasy dark carbon
Candle *non*-perception
Lurks a sudden sparkle
That hark! it will
Delight
Ignite![504]

This glosses the Boehme horse on the merry-go-round of philosophers throughout history in *A Suit of Nettles*. Boehme is clearly Reaney's favourite of all the philosophers précised there: 'what a pretty snow white horse tattooed with stars, mountains meadows real sheep moving on them it seems & fiery comets & ships in a harbour & little horses dancing in a barnyard. This horse's eyes—oh the angelic aurora wonder of its gold red mane. Every once in a while this horse's colour completely changes. People shy away then I can tell you! Storms break out in the tattooed skies and a fiery fire burns in the eyes. However, it bubbles over—a light comes into his eyes and the world changes back again.'[505]

Boehme's first book (begun in 1612) is called *The Aurora*. Its subtitle is *The Day-Spring or Redness of the Morning*. As published in English translation it bears epigraphs from Revelations, about beasts (angels) praising the Lord on his throne, and, from Isaiah and Matthew, two versions of the same passage. Isaiah 9:2: '*The People that walked in* Darkness, *have seen a* great Light: *they that dwell in the Land of the* shadow of Death, *upon them hath the* Light shined.'[506] Light, a sudden sparkle, Vision. Introducing Boehme's *Six Theosophic Points*, Nicholas Berdyaev shows why Boehme's thought would appeal to Reaney (besides the fact that Boehme was by profession a working man, a shoemaker, and later a seller of gloves). He has 'a wisdom grounded in revelation and employing myths and symbols rather than concepts—a wisdom much more contemplative than discursive. Such is religious philosophy, or theosophy.'[507]

Though the news he got is the sort that angels have been entrusted to carry, Richard Maurice Bucke was not visited by an angel (he *was* 'wrapped around as it were by a flame-colored cloud') but David Willson was. 'I was called to retire into secret from all men,' he says, in a passage from Reaney's *Serinette* about his call to a ministry.

Accordingly I obeyed the call and came forth by myself into the forest. It was expressly spoken to me that if I would go I should see the angel of God. Half believing that such a thing should be and still fearing the event of not going, I obeyed the command.

According to divine promise, I saw a beautiful young man clothed in a scarlet robe.

This robe was the blood of Christ Jesus and a mission for me.

He stood at my left hand, I could have touched him and he signified by motion this covering was for me.

He gently stripped the garment from his own shoulders and laid it on mine and told me that through the sorrows of his sin I must minister to the Christian Church—this redeeming blood was laid upon me, which I must be baptized in.

He disappeared from me naked and beautiful and I saw him no more. [508]

To encourage others to take Reaney's angels as seriously as I do, it may help to translate them into a discourse that offers less poetry and more precision, at least a different sort of precision than poetry renders. Jan Zwicky mentions angels just the once, in passing, but the angel thought comes to her through an association with Gestalt. 'Gestalt comprehension is insight into how things hang together. It is perception *that* a thing or situation hangs together; and it is sensitivity to structural echoes between that thing or situation and others.' [509] It is 'an attempt to perceive the shape of things, their inner and outer attunements, their melody.' [510] The Reaney line that immediately comes to mind again (the William Dale line in *The Dismissal*) is 'the integral versus the fractional life.' [511] Here is Loren Eiseley on the difference between the two:

The technology which, in our culture, has released urban and even rural man from the quiet before his hearth log has debauched his taste. Man no longer dreams over a book in which a soft voice, a constant companion, observes, exhorts, or sighs with him through the pangs of youth and age. Today he is more likely to sit before a screen and dream the mass dream which comes from outside.

No one need object to the elucidation of scientific principles in clear, unornamental prose. What concerns us is the fact that there exists a new class of highly skilled barbarians—not representing the very great in science—who would confine men entirely to this diet. Once more there is revealed the curious and unappetizing puritanism which attaches itself all too readily to those who, without grace or humor, have found their salvation in 'facts.' [512]

The Night Country, from which that passage comes, was published in 1971, much of it assembled from even earlier writings. Eiseley could not have known then what the word 'screen' would mean to us now. Some of us do still dream over a book, but the 'mass dream' has spread like a virus.

'In our time,' said C. G. Jung in 1959, 'it's the intellect that is making darkness, because we've let it take too big a place. Consciousness discriminates, judges, analyzes, and emphasizes the contradictions. It's necessary work up to a point. But analysis kills and synthesis brings to life. We must find out how to get everything back into connection with everything else. We must resist the vice of intellectualism, and get it understood that we cannot only understand.'[513] Elsewhere he is blunter: 'one-sided cerebral thinking' produces 'many cultural cripples.'[514] Albert Einstein: 'The intuitive mind is a sacred gift and the rational mind is a faithful servant. We have created a society that honours the servant and has forgotten the gift.'[515]

In the eyes of his colleague Charles Baudouin, Jung was much more than a mind: '[W]atching him live, one perceives that these disparate expressions are organized into a coherent whole. One feels that he denies none of them, that being and appearance (the self and the persona) have found their *modus vivendi*, that his teaching about "integrating all the functions" to form a totality is not book knowledge but lived, which amounts to affirming that he belongs not only among the scholars but among the sages.'[516] Reading that, I think again of William Dale, another professor who lives what he knows. Dismissed from the University of Toronto for standing on principle, he has fallback resources. He can and does take the train back to his father's farm near St. Mary's, Ontario, the place where his character was formed. 'When I was a boy I'd had a vision while working in the fields, such a vision that I had been made independent of the literal for life. That had ruined me. Because others hated you if you tried to take away the crutches they had to have. But I didn't need crutches. So I spoke out and said embarrassing things.'[517] Ruined him for work in a corrupt institution, fitted him for the larger life. Integral: 'of or pertaining to a whole.' Integrity: 'The condition of having no

James Reaney at the farm near Stratford, Ontario, Summer 1979.

Photograph by Lester Kohalmi.

part or element taken away or wanting; undivided or unbroken state; material wholeness, completeness, entirety.' (*OED*)

'[H]ere you are safe and sound at your father's place,' says Dale's father, 'where they can't get at you and where you can finish your history of Rome in between teaching the cows Latin and my horses some Greek, but first—[here comes a reminder of Dale's grounding; where he comes from is who he is] the pump's froze, no amount of tea kettles is going to unfreeze it—take that crowbar and go down to the creek and chop a hole in the ice. When the hole's big enough, lots of water—wave back at me with your scarf and I'll let the cattle out of the barn. They're thirsting out of their minds and the silly old pump's broke.'[518] Two photographs, both captioned 'Locale of Dale Farm, Winter 1977, courtesy James Reaney,' illustrate the pages where these speeches appear in the published play. They recall two things for me: first, the photographs taken by teachers of English 138 at locales of the Souwesto books we taught on the course; second, photographs I have seen of Professor Reaney standing in his ancestral front yard in overalls with a rake or hoe in his hand.

D. I. Brown finds the integral life operating in *Alphabet*: 'Evidence of Reaney's desire to synthesize may be seen throughout his work, but because of the nature of *Alphabet*, it is valuable to see him standing back from his own work and organizing other literary objects, the work of other writers. Focus and pattern, we have maintained, were the heart of the editorial approach to the magazine.'[519] The 'process of gridding the documented world into smaller and smaller areas,' Brown goes on, 'was Reaney's investigation into dimensions of the imaginative world. The relation between the syncretized world and its apparently dissimilar parts was consistently his concern; the resolution was in the ability to take a grand overview—stand far back—so that the pattern governing the elements could be discerned.'[520]

In Reaney, the gestalt life is made of metaphor, and in his work those who reject metaphor sound very like the rationalist sceptics Zwicky is rebutting: 'No metaphors! Literal analysis! Objectivity!—This is not a critique of Gestalt theory but a statement that it must be wrong.'[521] 'Our way of talking in literate post-Enlightenment society is epistemologically loaded: reductionism, and the ideal of context-independent, algorithmically specifiable processes that reductionism subserves, are part of the texture of "educated" speech.'[522] If Google had been true to its ideal of 'Mirroring the world,'[523] rather than harvesting data for profit and permitting the spread of skewed information, users might be less skeptical about the (certainly useful) search function of artificial intelligence. A disinterested archival supermind would have its value. But 'Google has monopolized the act of asking a question as it whittles down possible answers and influences to determine which is the "right" one.'[524] 'There was a time when we searched Google and Amazon,' says Marshall Soules, paraphrasing Shoshana Zuboff, 'now, they search and render us. Big Data is stitching together the lives we are weaving, one query at a time.'[525] And 'the fundamental problems of social media still remain. Creepy surveillance, dissolution of civic norms, widening unease, infectious rage, a tilt toward autocracy in several formerly placid liberal democracies—these are starting to seem like inherent features, not bugs.'[526]

It would be well, now, to bring in some words about Blake by Susanne M. Sklar in a book notable—though perhaps only to a Reaneyite Canadian—for acknowledging many scholars, mentors and friends but not Northrop Frye: 'Blake wants us to experience imaginatively how we and all things are interconnected, "divine members of a Divine Body". We can move (with Blake's characters) from a state of rationality and isolation (which he calls Ulro) to one of creative interconnectedness (called Eden/Eternity). In Eden/Eternity forgiveness is a spiritual and social structuring principle—which Blake advocates as the basis for all human and political relationships.'[527] About thirty years before writing her book, *Blake's* Jerusalem *as Visionary Theatre: Entering the Divine Body* (2011), but already fascinated by *Jerusalem*, Sklar had 'an extraordinary experience. The last great scene of *Jerusalem*, in which all living creatures enter the Divine Body, seemed to leap off its pages at me. I was inside the scene.

I was reading as many children read; Blake's characters (especially his Jesus) were more real to me than the furniture in my room. Something had happened to me on a fundamental level.' No angel, no vision as such, but 'something' had brought Sklar 'into the presence of God.'[528] A secular reader like myself, not (yet?) having encountered Presence, may still respect such testimony. Those who care deeply for literature will surely hear a resonance.

In the March eclogue of Reaney's *A Suit of Nettles*, the sensible visionary Effie 'recites a fable about the doorknob and the door which argues for having some sort of handle to your life whether you believe in it or not.'[529] She is trying to rouse nettled Branwell out of his melancholy, his sense that life is meaningless. What good is a door without a knob? That is the basic lesson of the fable. Knob understands its function; Door thinks it can do nicely without. 'I turn as smoothly as I can,' says Doorknob, 'To hand of wife and child and man.' But this Knob is more than a knob responsible for opening and closing a door. It's also a kind of antenna receiving news of what's out there and calculating how to react on the basis of that:

'When day is over then neap tide
Of dreams drowns all my day's neat pride;
Whales of Lust and Rays of Hate,
Madness like Eel and Fear like Skate
Swim rough and tumble in my mind;
Devouring all sane things they find
They warn me what net I must choose,
What hook & trident, leaden shoes,
Harpoons or cages I must use
When I do wake the following day
Beside the day-sea's voyage way
That leads through clouds of thoughts & hands
Unto again these dreamy sands
Where how to progress, how retreat
I learn for climbing world-life's street.'[530]

That's part of it: a highly developed sensitivity to the dangerous depths of life, with practical applications for actual behaviour. What else Knob is becomes clear after 'The door convulsed and shook/ Knob snapped in two and Door forsook.'[531] Without its knob the door ends up as firewood, but

> Its knob was toy to children dear,
> Still thinking, dreaming, showing them
> How to be Ham, Japhet and Shem
> And drunken Noah as all men must
> Who for the height of being lust.[532]

Both Branwell and Mopsus have been listening to this story. Mopsus doesn't follow, not at this point, but Branwell knows there's good in it because, despite his demoralizing skepticism, he does possess intuition. 'The meaning's felt often before it's seen;' he says,

> My heart knows what my rusted mind does not.
> Thank you Effie. Such moments have I sought
> When I might smile or pick at such a knot
> As logic fingers could not ravel out at once.[533]

The fable comes to mind while reading Zwicky on the limits of logic. With Noah and his sons, each son destined to be a patriarch and a nation, we are back to the containing figures of anagogy, of which 'the height of being' might be a decent plain definition. Craig Stewart Walker says that '[Reaney] effectively makes the simple doorknob into what Northrop Frye calls a "monad": a symbol that, viewed from an anagogic perspective, becomes the centre of one's total literary experience,'[534] though I don't think Reaney wanted his meaning limited to literary experience.

To illustrate a point about 'how empiricism leads to certain discoveries,'[535] Jung tells a story to interviewer Georges Duplain about a woman suffering from 'incurable insomnia' who was referred to him by another doctor. Jung could see that she needed 'psychic relaxation.'[536]

I tried to explain to her that relaxation was necessary, that I, for example, found relaxation by sailing on the lake, by letting myself go with the wind; that this was good for one, necessary for everybody. But I could see by her eyes that she didn't understand. She got it intellectually, that's as far as it went, though. Reason had no effect.

Then, as I talked of sailing and of the wind, I heard the voice of my mother singing a lullaby to my little sister as she used to do when I was eight or nine, a story of a little girl in a little boat, on the Rhine, with little fishes. And I began, almost without doing it on purpose, to hum what I was telling her about the wind, the waves, the sailing, and relaxation, to the tune of the little lullaby. I hummed those sensations, and I could see that she was 'enchanted.'[537]

But that was it. The hour was up and the woman had to be sent away. Even Jung was on a tight schedule. I said above that insofar as Jung had a system, it was flexible. This beautiful anecdote is one of my reasons for saying so. But his response to the woman's malady was *hors* system, outside book knowledge. It reached out beyond words. It was intuition at work—that and a personal centredness that raised this eminent man above any concern with making a fool of himself or appearing childish.

Years later, at a conference, Jung met the doctor who had made the referral. He wanted to know what Jung had done, because the patient had come home cured. 'How was I to explain to him that I had simply listened to something within myself? I had been quite at sea. How was I to tell him that I had sung her a lullaby with my mother's voice? Enchantment like that is the oldest form of medicine. But it all happened outside of my reason: it was not until later that I thought about it rationally [this must be where the empiricism comes in] and tried to arrive at the laws behind it. She was cured by the grace of God.'[538] 'How can you speak of the grace of God,' exclaims Duplain. 'It makes little difference what I call it,' Jung responds: 'God, Tao, the Great Voice, the Great Spirit. But for people of our time God is the most comprehensible name with which to designate the Power beyond us.'[539]

Jan Zwicky might have introduced Jung as an instance of left brain/right brain integration. '[T]he left hemisphere,' she writes, 'doesn't know that there is anything that it doesn't know. Its temporal range is short-term; it analyses its local environment for immediate use.... By contrast, the larger of the two hemispheres (usually the right, which controls the left side of the human body) attends to relationships, to patterns of interconnection, to context. Its world is the world at large, the world in which I experience myself "in relation to others, whether they be friend or foe."'[540] Zwicky wants to right the imbalance in conventional thinking which scants right hemisphere/gestalt comprehension. '[A]s Frye ... points out,' says Reaney, 'we live in the Age of the Tiger where the claws of scepticism are into everything visionary.'[541] I want to read gestalt as Vision. Both have been discounted; both are given too little credence in a world given to 'thinking as calculation—which has itself eroded our ability to see its limitations.'[542] 'One of my aims,' says Zwicky,

is to establish the *reality* of lyric, gestalt—based comprehension for an intellectual culture that has sidelined it for centuries: to establish not only that it is itself a real phenomenon, but that it perceives and understands the real world. We do not stand a chance of producing a viable epistemology or a viable metaphysics, ontology, or ethics, until we open a genuine dialogue between the two ways of knowing. And the problem is urgent. In the absence of that dialogue, I believe we are fated to continue to ignore the facts of ecological cataclysm and to imagine they'll be fixable by piecemeal measures. They won't be. The fate of the species depends on the left hemisphere coming to the table.[543]

Iain McGilchrist would say that the left hemisphere is already at the table, but dominating the discussion. 'The left hemisphere is competitive, and its concern, its prime motivation, is *power*.'[544] But, after all, every normally functioning brain *has* the two hemispheres, two independent cognitive processors, and they *can* work together productively. 'Both of these drives or tendencies can serve us well, and each expresses an aspect of the human condition that goes right to the core. It is not inevitable, ultimately, that they should be in conflict; and in fact it is best that they should not be. In some human brains, it appears that they can more closely co-exist....'[545]

What is offered by the right hemisphere to the left hemisphere is offered back again and taken up into a synthesis involving both hemispheres. This must be true of the processes of creativity, of the understanding of works of art, of the development of the religious sense. In each there is a progress from an intuitive [gestalt, right hemisphere] apprehension of whatever it may be, via a more formal process of enrichment through conscious, detailed analytic [left hemisphere] understanding, to a new, enhanced intuitive understanding of this whole, now transformed by the process that it has undergone.[546]

This is how parties at that table *should* behave, and sometimes they do. After delightedly watching a 2002 performance of *One Man Masque* that he wrote for himself forty-two years earlier, a revival directed and acted by Jeff Culbert, Reaney wrote that 'Jeff's convincing, continuous riot of progressive visual images reminded me of a spiritual Yin and Yang, where the left side and right side of the brain curve in upon each other with startling effects.'[547] One interesting feature of *The Bicameral Review* is that it takes its title from Julian Jaynes's 1976 book, *The Origin of Consciousness in the Breakdown of the Bicameral Mind*, a version of the left-hemisphere/right-hemisphere theory based on Roger W. Sperry's Nobel Prize-winning research. Sperry himself is quoted on the back cover of the *Review*, and other related passages, cut out of various books, comprise a sort of bicameral marginalia to many pages in the magazine. I would say that the *Review* is mainly a right hemisphere sort of organ, but that the editor is also pushing hemispheric collaboration. In 'Brain Waves,' James Weeny's work is lauded as the left-right sort: 'Professor Weeny won the G.G. Award for Poetary and again for Playmaking while he was crawling out from undergraduating. Secretly and not so secretly he was also scribbling images as these pages so proudly reveal. If only more scribblers could get into bothbrain drive and illusterate their wordwork with straight from the cortex cognition, the whirled would be a more undizzylike space.'[548]

Well, yes. If only it were that straightforward. But 'there has been a tendency for the left hemisphere to see the workings of the right hemisphere as purely incompatible, antagonistic, as a threat to its dominion—the emissary perceiving the Master to be a tyrant. This is an inevitable consequence of the fact that the left hemisphere can support only a mechanistic view of the world....'[549] The 'particular danger of the modern world view' is that 'the hemispheres are ... out of kilter.'[550] Like Zwicky, McGilchrist brings philosophy, literature, visual art, history and music to bear on his subject, trying 'to make links outside and across the boundaries of the disciplines,'[551] but he is a neuroscientist by training. In his book a reader finds that the workings of consciousness, what seems a pretty straightforward matter to most of us, are intricately complex, astonishingly so. Inside the skull, a constant struggle is going on. He delves deep into experimental research into the workings of the brain to make his own passionate, complex, nuanced version of the case that, since the Renaissance, the limited, reasoning left hemisphere of the brain has increasingly become the default—the tyrant—brain of Western civilization, and that is why so much of 'progress' has gone wrong.

All this places Reaney on the 'wrong' side of 'progress.' His world is that of the right hemisphere of the brain, sponsor of the holistic view of things, the sector that understands metaphor, paradox, irony, humour, ambiguity, symbolism, that sponsors intuition, empathy, individuality and aesthetic appreciation. Such capacities favour a view of life as process ('betweenness' is a word for this that recurs in McGilchrist), even, ultimately, as ineffable. For claims of the left hemisphere, the side par excellence of science—though distancing reason and calculation do play significant roles in consciousness as a whole, and even in creation—Reaney had very little use. Perhaps his unsatisfactory encounter with his high school science teacher was formative in this regard. Reading that the atom is structured like the solar system, he immediately took the one as metaphor for the other. 'Go deep enough into ourselves,' he says, 'and you came to outer space filled with stars; go far enough out of yourself beyond your so-called real world, beyond our sun, and you came to the same starscape! My response was "Wow! Vision!"' He was already in Blake territory ('To see a World in a Grain of Sand/ And a Heaven in a Wild Flower'[552]). 'So excited was I by this idea,' he continues,

that I made the mistake of telling Mr. Bissonnette about it. He gave me a look of deep and scientific scorn:

'None of that now, Reaney!'

'But sir, the planets go around the ... so do the little equivalent things in us.' But 'None of that now' was his reaction, and as I biked home to the farm I rather wondered why he had lost his temper at me.[553]

A 'crackerjack teacher of Biology and natural science'[554] was Mr. Bissonnette, but no gestalt thinker. To this moment of rebuff can we trace Reaney's antipathy to science? Henceforth, he will not be inviting science to the table. 'Finally,' he goes on,

I concluded that scientists and poets are never going to get along. The poet's metaphors are regarded as lies although the mathematician has similar equations that say the most unlikely things are equal to other unlikely things, and boom!—a hydrogen bomb is possible thereby! But the poet's equations, in words not in numbers, of course, are not all right, not to be taken seriously? The kind of vision that involves stories, myths, and imagery, that also involve speech, letters, and words, is, today, constantly in trouble; the kind of vision that involves numbers equations, chemical formulae, etc is worshipped as the root of our progress, 'progress' yes, and our consumeristic successes, our medicine, our health, despite the fact that the obverse side of these accomplishments is—atom bombs, materialism, slaughter, nerve gas, you name it. It's a treadmill in a squirrel cage.[555]

(Grace Paley: 'I haven't needed to iron in years because of American science, which gives us wash-and-wear in one test tube and nerve gas in the other. Its right test tube doesn't know what its left test tube is doing.'[556])

In *Science and Poetry*, Mary Midgley argues, like McGilchrist and Zwicky and others, that scientists and poets *must* get along. Beginning with 'the alleged clash between "the two cultures" (humanities and science),'[557] she writes to resist the 'conviction that there must be a single human faculty that is finally able to solve all our problems and arbitrate all our disputes. And today the intellect, as exercised in science [and analytic philosophy], is most often thought to be that faculty. It seemed to follow, then, that other human powers and pursuits ought not to be allowed to compete with it and that we probably should not waste too much time in exercising them. Science should simply be acknowledged as a benign and absolute ruler.'[558] 'One very deplorable feature of the simple, one-sided, reductive attitude that we have inherited from the seventeenth century has been a detached, contemptuous attitude to the natural world—a vision of ourselves as something quite distinct from that world, superior to it, able to study it and use it just as we please. As we are now beginning to realize, this is a point on which Enlightenment thinking has been terribly faulty.'[559]

Metaphor, poetry, vision. Gestalt. Badly needed now. It's worth emphasizing that a good many scientists like Jane Bennett, Suzanne Simard, Iain McGilchrist and Jesper Hoffmeyer are already at the table. Like Bennett and McGilchrist and other 'enquirers into many things indeed' (Heraclitus), Hoffmeyer brings together a vast network of disciplines, a confluence of sciences, philosophy, linguistics, literature and so on. He finds cellular sources for our 'yearning for meaningfulness'[560] and outlines an ethics meant to heal the rift between humans and nature. *Signs of Meaning in the Universe* is a work of great humanity and common sense. So is McGilchrist's *The Master and His Emissary*, a book which returns again and again to the notion 'that there is a *something* apart from ourselves, which we can influence to *some* degree. And the evidence is that how we do so matters.'[561]

But, alas, Reaney saw that hard scientists were not the only ones who discouraged cultivation of the integrating imagination. Some of his English teachers at the fictional Rupertsland College in *Three Desks* represent the vision-denying, anti-intellectual wing of academic humanities. No need to bring up the nihilistic seam of post-structuralism, as Reaney might; Niles, in *Three Desks*, will do. It's no accident that Niles's name suggests nihilist. He takes the sexy approach to teaching, as in his course 'From Moll Flanders to Lady Chatterley.' Believing only in his own well-being and courting personal popularity, he fools smart and committed students for a time. Deborah and her boyfriend Tuckersmith had left Jacob Waterman's Old English class—his 'camp,' actually—for that of Niles, but they have wised up. Deborah returns to Waterman to find out what he meant by saying that 'the legends about [King] Arthur were true.'[562] She desperately needs them to be true. 'Dr. Waterman; if you can convince me that King Arthur is still alive I'll be able to—exist.... You see when I go to Mr. Niles' lectures he's always saying that, well, in effect, King Arthur is dead. Dead as a doornail. Milton was a fool. What's the difference between reading a play by Shakespeare and a Salesmanship Manual? Nil. Except the latter has more relevance to life as it is actually lived. The fraud!'[563] This is worse than science narrowly construed. This is soul-denying cynicism. Invited to the table, Niles would say what for? What's the point? We're all going to have our heads chopped off anyway. And this guy is about to become the next principal of Rupertsland College.

In *The Dismissal*, as in *Three Desks*, (and too often in life outside of plays), the narrow rather than the expansive thinkers are the ones who worm their way into running educational institutions. The new president of the University of Toronto in *The Dismissal* is a physicist by the name of Fury. Immediately after his installation, he demonstrates his priorities: '[W]e must see what we may accomplish by running as trim a ship as possible.... For example, the Men's Residence is said to have forty-three chairs in the dining hall, yet only forty residents. Thirty dessert plates and yet there are fifty-two butter dishes.'[564] Later in the play he is upset by the cost of running the men's lavatory. Fury is a 'bean counter,' as academics devoted to teaching and research call such anti-intellectual administrators. Another way to assess Fury would be to say that he is fractional, not integral, fractional in spades.

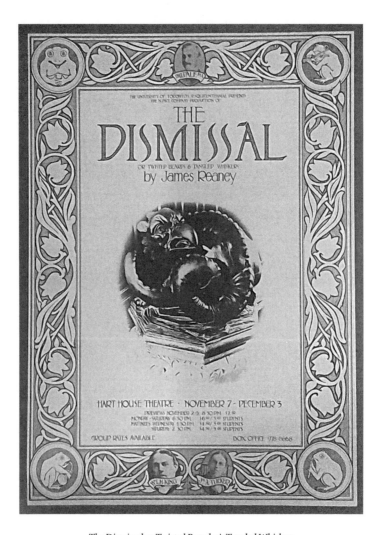

The Dismissal or Twisted Beards & Tangled Whiskers.
Poster for the NDWT Company Hart House production,
November 7 to December 3, 1977. Generations of undergraduates will
remember the fanciful sculpture that sits on the newel of the staircase in the east wing of University College that has been variously
described as a Gryphon, a Gargoyle and a Chimera.
James Reaney would have known it well.

I remember a Western English department meeting sometime in the 1980s during which criteria for advancement—raises and promotion—were being discussed. Possible ways of arriving at some sort of assessment number were being kicked around. Reaney erupted with 'How much for an epic poem!' It wasn't a question and the talk went on as if the outburst hadn't happened. In a department meeting one raises a hand, secures recognition from the chair, is then permitted to speak. *Robert's Rules of Order* keeps anarchy at bay, and a good thing too. But in this case the underlying assumption—performance is quantifiable—went unchallenged. Discussing *that* would have been a better waste of our time, though it would have interminably prolonged an already insufferable meeting. That was in the twentieth century.

'One of the strangest projects of privatization and commodification in the early twenty-first century,' says Anna Lowenhaupt Tsing, 'has been the movement to commoditize scholarship. Two versions have been surprisingly powerful. In Europe, administrators demand assessment exercises that reduce the work of scholars to a number, a sum total for a life of intellectual exchange. In the United States, scholars are asked to become entrepreneurs, producing ourselves as brands and seeking stardom from the very first days of our studies, when we know nothing.'[565] Add up the numbers of your books and articles and reviews and whatnot, assign a number to the lot: that's you, and that's how your position on the great chain of academic being may be fixed. Universities are ecologies; they have pretty well the whole range of human beings. Thirty years of academic life showed me that true scholars and idealists still enter the system and resist commodification as best they can. Even business schools need to be about more than business, but universities are now competitive businesses. Working within the contemporary academy means rolling with one of those human compromises that prop up flawed but necessary structures. The only way to do so with integrity is to keep the gaze fixed on something ancient and bright: the ideal of unfettered learning.

Reaney worked the theme of mistaken priorities for a long time. 'What is truth but a game, eh,' asks Harry Gardner in *The Killdeer*. 'It isn't what's true that matters but who/ Is the more powerful.'[566] 'Look at all these books they teach,' says Tucker, a U of T student in *The Dismissal*, 'but when it comes to practising what the books say—it's the same old privilege and power grab game with our college as it is with the money people downtown.'[567] And it's the same with politics. Another student, William Lyon MacKenzie King, will become Prime Minister of Canada; the wiles he used to achieve and occupy that position are on display in the play. Like Professor Dale, Tucker stands for real learning, the integral life. Dale will be dismissed, Tucker expelled. King will thrive.

The equivalent of Niles and Fury in *Colours in the Dark* is Dr. Button, of University College, Toronto. His class in Old Testament Studies debunks everything in the Bible that might foster belief 'in a holy creative force which bonds the Universe together, inspires people to believe in something.... All wrong of course....'[568] In this play, the Deborah figure is Son, who has brought his high school friend Bible Sal to one of Button's lectures. Son has the instincts of a poet. He usually retreats from Dr. Button's antivision sentiments by going to sleep on the coats at the back of the lecture hall. On this day, Dr. Button provokes him into making his 'usual outburst.'

SON: A flower is like a star.

BUTTON: Oachghwkwk! A flower is not like a star! Nothing is like anyone else. Anything else. You've got to get over thinking things are like other things.

SON: Then if a flower is not like a star, and nothing is like anything else then—all the spring goes out of me. I used to take such pleasure in little things—images, stones, pebbles, leaves, grasses, sedges—the grass is like a pen, its nib filled with seed—but it all seems—lies. I can't go on. There seems no reason to go on living or thinking.[569]

Deborah and Son are versions of Reaney himself, as he shows in the 'Editorial' to *Alphabet* 1: 'I can remember about twelve years ago at Toronto feeling the final clutch of the so-called scientific world. Metaphors seemed lies. Poetry seemed to have no use at all. The moon looked enchanting through the trees on Charles Street, but the enchantment was really nothing but an illusion of clouds and fantasy covering up a hideous pock-marked spherical desert. When I told this part of my problem to a friend, whose work appears in this issue [Richard Stingle], he showed me a passage from [Blake's] *The Marriage of Heaven and Hell* which had the effect of starting me back to the belief I had held as a child that metaphor is reality.'[570]

In *Colours in the Dark* that affirmation is dramatized after Bible Sal is provoked into a linguistic/spiritual competition with Dr. Button. The professor has heard of this young girl who works in the university kitchens, has been writing out the Bible in longhand, and takes it all literally. He makes the mistake of scornfully referring to her in the class, she identifies herself, he proposes a test of her faith. He first tests her on Bible passages. She recites them all from memory. All right. Having established that she knows only English, he ups the ante. 'I will ask you a question in a foreign tongue,' he says. 'The Holy Spirit will give you the power no doubt to reply to me in that tongue.'[571] He poses three questions, one in French (Claudel's version of *Electra*), one in German (Grimm's 'Red Riding Hood') and one in Ancient Babylonian (the first words of the Bible) and lo! the unilingual Bible Sal answers them all in the original languages. 'Highly significant things are often rejected,' says Jung, 'because they seem to contradict reason and thus set it too arduous a test.'[572] Bible Sal's success empowers Son to promote his simile ('A flower is like a star') to a metaphor: 'A flower is a star.'[573] After Dr. Button exits 'in shame and wrath,'[574] Son gets the whole class chanting that. Presumably they are now all proponents of identity that passeth beyond mere likeness, all empowered to merge radically different things in imagination. Imagination over reason, spirit over matter.

The view of metaphor advanced here is simplistic, but the play works well with such simple images. The complexity is created by their layered multiplicity. 'Metaphor is reality' is itself a kind of flat metaphor. It only half works. As a flower is also *not* a star (Dr. Button is half right), reality is also *not* metaphor. The most interesting metaphors have the yes-no torque of paradox. Whether the 'is' of 'this is that' be overt or implicit, metaphors defy logic or illogic in the link. They release an energy greater than the sum of this + that. In any case, there are non-metaphorical ways of representing reality. I wonder if faith in metaphor narrowly construed had something to do with Reaney's dismissal of realism.

Realism Reconsidered

If Reaney had been able to see a bridge between science and poetry, would he also have been more open to the various arts of realism? Might he have been more receptive to some of the renditions of 'real life' that he found limited and boring? Almost anywhere you look in his work—overtly in the essays—he dismisses realism. Margaret Avison's poem 'Perspective,' he says, refutes the artistic convention of converging lines, and out with that convention, for him, also goes 'tedious photographic realism.'[575] One of the distinctive features of Lewis Carroll's *Through the Looking-Glass* that Reaney adapted for the stage is that 'in Looking-glass Land time flows backward. Could this ever be so? Yes, it is so every time a great artist such as Lewis Carroll gets tired of our always predictable world and decides to liven things up a bit by suggesting other possibilities.'[576] Carroll himself is 'eccentric, donnish, obsessed with fantastic "elsewheres" quite unlike our couch-potato kitchen-sink scenarios.'[577] 'What both the *Wonderland* and *Looking-glass* books imply, is that there is another level of consciousness altogether different from the one with which we see only "dull reality."'[578]

I hope it's clear by now that I understand Reaney's ardent sponsorship of romance and myth. He is always making the case for it against those who dismiss it all as child's play. He is always pressing its claim to be a true way—besides a dramatic and exciting way—of representing the world as it is. As I have said, he is also against the one-side-only way of viewing anything, but that openness has limits. The limits may have been those of his mentor. 'Cosmology is a literary art,' says Frye, 'but there are two kinds of cosmology, the kind designed to understand the world as it is, and the kind designed to transform it into the form of human desire. Platonists and occultists deal with the former kind, which after Newton's time, according to Blake, became the accepted form of science. Cosmology of this type is speculative, which, as the etymology of that word shows, is ultimately intellectual narcissism, staring into nature as the mirror of our ordinary selves. What the mirror shows us is what Blake calls "mathematic form," the automatic and mindless universe that has no beginning nor end, no up nor down. What such a universe suggests to us is resignation, acceptance of what is, approval of what is predictable, fear of whatever is unpredictable.'[579] Two kinds: one bad, one good. If world views could really be so sharply differentiated, it would be easy to choose which way to go. But it's not so clear. It's not either/or—as Frye knows; his dualities are meant to hold shifty complex matters still for a bit.

In Elizabeth Strout's novel, *Olive, Again*, her sequel to *Olive Kitteridge*, there is a scene that bears on what I've just been saying, a discussion between Suzanne and Bernie, both lawyers, though Bernie is the elder of the two. Suzanne has just been through a family trauma. She is feeling a childlike vulnerability that opens her up to Bernie. At the end of a phone discussion between the two, she asks him if he has any faith. 'Religious faith, I mean.' '"[Y]ou know,"' he replies, '"I've lived for many years as a secular Jew, and I don't believe I have any faith in that sense."' Suzanne hears a 'but' in his voice, so she presses him further and he admits that he has a faith, though '"I don't have words to describe it. It's more an understanding—I've had it most of my life—that there is something much larger than we are."' He is describing a sensation that Suzanne has also had, but not for years.' Still, she responds, '"whenever someone says they're an atheist, I always privately have this bad reaction, and they give all the obvious reasons, you know, kids get cancer, earthquakes kill people, all that kind of stuff. But when I hear them I think: But you are barking up the wrong tree." She added, "But I couldn't say what the right tree is—or how to bark up it."' Assured by Bernie that she *will* have her deep sensation again, Suzanne shares this: '"You know what, Bernie? I've thought about this a lot. A *lot*. And here is the—well, the phrase I've come up with, I mean just for myself, but this is the phrase that goes through my head. I think our job—maybe even our duty—is to—" her voice became calm, adultlike. "To bear the burden of the mystery with as much grace as we can."'[580]

Other than the fact that Bernie and Suzanne both invoke 'something much larger than we are,' which recalls Reaney's 'there has to be something outside ourselves that inspires and orders' (I'll have one more kick at this can later), what is this passage doing here? First let me say that the impact of the exchange depends on what precedes and follows it in the chapter it comes from. The force of that chapter depends on what has preceded and what will follow it in the book. *Olive, Again* is either a novel or an articulated sequence of short stories. The experience of Olive Kitteridge, in her advanced years, is central. Some of the chapters are focused on her; in others, she is secondary, making brief but significant appearances in the lives of others who live in the town of Crosby, Maine. She is literally absent from 'Helped,' Suzanne and Bernie's chapter (Suzanne and Bernie have a walk-on in the last chapter of the book), but her presence hovers even there. The book is plainly written, local effects are quiet, but a particular world is patiently being built up. It's carefully created of 'ordinary' people who feel real. They interact in commonplace situations that are made to feel plausibly human. They inhabit an unexceptional but convincingly realistic American town. The book is a realist work of art.

By bringing Elizabeth Strout to bear, I have in mind to say something to James Reaney that he can no longer hear, might not even have wanted to hear: take a good look at the medium in which Bernie and Suzanne say they believe what you do; a reader may live inside that worthy book, may inhabit many others so painstakingly and convincingly written, may find those works joining all other important inner things that create the very fabric of a mind—so surely the possibilities of realist microcosm have to be respected. Romance and realism are opposites at odds only in their extremes. Merging their resources may generate enormous power. Well, we have only to look at *The Donnellys* to see Reaney rooting his archetypes in all kinds of aural and visual detail drawn from life outside of books. I might be inclined to chalk up all my prorealism palaver to private axe-grinding—and I do sometimes ask myself: why not just deal with the work as it is, not get exercised about what it is not—if so many of the valuable resources of realism hadn't been so marvellously mobilized in the trilogy. (I'm not a proponent of realism to the exclusion of literary assaults on it, as in so-called postmodernist novels. I've written a book called *The Difficult* which takes all that very seriously.)

Back with *Olive, Again,* back to Suzanne and Bernie, to haul this part of the argument all the way back into Reaney territory: all of the ordinariness I've mentioned does not mask the fact that Suzanne has her finger on something very important. She is not presented as any kind of intellectual. She is a plain citizen, but she gives serious thought to the numinous surround of her existence. She feels no urge to explain the source of her sense of reverence. As Bernie marvels, despite a familial background that could easily have made her as dysfunctional as her parents and her brother, she is still an 'innocent.' She is innocent of the agonized thinking that has for centuries argued about the nature and the object of belief. She can just do it. She possesses an understanding that Jan Zwicky, invoking the gestalt thinking of Max Wertheimer, says so many smart people have lost: '"Piecewise" methods in logic, science, and mathematics, [Wertheimer] argues, have obscured what any intelligent *unschooled* child can see. Members of post-Enlightenment European and colonial cultures can't, anymore, see the facts for what they are because we have so profoundly committed ourselves to an erroneous view of what the facts must be.'[581] 'Wertheimer suspects (as do I),' Zwicky goes on, 'that a full appreciation of the facts will necessitate a fundamental overhaul of a great deal of philosophical vocabulary.'[582] Here again is the wisdom of a child that Reaney wants active in the adult.

'Pick any of the notions that Enlightenment philosophy has been unable to crack,' says Zwicky, 'but which, equally, it hasn't been able to make go away—meaning, certainly, and beauty, but also goodness, identity, being—and you'll find that it's an idea or an experience that depends on gestalt rather than on piecemeal thinking.'[583] Various critics have called Reaney childlike, naive. I've said above that such observations completely miss his sophistication. Also his fierce, assertive combativeness. ('Naturally, there were some people to whom the whole idea of *Alphabet* was red flag/bull! Good! I was always aware that what I was doing went counter to the stream of the Whitman influence on our poetics and, surely, so powerful is that influence—life is a poem—that some opposition should be set up like a time-bomb, if only in library shelves.'[584]) Reaney will typically begin an assertion with 'I happen to believe,' an expression with more chip-on-the-shoulder heat than plain old 'I think,' or 'I believe.'

Such critics also miss how clearly he sees the necessity of thinking in wholes. He was an intelligent, educated, adult child. He knew how to play, and he knew the meaning of play. Childlike innocence maintained into adulthood, informed by education and experience, may mature into wisdom. But here it is in the plain voice of an adolescent in Dennis Lee's poem, 'The Mystery':

> Can't talk about it,
> don't know if anybody else even gets it,
> animals live in it, maybe they don't know it's there,
> little kids the same;
> grownups act oblivious—situation normal.
> Half the time I just mooch along, then I laugh too loud.
> But it catches me late at night, or in winter when
> branches glow with snow against the bark, or some dumb old
> song cracks me up and I want to go
> howl in the city, or smash windows, or make my
> life sheer shine in this miracle ache of a world.[585]

The last line, particularly 'miracle ache,' firmly identifies the speaker as a mask of his author. Throughout his career, Lee has found many ways of saying 'to / be is a bare-assed wonder....'[586]

There is a lot of good writing in resistance to the dominant discourse that feeds technocracy and leads in turn to life-threatening innovations. Humanist Northrop Frye could see trouble coming a long way off: 'I understand the fear that our civilization will fail to adapt in time to the changes which its technology has already started. But the word "adapt" may be misleading, because there is no environment to adapt to except the one we have created. Man is the one animal that has stopped playing the Darwinian game of adaptation, and has tried to transform the environment instead. Much of his transformation so far has been pollution, waste, overcrowding and destruction, and there is a limit beyond which he can't go on doing this. At least I hope there's a limit: there are movies like "Star Wars" which suggest that we can learn to visit distant galaxies and smash them up too; but I'd prefer not to think of that as our future.'[587] We haven't started smashing up planets in our own solar system, let alone distant galaxies, but our off-earth efforts are showing promise. Millions of objects of space junk are now orbiting the earth.[588]

As I've been saying in various ways, there *is* an environment other than the one created by humans. Otherwise, I'm with Frye. It's interesting to note that in 1959 C. P. Snow, a novelist among other things, was blaming British universities for neglecting scientific literacy among humanities students while, not so much later, Reaney and others began criticizing North American subjugation of the humanities. Particulars of each time and place aside, Snow's term, 'the two cultures,' still resonates, though each of those 'cultures' embraces many disciplines—'Biology,' for instance, 'is a loosely constructed network of fifty or more different sciences'[589]—and, increasingly, they are not competing but collaborating. There is much agreement between quite different thinkers, much fine writing these days from scientists agreeing with poets on what must be done to save the biosphere: more holistic ways of thinking must lead to better ways of doing. A lot of thinkers are convinced that we must change our ways and hope that it's not too late.

There is a huge assumption shared among such writers and others who are more directly advocating a Green New Deal, or maybe it's a wish: what intellectuals say will influence what so-called ordinary people think and do. A question has to be asked, today, that once was not so burning: if the citizenry can't think in enlightened ways, and if, rather than having the principles and the guts to do what is right and necessary, politicians go on pandering to their constituencies, first to get elected, then to stay in power, how can any change be made, let alone change requiring decisiveness and dispatch? Not even all the so-called intellectuals are on board. Some just don't care about anything other than themselves. Let Reaney's Niles stand for the likes of them. Many citizens have no capacity for thinking beyond what they can see with their own two eyes, and, apparently, no way of entertaining two ideas at once, or else they would never have voted for Donald Trump; nor would they have been in 2020 giving the malocchio to Americans of oriental descent because COVID-19 started in China. And how to counter the tremendous inertia of the 'progress' responsible for so much of the way things are now that so many of us take for granted.

The lives of so many people, their incomes and lifestyles, depend so much on what has been put in place and fixed there that resistance to healthy change is endemic. Take two aspects of one unlikely polluter: the cow. 1) Dairy cattle in Wisconsin, USA: 'Manure runoff from industrial dairy farming has contributed to a dramatic increase in bacteria and nitrates in the state's groundwater, according to a study funded in part by Wisconsin's Department of Natural Resources. (A farm with twenty-five hundred cows produces as much waste as a city of four hundred thousand people.) The E.P.A. recently sampled the groundwater in a thirty-mile area of Juneau County that's dense with dairy cows and found that sixty-five per cent of the sites had elevated levels of nitrates, which have been linked to birth defects, colon cancer, and "blue-baby syndrome," a condition that reduces oxygen in an infant's blood and can be fatal.'[590]

The waste goes down, and it goes up: 2) 'When the world's one and a half billion beef and dairy cows ruminate, the microbes in their bathtub-sized stomachs generate methane as a by-product. Because methane is a powerful greenhouse gas, some twenty-five times more heat-trapping than carbon dioxide, cattle are responsible for two-thirds of the livestock sector's G.H.G. [greenhouse gas] emissions.... Steven Chu, a former Secretary of Energy who often gives talks on climate change, tells audiences that if cows were a country their emissions "would be greater than all of the E.U., and behind only China and America." Every four pounds of beef you eat contributes to as much global warming as flying from New York to London—and the average American eats that much each month.'[591] Cattle have to go? We all have to become vegetarian? If so, by when? The meatless burger is now in production—it's in an article about Pat Brown, the scientist who developed one meatless burger, that I found out how bad for the planet is the plain old inoffensive bovine—so, if ground beef were all we wanted from a cow, a future without cows might be possible. Though actual cows and chickens may eventually disappear in favour of real but 'cultured' or 'cultivated' meat. Still, like Greta Thunberg, we ought to stop flying anywhere, we should all buy electric cars (or resort to bicycles, or shank's mare, à la Reaney), all opt for solar power....

Because the sixth extinction is in progress, everything I write now must acknowledge that and stand against it, whether or not the gesture is futile. Some of what Reaney said and did—like his sustained critique of technology—is allied with that stand. In that respect, he was prophetic. And everything I've just said notwithstanding, there is no choice but to keep on plugging away. As long as there is hope, I'll keep on doing this. Maybe even after. But read on to find out how very little hope may possibly suffice to press on.

To return to my main theme in this chapter, it's ironic that Reaney regularly took such a scunner to realism when so much of the fine texture of *The Donnellys* is rooted in realistic detail. The world of the trilogy feels complete because it's built from the ground up. During the summer and fall of 2019, as I read though *The Donnellys*, one thing that stood out in very high relief was its many voices, the sounds made both by props and by actors, the latter including songs, poetry, animal noises, Latin liturgy, formal and demotic speech of many sorts, English with Irish rhythm and diction, stage Irish, ignorant speech, elegant language, sophisticated rhetoric, salty language, creative cursing, the spiel of a showman, narrative addressed to the audience, litanies of place names (to carry a character from town to town) and dates (counting days of the week, months of a year, years of a life, compact expressions of passing time and also, in Mrs.

Donnelly's version, 'crossing times and places as I please'[592]); passages from letters, inquest voices, choral speech and sound effect, newspaper headlines and period prose, items on bills, trial transcripts, legal jargon, et cetera, et cetera. Such a list may suggest the manyness and extraordinary economy of the technique but it omits what was seen as well as heard, and can't begin to express how everything was woven together, myth and documentary, humour and pathos, scene dissolving into tightly woven scene, all gorgeously designed. The list of humble props at the beginning of *14 Barrels from Sea to Sea* is a page long. I say again: it's a marvel that, despite the extraordinary complexity, the storyline is kept perfectly clear.

But I've been stressing only the human content of all these voices. In an article which traces Reaney's preoccupation with sounds back to his early plays, *The Killdeer*, *The Sun and the Moon* and the rest, Gerald Parker discusses what Reaney has called the 'rapids' of the later plays in terms of their orchestration of all sorts of sound. 'All of Reaney's plays since *Colours in the Dark*,' he writes, (and he might have included *Listen to the Wind*) '—*Sticks & Stones*, *St. Nicholas Hotel*, *Handcuffs*, *Baldoon*, *Wacousta*, *The Dismissal*, *King Whistle*, *Gyroscope*, *Antler River* and *Traps* possess, to one degree or another, a sonic score of "big and little sounds." '[593] It's in *The Donnellys*, however, that the sonic environment is at its richest and most polyphonic. '[S]ongs and dances and melodic fragments' in the trilogy 'contribute to a general musical atmosphere and rhythm, and assist in the transitions between episodes in the story.' They 'are also designed to function as important signs of the social, religious and racial life and history of the Biddulph community. That is, they possess a documentary as well as an esthetic life in the plays....'[594] What else? Quoting liberally from Reaney's stage directions, Parker makes quite a full list of 'the extraordinary range of Reaney's vocabulary of expressive sounds in the theatre':[595]

There are the sounds of the 'deep forest bird—the peewee' (which, after the choric rendering of stanzas from the Barleycorn Ballad, is the first sound of the trilogy...); the church bells; wood-chopping sounds; the missals which 'rustle shut'; 'scythe sounds at harvest time'; bell and jug sounds; Grace's sawing sounds; 'stick, stone, reel sounds'; cowbells; sticks and stones percussion effects; sleigh bells; 'road sounds—barking of dogs etc.'; hot summer sounds ('cicadas strumming'); train whistles; the buzzing of a fly against the church window; night sounds—crickets; the sound of a pen scratching as Donnelly signs his name to a deed; the 'drumming of invisible hooves' at the London race-track; the sound effects at the race-track when 'wind and distance play tricks with announcements'; the pounding of the anvil; cows mooing; wind sounds; the sound of coins in a tin box; a 'blast of sound'—buzzsaw, guns, drums, fiddles etc.; Tom Ryan sawing a rail; the triangle and anvil sounds which accompany some of Mrs. Donnelly's journey; the clock striking twelve, fusing (as in *Night Blooming Cereus*) with the sound of the train; the sewing machine ('Its whirring sound rises and falls as part of the play's spirit' in *Handcuffs*); the sound of stamping and clapping ('Vary with toe taps and finger snaps'); the 'concrete sound chorus ending with an exhausted slurp'; the sound of the threshing machine; the sleighbells juxtaposed with the 'chuff chuff of the gramophone'; the various bird sounds ('vicious chirping,' 'bird starling sounds'); 'organ chord out of horror movies'; 'We hear the cane of an old, yet tough, strong farmer tapping on the frozen ground'; crow sounds; a tiny bell; 'sewing machine sound here should help us transfer our mind back to the earlier shebeen scenes'; Cassleigh whetting the knife on a stone; the sounds of the 'pig chorus'; the sound of beating stones with pickaxes; a plate cracking; the sound of beating 'handcuffs apart with a hammer.'[596]

Along with word and action, each of these plain sounds thickens up the atmosphere of particular times and places for each scene. Along with the music of song and dance, they operate like the sound-effect score of a movie: sometimes overtly, sometimes subliminally colouring each scene with emotion. Each sound is a kind of aural metaphor, a word in a nonverbal language, like those drum rolls and taps mentioned above. I said before that while the word 'biosphere' was not in Reaney's vocabulary, he was on the edge of a deeper understanding of biosphere than his ingrained humanism permitted. He was paying attention to particulars in his own environment as a way of firmly rooting himself and others in it, looking where many others did not for significance outside the strictly human sphere. And he was using his ears as well as his eyes, attending very carefully to what he heard around him, much of it non-human, so as to fold it all into his dense theatrical language. In this other way, he was on the edge of such sensitivity to the extra-human context of human life as might have prepared him to meet the scientists half way. If that 'verbal universe' hadn't predominated....

During the Winnipeg leg of the national tour of the Donnelly trilogy, Reaney says he was excited to meet 'Two separate families whose ancestors had come West from Biddulph township in the nineteenth century.' He had found references to those ancestors during his Donnelly research; 'now in Row S of the Salle Pauline Boutal,' the St. Boniface theatre where the plays were performed, 'the verbal universe dissolves into human figures and faces telling me things that enable me to go back into the patterns I am weaving in the world of words and adjust here, shade more there.'[597] Those shadings, some of them minute, set *The Donnellys* apart from and, to my mind, above all of Reaney's other drama. I don't sell that other drama short—in fact the later *Gyroscope* is one of my favourite Reaney plays—I merely register how very far Reaney has pushed all the levels of his art in creating his masterpiece.

Something else: in many of his other plays, antagonists are quite sharply defined: good guys and bad guys, so to speak, often with some character caught or drawn between them. The stark black-and-whiteness is perfectly appropriate to romance. But the Donnelly family is mixed. Mother and father and their son Will, in their different ways, though not perfect, are nevertheless noble, 'part of the indomitable spirit of man in all ages,' according to James Noonan,[598] but some of the other six boys are too energetic and wild for the good of the family's standing in the community, and a couple of them, 'genuinely bad,'[599] make it worse. The Donnelly males are 'men filled with verbs, very nearly pulverizing their enemies,'[600] though Mrs. Donnelly is the matriarch who towers above them all. She is intelligent, imaginative, personally powerful. As such, she contrasts with other characters, some powerful and narrow-minded, some too weak to act on their own convictions, some ignorant, some even stupid. *The Donnellys* contains pretty much the whole human mental and moral panoply.

Which is to say that the trilogy incorporates many of the plot and character shadings of realism that Reaney was mostly inclined to disdain. 'We live in a fairy tale, not in "real-life" novels!' he wrote in *Souwesto Home*, many years after he'd written *The Donnellys*. 'The Brothers Grimm are right/ Dreiser, Farrell and Zola ain't!' [601] He names some of his culprits here; usually he doesn't bother. Would he add Elizabeth Strout to the list, had he been aware of her work? I think so. Who else? While working on Reaney, I have been enjoying the wonderful short stories of Grace Paley; nary a myth in sight (well, on page 383 of 386, 'all-refusing Zeus and jealous Hera' [602] are mentioned in passing.) Reaney was asserting and defending an aesthetic he often felt was undervalued and demeaned in his time. Perhaps it shouldn't be surprising that he was inclined to overstate the case. The Brothers Grimm are right *too*. And let's remember what Frye says about what might first impress a reader of *Ulysses*: 'the clarity with which the sights and sounds and smells of Dublin come to life, the rotundity of the character drawing, and the naturalness of the dialogue.' Frye is much more tolerant of writing across the genres than his student was. But the student worked the nuancing detail of realism into *The Donnellys*. He needed it to delve into the story of what he has called 'a demonic atrocity alive with all sorts of moral complexities that challenge one's capacity to really understand them.' [603]

The Book of Life

Can we change, as Reaney thought we could? Not without coming to see the kinds of structure that enclose us unawares. Let me move back into *The Donnellys* through the subject of grids that imprison, like the Protestant-Catholic divide that came, pretty much intact, from Tipperary, Ireland to Biddulph Township, Souwesto, and, even before that, something more neutral but nevertheless a decisive contribution to the Donnelly tragedy.

There is a literal grid in a scene early in *Sticks & Stones*, the first play of the trilogy. It involves a surveyor and the son he has along for company. Preceding the settlers in Biddulph Township, he lays his grid over the township, just as he and his like have gridded the world's topography. Boy asks father why the people who will come to live on Concession Six, Lot Eighteen, eventually to be the Donnelly farm, will be fighting over that particular bit of ground. 'Well,' the surveyor replies, 'to begin with the way this lot is laid out, there's a small creek enters it from the next farm, crosses it and then flows into the next farm. Farm that is to be. It'll be the subject of a lawsuit, quarrels about water rights, flooding—they'll love that little creek.'[604]

BOY Couldn't you stop that?

SURVEYOR Well now, what would you suggest?

BOY Make the farms a different shape?

SURVEYOR I'm not allowed to do that, Davie. The laws of geometry are the laws of geometry.... No, people must make do with what right angles and Euclid and we surveyors and measurers provide for them.[605]

This is a far cry from cowpaths following 'the lie of the land.' It's reminiscent of one of the main settings in *Wacousta!*—Fort Detroit plunked down in a sprawling forest that it repudiates by its enclosure and its square shape. In fact it has obliviously been erected over an Indian burial ground. For Pontiac, whose uprising is one of the dramatic cores of the play, this fort and nine others in his territory are eggs to be crushed. 'These nine eggs,' he says, 'are filled with straight lines, freeways, heartlessness, long knives, minuets, harpsichords, hoopskirts, death, disease, right-angled extermination.'[606] Minuets, harpsichords and hoopskirts are just foreign. The rest of his list is a capsule of colonial inroads on his culture.

'We have to deal with the fact that we had a cadastral survey, that did everything at right angles,' says Reaney to Wanda Campbell, 'and you don't get a very interesting landscape when everything is chopped up into 90 degree angles. You have to fight that.... Our lane, for example, at home, our lane is not at right angles with anything. My theory about culture is that you have to have a crooked road, which is the road in front of our farm, because there were three families that were very interested in art there....'[607] William Blake may be behind this theory: 'Improvement makes strait roads, but the crooked roads without/ Improvement, are roads of Genius.'[608] Theory becomes poem in *Souwesto Home*: one section of 'Little Lake District (Where I Was Born) Poems':

Huron Road
In all its straight surveyed push
From Wilmot to Goderich
The Old Huron Road curved only once,
Defeated by the Little Lakes
With their hemlock swamps
Bottomless
Where they bent him south & then north
And caught, therefore, in their crooked snare
Painters & poets, storytellers, eccentrics
Who were born & lived & died there[609]

Perhaps the most extreme form this environmental determinism took was in Reaney's hilarious (but serious) response to the problem his Ontario Literature and Culture students had with Harold Innis's *The Bias of Communication*, a text on the course. 'We went in the week after it was assigned,' says Jean McKay, 'and said, "This guy's prose style is impenetrable!" And he said, "Of course he's got an impenetrable prose style! He was raised on a stony ridge in Oxford County"!'[610] Good answer? It would have been tough to think of a comeback. Reaney 'walked through the same world,' Jean says, 'in a totally different way.'[611]

As I understand it, cadastral surveying has to do with determining legal ownership of land, and thus postdates the work of surveyors like the one in *The Donnellys*. He is an instrument of the Geological Survey of Canada. The Geological Survey caused plenty of disturbance to peoples, lord knows, Indigenous and Metis people in particular, who had occupied the land before the survey retroactively, disastrously, decided certain things these peoples had already decided for themselves. Reaney's terminology is not precise, in this case, but it still catches the issue of colonialism in a nutshell.

Meanwhile, speaking in *The Donnelly Documents* of Concession Six, Lot Eighteen, the Donnelly farm, Reaney refers to 'the emotive power of one factor to all involved: land.'[612] 'This embattled farm and the Donnellys' relationship with land and property,' he says 'should be seen as one of the most important features in this dramatic story.'[613] One other take on this survey grid appears in the first section of 'Entire Horse (Poems Written About The Donnellys To Assist in the Renewal Of The Townhall At Exeter, Highway # 4)':

Around Borrisokane, in Eire, the roads twist
After cowherds with willow gads, after wise woman's spells,
After chariots and the widest go-around found in a mare's skin.
But in Biddulph, Canada, in Mount Carmel's brooder stove,
  St Peter's fields,
The roads cross at right angles, a careful Euclidean net, roods, rods

Spun by surveyors out of Spider stars—Mirzak, Spicula,
Thuban, Antares.
Like serpents, twitchgrass roots, dragons—the Irish roads twist,
The old crooked roads twist in the cage of the straight new.[614]

The speaker of this poem (one of three, the other sections voiced by Tom Donnelly and Mrs. Donnelly) is identified in a note as William Porte, Lucan postmaster.

The grid of geometry is probably the most neutral source of the conflict that eventually overwhelms the Donnellys. The Catholic church is, at first, either neutral or aligned with the Donnellys. At least the first priests at St. Patrick's church, Lucan, regard the Donnellys as fascinating people, anything but the devils they are already beginning to be made out as. But a change takes place at St. Patrick's, mainly because the bishop of a later era wishes to use his power to sway the Donnellys to vote conservative. The Catholic church and the McDonald government are in cahoots. So Father Connolly is sent to Lucan. Connolly is a powerful man, a man of extremes and little common sense. He visits every family in the parish shortly after his appointment, first the O'Hallorans, Donnelly enemies and, by superficial standards, the most respectable family in the parish. 'Why is it,' says Mrs. Donnelly, addressing the man who is supposed to be her priest, 'that you have a face for our deeds but no face at all for the lives that are explainers of these deeds.... Is it that when you first came to our neighbourhood—her farm on the road is before our farm and with her sable coat and her sable muff and her fur hat driving down to the church to suck the toes of Jesus in her jet black cutter, the soul of respectability ... Mrs. O'Halloran.'[615] When Connolly finally reaches a Donnelly household, he already has a fixed sense that Donnellys don't subscribe to the values he is supposed to represent, so his visit is confrontational. When Norah Donnelly, wife of Will, says to him 'there are always two sides to a story,' his reply is chilling: 'Well, Mrs. William Donnelly, in that supposition you are wrong. There are not always two sides to a story. There is one side, mark this, and one side only.'[616] He already knows what side he is on. He will eventually hound the Donnellys out of his church. Equally chilling is the self-righteous bishop to whom William Donnelly addresses himself in a letter, a cry for arbitration between himself and Father Connolly, priest and parishioner having become rivals in the community. Very early in the first play of the trilogy we see the young William Donnelly being tutored for confirmation by his mother. One of her questions ('would you know then how to address the bishop with the proper form of his title'[617]) is interrupted and goes unanswered, and that hiatus comes back to haunt in the third play. Here, after reading Will's letter asking him to 'do something before it is too late,' the bishop first has two positive reactions: 'what beautiful handwriting,' he says, and 'The man should have been a priest.'[618] 'But he doesn't know how to address his bishop. No, I am not Your Reverence, William Donnelly. I am Your Excellency. And. He doesn't know that before you can stand you must learn to kneel.'[619] In his ivory tower high above and remote from the lives of the people whose shepherd he is supposed to be, the bishop has no way of knowing that Donnellys do not kneel, and he has no clue that they are too smart to be taken in by his clumsy strategy to sway them to the conservative side. They are proud, independent, democratic people who do not submit to those whose vision of things is less complex and tolerant than their own, not even when compromise with wrong, even evil, would smooth their way in life. Part of what gets others up in arms about them, after all, is jealousy of that proud independence.

One fascinating thing about the construction of the *Donnelly Trilogy* is that there is never any doubt about the fate of the family. Their murder is first spoken of, by Mr. Donnelly, early in Act I of *Sticks & Stones*, and it's brought up again and again—by Donnellys—before the moment in *Handcuffs* when the actual massacre happens. The focus throughout is on how such an atrocity could, step by isolating step, come to be. In a sense, the Donnellys are speaking from beyond death from beginning to end of the trilogy. Whether on the page or on the stage, the plays establish that they are living, by turns, in past, present and future. 'The living must obey

the dead,' one of them will say from time to time, often before command-
ing some play-within-the-play about the Black Donnelly story, to show
how gothic-unreal it is. The Donnellys have lasted. They have passed into
story both false and true, and also mixed, because fiction is shaped differently than history. In his introduction to *The Donnelly Documents*
Reaney takes 145 pages of nonfiction prose to tell the story another way.
That is a digest of the 287 pages of documents that follow, and those documents, Reaney says, 'are but part of a much larger collection of material I
have assembled over the years, which has informed my understanding of
this story.'[620] The Donnellys have lasted, the trilogy demonstrates, because
they were special, charismatic people, and also because of human fascination with the darkness that engulfed them.

The massacre is never staged, not directly. It need be represented by
nothing more than violent sounds and shadows, because direct, but
retrospective, narration tells what is happening. And how it is that the vic-
tims go clear of the savage brutality inflicted on them is made clear in the
last words of Bridget, the niece whose visit from Ireland was so very poorly
timed. She has fled the slaughter that is going on below: '"When I got
upstairs I went to the window and knelt by it hoping to see a star if the one
cloud that covered the whole sky now would lift. I knew they would come
to get me and they did. They dragged me down the stairs. The star came
closer as they beat me with the flail that unhusks your soul. At last I could
see the star close by; it was my aunt and uncle's burning house in Ontario
where—and in that star James and Judith and Tom and Bridget Donnelly
may be seen walking as in a fiery furnace calmly and happily forever. Free
at last."'[621] Donnellys may have company in that fiery furnace, just as, in
the book of Daniel, Chapter 3, Shadrach, Meshach and Abednego are
joined by another who was not thrust into the furnace by Nebuchadnez-
zar. The three are 'walking in the midst of the fire, and they have no hurt;
and the form of the fourth is like the Son of God.'

The reader or viewer or listener to Reaney, from beginning to end, will
recognize the fiery furnace speech as a beautiful instance of what he has

been reaching for and sponsoring just about all his writing life, reaching for it and trying to spread it—the loving spirit that is deepest and best of all the tangle that makes us human. First among other sources, he found that spirit in the Bible, which promises a life beyond death. Let me bring in *The Dance of Death at London, Ontario*, a book of Reaney poems based on the danse macabre of medieval tradition and wonderfully illustrated with pointillist drawings by Jack Chambers. 'The poet's idea for this chapbook,' says Reaney on the back cover, 'came from an old German book called *The Dance of Death at Basle*. This "totentanz" book was not the only impetus though, for it was only after seeing some burdocks in an old graveyard at the edge of the city that the book really began to get going.' The first poem, 'Invitation to a Dance,' has Death introducing his 'dancing regiment':

Executive Esquire & Grocery Boy
Man, Woman, Doctor, Child, Bishop
The Scavenger & the Rich Young Lady
Painter & Poet & Cop [622]

Each of these individuals, and a few others, will speak in a quatrain, then

Jack Chambers, 'The Poet' from Jack Chambers and James Reaney,
The Dance of Death at London, Ontario.

Death will have the last word in a following quatrain of his own. In various guises, skeletal Death shadows each member of his regiment in the Chambers picture on each facing page. Poet and professor Reaney holds forth behind a lectern, for instance, while Death fiddles ironic accompaniment.

THE POET

Since I write you I well know
  What you will doubtless say
That every word I write must go
  The dusty change of vowel way.

DEATH

Of course. All your tropes and iambics
  Become my leaden fiddlesticks.
My laurel soon will make you dull,
  And your tongue dust pepper in your skull. [623]

Everyone is mortal, okay. But is that it? Summing up the book, 'CON-CLUSIO' talks back:

'Death's Head Moth, King of the Tower of Burs
  With streets and avenues written on your wings,
I shall come to London and join your dancing.
  I will be one of your things,

Yet stand not in dread of you,
  Thy tumble drum, nor thy hollow fife.
For I know a Holy One who some day will
  Shut up thy book with the hands of Life.' [624]

You may recall me observing, many pages back, that Mopsus did not understand Effie's fable of the doorknob and the door. He didn't follow the story when it was being told, no, but eventually he sees that it offers him victory over the relentless march of time toward our common fate represented by the calendar year that structures *A Suit of Nettles*. In a passage that recalls the cradle/source in *One Man Masque*, and all the anagogic passages discussed above, it gives him a saviour and release from Death.

> A sun, a moon, a crowd of stars,
> A calendar nor clock is he
> > By whom I start my year.
> He is most like a sun for he
> Makes his beholders into suns,
> > Shadowless and timeless.
> At the winter sunstill some say
> He dared be born; on darkest day
> > A babe of seven hours
> He crushed the four proud and great directions
> Into the four corners of his small cradle.
> He made it what time of year he pleased, changed
> Snow into grass and gave to all such powers. [625]

Reading and rereading Reaney after having left most of it be for decades, I have again been immersed in his writing. Some of it has helped guide my thinking for over forty years. Some of it has been new to me, like the very fascinating *Box Social and Other Stories*. With some of it I have formed a new and warmer relationship. *Listen to the Wind* touched me deeply, even just the reading. (I haven't been encountering the dramatic works in the proper way: on the stage. 'However important what is heard in a theatre may be,' says Northrop Frye, 'the theatre itself is primarily a visual experience, as the origin of the word "theatre" (*theasthai*, "to see") indicates.'[626]) 'Art is made by subtracting from reality and letting the viewer imagine or "dream it out" (as Owen is told to do in the play)' says Reaney in his 'Production Notes' for *Listen to the Wind*. 'The simpler art is—the richer it is. Words, gestures, a few rhythm band instruments create a world that turns Cinerama around and makes you the movie projector.'[627] I loved again the scene in *Colours in the Dark* in which believer Bible Sal defeats materialist Professor Button by drawing on the Holy Spirit to match him language for language, though she has never learned the languages with which he challenges her faith. I found *Imprecations: The Art of Swearing* a much finer poem than I did when I first read it. And here's one more plug for *Gyroscope*.

I have said why I believe Reaney's work is important today, despite my reservations about some of it. I envy his faith. I would love to be able to assert, as confidently as he did, 'I do believe with Blake that you can transform this world we live in....'[628] I struggle to find the BALANCE he thought might be achieved. While rereading *Alphabet* 3, on August 24, 2019, Thomas Hardy's poem 'The Darkling Thrush' slipped into my mind. I don't think the prompt was anything in that particular *Alphabet*; I think it was cumulative Reaney. Anyway, I looked the poem up and wrote it down in my reading notes. It begins sadly, in pessimism, as well it might, given Hardy's atheism: 'The land's sharp features seemed to be/ The Century's corpse outleant' (the nineteenth century is just about to end). But then the speaker hears the voice of a thrush 'In a full-hearted evensong/ Of joy illimited;'[629] and his own sad heart rises in response.

> So little cause for carolings
> Of such ecstatic sound
> Was written on terrestrial things
> 　　Afar or nigh around,
> That I could think there trembled through
> 　　His happy good-night air
> Some blessed Hope, whereof he knew
> 　　And I was unaware.[630]

There may have been no particular joy in the breast of that thrush. It was probably delimiting territory or addressing a mate—though it's worth observing that 'music is and always will be the exclusive privilege of birds and humans.'[631] Letting the thrush sing as for him, Hardy naturally anthropomorphizes. It allows him to release something inside himself that another part feels obliged to deny. Even a fatalist like him, for whom an uncaring 'President of the Immortals'[632] just sports with human beings, as in the tragedy of *Tess of the D'Urbervilles*—even such a man may have inklings of something redemptive. In those ecstatic carolings I seemed to hear Effie all but relieving Branwell of his melancholy. I was hearing Reaney too. From a long way off, yes, but very clearly.

Where to find the blessed hope in these much darker days? 'Hope, you illicit/ imperative,' writes Dennis Lee, 'throw me a bone.'[633] In this writing I've been hanging out with angels, prophets, visionaries. Perhaps it's inevitable that a certain longing would develop, a certain nostalgia for a mind-space not my own. It makes me wonder about the minimum amount of hope a person might require to keep on with this kind of work. It takes me back to Nobody in Reaney's poem about the book that

> makes so sharp [people's] eyes
> That East or West
> They can spot Nobody coming up the Road

When I quoted that before, I was thinking Bible. Never mind that now. Now I'm looking right at Nobody. A single capital letter elevates the word into a proper noun. It dresses Nobody up as Somebody. Somebody of significance, in fact. Nobody is personified and set into motion, yet nothing is visible. There is nothing to be seen with plain old eyes. To get this poem, it's necessary to accept as real and present something whose existence cannot be demonstrated. To accept that, to see it, you need a third eye. 'Of three eyes,' says the speaker in Jay Macpherson's poem, 'The Third Eye,'

> I would still give two for one.
> The third eye clouds: its light is nearly gone.
> The two saw green, saw sky, saw people pass:

The third eye saw through order like a glass
To concentrate, refine and rarify
And make a Cosmos of miscellany.
Sight, world and all to save alive that one
Fading so fast! Ah love, its light is done. [634]

'The Third Eye' is in the first section of *The Boatman*, where the fall into single vision is just happening. The book moves from there into the fallen world of irony before climbing, by degrees, back up to Cosmos, anagogy.

Reaney is also always toiling toward Cosmos; I am mostly stuck with miscellany, if stuck is the word, because I love so much of what I see with my own two eyes. Still, I'm extremely interested in Nobody and its cognate, nothing. Nobody in Reaney's poem sends me over to W.H. Auden's poem, 'In Memory of W.B. Yeats,' where I read that 'poetry makes nothing happen.'

Take that line out of context, as has often enough been done, and you get poetry as useless, dispensable, as in the utilitarian schemes of 'progressive' educationists. Or you get an academic of my acquaintance, citing Auden while marking his promotion to a position of eminence in the university, saying, in effect, 'poetry makes plenty happen; look at the cushy job it got me!' No. Let's look at the context in Auden's elegy for a much-esteemed and much-loved Irish poet:

Mad Ireland hurt you into poetry.
Now Ireland has her madness and her weather still,
For poetry makes nothing happen: it survives
In the valley of its making where executives
Would never want to tamper, flows on south
From ranches of isolation and the busy griefs,
Raw towns that we believe and die in; it survives,
A way of happening, a mouth. [635]

Poetry 'survives,' it 'flows,' it's 'happening,' it voices. This may remind you of Robert Bringhurst's definition of meaning: 'Meaning keeps going.' So poetry makes nothing *happen*.

I first saw this way of looking at the Auden poem in Don McKay's brief essay, 'Some Remarks on Poetry and Poetic Attention.' 'In one version of our evolution as a species,' he writes, 'we become outfitted with a capacity for poetry (all the arts, maybe) as a natural check on our genius for technology: for making things, for control and reduction, for converting the world to human categories. Poetry, that wonderful useless musical machine, performs the actions of technology but undoes the consequences. In this version, Auden gets modified; poetry makes nothing *happen*.'[636]

That was in 1980. In 2012, nothing enters a McKay poem called 'Sleeping Places.' The poem ruminates on an 'artwork by Marlene Creates comprised of twenty-five black-and-white photographs of ground she slept on around the island of Newfoundland.'[637] Environmentally responsible campers do their best to pack up and leave no trace of where they've been, but it takes an environmental artist like Creates to think about documenting no trace. There is scarcely a vestige of human contact to be descried in her day-after photographs. In about one more day, once the obliging grasses and reeds have perked right up again, there would have been nothing whatever of the human to be seen.

> What is nothing doing,
> there in the pressed grass,
> there in the bent-over reeds,
> in the slightly scuffed ground
> and four-leaved cruciform
> bunchberries? Something whispers here
> so softly it's dissolving
> even as the camera clicks.

Here is nothing as something again, a barely audible voice saying things like 'this memory is earth's/ not ours,'[638] before gently sliding into the imperative to erase plot and hero of the dominating human story, to

Let them slip—
        practice this—
                slip
back to the unwritten:
                that place where place
sleeps, where sleep itself
seeps into the landscape, having scrawled
in the pressed grass, in the bent-over reeds
its auto-erasing name.
What is nothing doing? The antique
riddle. The old
ungettable joke. [639]

'Doing' is a verb. Nothing is making things happen again. That question regarding the agency of nothing frames the poem. Is there an answer? Is nothing *doing* the riddle, *doing* the joke? Not exactly. Those almost-answers are oblique, because the syntax has shifted into a couple of sentence fragments touching things unfathomable. This is human language about rolling back language—so as quietly to usher the human out of the picture, leave the land to itself. Who's *doing* nothing? The poet.

'Sleeping Places' is a summer poem that, for me, echoes a winter poem, Wallace Stevens's 'The Snow Man,' which begins with an imperative: 'One must have a mind of winter' to 'regard,' to 'behold' a winter landscape, to be a 'listener' to the winter wind, one

        who listens in the snow,
    And, nothing himself, beholds
    Nothing that is not there and the nothing that is. [640]

There the poem ends. This perception of what is out there, in a season often called bleak, seems pure because the snow man, being nothing (not

— 252 —

thinking, that is, placing himself on an equal basis with the winter scene he views), imposes nothing on the landscape. That seems clear enough. But what is 'the nothing that is'? The nothings in the poem, including the double negative ('nothing that is not there') may be expressed in other ways so as to make them appear fully intelligible. 'Nothing that is not there,' for instance, could be everything that *is* there. It may also be tempting to hear a silent 'there' after the last word of the poem—so it would read 'the nothing that is there'—and feel as though we've got it. But that would be to disregard all the particulars of winter landscape already introduced: 'the boughs/ Of the pine-trees crusted with snow,' 'the junipers shagged with ice,/ The spruces rough in the distant glitter // Of the January sun.'[641] There is plenty out there. It's not nothing. I've read a number of tone-deaf paraphrases of the poem whose aim is to get that final 'nothing' to lie still and mean one thing. It won't. It's not just nothing, after all, it's '*the* nothing' and it *is*. The noun acts. Stretch the explanations out and out, still the ending of the poem snaps back into enigma. The potency of the life in that one word can be felt but not expressed, not once and for all. Here is another fullness that passeth understanding.

How much does a person really need to keep on going, then? Nothing—whenever it's something doing, whenever it *is*.

'I was trained,' says Anne Carson, 'to strive for exactness and to believe that rigorous knowledge of the world without any residue is possible for us. This residue, which does not exist—just to think of it refreshes me. To think of its position, how it shares its position with drenched layers of nothing, to think of its motion, how it can never stop moving because I am in motion with it, to think of its tone of voice, which is casual (in fact it forgets my existence almost immediately) but every so often betrays a sort of raw pity I don't understand, to think of its shadow, which is cast by nothing and so has no death in it (or very little)—to think of these things is like a crack of light showing under the door of a room where I've been locked for years.'[642] This nonexistent residue has position, motion, voice, shadow: a plenitude of attributes. Executives might not tamper with it, but for me that second sentence is itself a crack of light. It's *much* ado about nothing.

'After its death,' says Charles Simic in a poem called 'The Point,'

They opened the story
Afraid to go on.
And found nothing.

Inside nothing
They found a slip
Of the tongue.
Inside the tongue
A loose hair.
Inside the hair
They found

Whatever
Is destroyed
Each time
It is named. [643]

Another nothing turns out to be something, what with all those items inside it, including, ultimately, again, a residue that eludes language. That residue actually can't be killed, not literally, but I've found few more striking ways of throwing doubt on what language can do. It strongly reminds me of C.G. Jung, very early in *The Red Book*, heeding 'the spirit of the depths' which, in a useful distinction, tells him different things than 'the spirit of this time.' 'To understand a thing is a bridge and possibility of returning to the path,' says the spirit of the depths. 'But to explain a matter is arbitrary and sometimes even murder. Have you counted the murderers among the scholars?' [644] Jung will return to explaining—he *was* a scholar—but his explanations will always honour a residue that passes understanding.

To pick up a thread introduced above—the 'multitude of non-linguistic messages active in the natural world'—here is Don McKay again, now trying to find the word for a sunken log over which he once saw a moose step quite unconsciously while its head was underwater, feeding. Lacking a precise term for what the moose was stepping over, how could he properly describe this graceful physical act by a member of a species he'd been accustomed to think of as clumsy? His symbol for the lacuna is [ ]. The category of [ ]—no word for it, 'an absence in symbolic language'[645]—gets him thinking along ecological lines he has followed before, but now he folds in new information about the intelligence of nature: 'An ecologist might remark that deferring the naming of [ ] increases our awareness of its *umwelt*, a term meaning "self-world." It was first coined by the biological thinker Jacob von Uexküll as a way to insist on the fact that organisms other than humans have interests, agency, relationships (including symbiotic ones), and lives that are valuable in themselves and integral to their communities. From the vantage point of language, we could say that an ecologically-minded writer often replaces the single-stroke fiat of nomination with the multiple relations of *umwelt*, a courtesy that implicitly acknowledges the limitations of language itself.'[646] There is so much more interwoven complexity than we can ever get our language to express that our limitations almost seem fortunate; we don't succumb to information overload like the low-IQ farmboy in Reaney's poem. Even the most compendious-minded and articulate among us may feel like blunt instruments of language in the face of the infinite all there really is to life. *All* naming, even of solely human perception and experience, is reductive.

Consider the vertiginous world of Jorge Luis Borges's character, Ireneo Funes. Funes is thrown by a horse and left paralysed, but with a strange, perhaps compensatory, omniscience. 'Now his perception and his memory were infallible,'[647] so much so that language is frustratingly inadequate to express all he sees and remembers. 'Not only was it difficult for him to comprehend that the generic symbol *dog* embraces so many unlike individuals of diverse size and form; it bothered him that the dog at three fourteen (seen from the side) should have the same name as the dog at three fifteen (seen from the front).... [He] could continuously discern the tranquil advances of corruption, of decay, of fatigue. He could note the progress of death, of dampness. He was the solitary and lucid spectator of a multiform, instantaneous and almost intolerably precise world.'[648]

Funes the Memorious is the invention of a writer dedicated to imagining conceptual labyrinths. There is something almost humorous about Funes's impossible omniscience—and the fact that, unlike most of us, he has zero capacity for generalizing. For me, Funes has always thrown a light on the shortfall of normal human language, but I think of him somewhat differently now that I've read *Sister Language*, a book in which two sisters, one schizophrenic and one functionally normal, communicate across a linguistic bridge made by their family bond. One blurse of Christina Baillie's schizophrenic existence is that language is not stable for her. It won't stay still. It keeps dividing and subdividing in ways that make it all but impossible to communicate with most other humans. 'I can't produce writing that locates anything,' she writes. 'I feel unlocatable, or located briefly, peremptorily, in some meaning-vessel outside myself—for instance, when un(der)medicated I experience myself as some random inanimate thing that has "stolen my brain" & is controlling me from a distance with its own cruel purposes in mind.'[649] She can't do what most people can with language, then, but what she *can* do opens up linguistic possibilities inaccessible to others, even her sister Martha, a sophisticated, published writer who reads Christina, then laments her own 'timidity, my law-abiding, linguistic prudery.'[650] There is a proliferating plenitude of information that most humans only graze with words. The vastness will crowd in and cloud the picture if a person isn't vigilant, if s/he doesn't pick and choose. So let me draw way back from the overcrowded semiotic field once again to dwell on those plain minimals, Nobody and nothing.

Is seeing Nobody like hearing Nothing? Not exactly, since, if John Cage is right, there never is nothing to hear. 'For certain engineering purposes,' he writes, 'it is desirable to have as silent a situation as possible. Such a room is called an anechoic chamber, its six walls made of special material, a room without echoes. I entered one at Harvard University several years ago and heard two sounds, one high and one low. When I described them to the engineer in charge, he informed me that the high one was my nervous system in operation, the low one my blood in circulation. Until I die there will be sounds. And they will continue following my death. One need not fear about the future of music.'[651] That last sentence will come as *non sequitur* to many. It takes us way back before middle C, and you will remember how absolutely basic Reaney found *that*. Cage's book *Silence* makes the connection between sound—any sounds—and music as he finds it and makes it. But leave that connection aside and turn back to the calm, declarative sentences that precede those you've just read: 'There is no such thing as an empty space or an empty time. There is always something to see, something to hear.'[652] Never mind the music, then; mind only the bare minimum of what is visible and audible. Mind or *body*, since deep 'silence' will take us *in* to our somatic being. Next to nothing: worth attention, faith to build on. (And I've been staying with the senses. Others posit a numinous silence well outside literal experience. Simone Weil, for example: 'There is a silence in the beauty of the universe which is like a noise when compared with the silence of God.'[653] I think *tha*t silence is Reaney's Nobody.)

For all the tussling that takes place among thinkers and writers over this or that view of reality and optimum ways of inscribing it—the fights can be vicious and they will continue—it may be possible for a good many of us, even if we come at it all from very different directions, to agree on some version of Reaney's 'there has to be something outside ourselves that inspires and orders.' This something is a thread throughout Iain McGilchrist's book. '[T]he right hemisphere,' he says in one place of many, 'delivers "the Other"—experience of whatever it is that exists apart from ourselves.'[654] He always capitalizes the Other, never tries to pin it down, though he clearly associates it with soul or spirit. In *Colours in the Dark*, this would be the 'holy creative force' which Dr. Button denies; Dr. Hoffmeyer, in *Signs of Meaning in the Universe*, does not. Well, he doesn't use the word 'holy,' and his primary focus is matter, not spirit, but he is familiar with creative force. There is even language in his book that one might be more likely to find in Reaney. For one thing, he is comfortable with the metaphor of story for theories such as his. Also, he says

I am somewhat skeptical of this worship of the God of Mathematics. I have a suspicion that, deep down, Galileo's credo ['the great Book of Nature is written in the language of mathematics' ... still the credo of the scientific world—its article of faith] is an expression of human reason's wish that the world should always resemble reason itself. But what if it does not? What if the world bears more resemblance to some crazy story, or a fairy tale? Might mathematics not conceivably be an unnecessary detour on the road to understanding it, rather than a shortcut?

Should we not at least keep open the option that the world is in the purest sense a creative place, the future of which, by that very token, is impossible to predict (after all, being predictable would mean being void of creativity)? [655]

Creativity is a concept that Hoffmeyer keeps coming back to. He wants to 'establish the creative dimension of the semiosphere.' [656] Of 'digital codes such as DNA sequences and texts,' he says, 'the digital code frees human beings from the chains of actuality; that is to say it opens the door to creativity and imagination.' [657] He speaks of the creativity of natural force(s), in units as tiny as the cell, which act in independent and apparently spontaneous ways that still elude explanation. 'Having been born as self-aware subjects,' he also writes, 'our forefathers were inevitably also implanted with the seeds of a longing for some greater meaning. The need arose for some kind of mystical fellowship to compensate for the affinity that had been lost.' [658] He understands human 'yearning for meaningfulness.' [659]

'Very few things in this world can be compared with one another, without something essential being lost,' [660] Hoffmeyer also says, and that's true. Selective quotation elides vast differences between biologist and poet. I introduced the one partly to critique the other, after all. Let them keep a distance, revolving back to back as it were, emblem of an urge to assemble but not merge.

I've tried to make a case for the biosphere as the outside other which is us, but just now I'm back to everything boiled down to the nothing which may be something. That is not just playing around with words. I'm talking about hope, terribly diminished even when Hardy wrote his lovely poem on the cusp of the previous millennium, but apparently inexhaustible. If something can be made out of nothing, or next to nothing, everything is possible, and will be so until such time as all of us are gone. That's our spark, our carolling thrush, our universe in a grain of sand. It's what has been called the indomitable spirit of man in all ages and might also be called irrepressible creativity. The Donnellys have it in spades.

Where I'm all in, then—heart, belly and mind—is with *The Don-nellys*. I place my entire trust in that masterpiece. With its embodied spirit of liveliness and love against narrowness and hatred, no grid but an organic web of adjusting visions, it holds me, dreaming it out. It's *the* Reaney book of Life that shuts up the book of Death for me.

That's where I left the Reaney lecture. I stand by what I said then, and I stand by what I've said here, but the conclusion just reached feels so bright that right away there's a shadow. It's too much like a last word. There are no last words. I need to dismantle; Dennis Lee will help: 'If hope disorders words, let/ here be where,'[661] he says in *testament*, a book of ardent responses to the current threat of apocalypse. It puts his English under such pressure that it all but shatters. One poem takes on nothing, takes it apart:

And are creatures of
nothing.
I noth you noth we
long have we nothed we
shall noth, staunch in true
nothing we
noth in extremis, noth until

habitat heartstead green galore & species

relinquish the terrene ghosthold;

crumble to alphadud; stutter to rumours of *ing*. [662]

There's something we haven't yet seen made of nothing [663]: cut the word in two: verb the front half, sever the *ing*, so noth never rises to the status of verbal noun, gerund, process word. Noth is less than nothing. It's what we humans were doing, are doing, shall be doing (I'd really like to be able to insert a question mark here), while our only home, 'habitat heartstead green galore' goes to shit. Alphabet? That was then, Jamie. Now is Alphadud. The news is very bad.

Even so, *even here and now*, in this poem and in all the other poems in *testament* (neither Old or New, lower case last will and covenant)— something anciently fecund is going on. Just give 'noth' a listen. Those monosyllabic 'noths' and short-line-ending 'we's punch out a verbal gusto that counters the negative content. Then strong rhythms release into something alliterative, gentler, sadder, elegiac, before the poem fetches up with two contrasting half lines. The first ends thud; the second offers a couple of pretty dactyls that my ear finds ironic, resigned, with *ing* reduced to rumour and still far from its better half. Each of the sounds has been weighed and patterned. That's your language and mine, dearly belovèd, rent open and sung back together strange. We have to rouse ourselves to read it.

Is this what we're reduced to now, making very much of very little? At the height of his powers, Reaney was having none of that. He thought— he *knew*—we could change society for the better by writing and by putting on plays. My expectations are much darkened, but I'm still scribbling. I'm still with him to that extent. 'burrow & sing,' [664] says another *testament* poem. Burrow & sing. I'm not on Facebook, so keep an eye skinned for that very watchword on the bumper sticker I'm having made.

Illustrations

---

3   Drawing by James Reaney from *The Essential James Reaney*, 2009.

8   Portrait of James Reaney by Barker Fairley, 1958.

10   Cover, *A Suit of Nettles*. Macmillan, 1958.

14   Cover design by Allan Fleming for the first issue of James Reaney's magazine, *Alphabet*, 1960.

26   Greg Curnoe, 'The Vision of Dr. Bucke, Nihilist Party Trilogy No. 1,' 1964.

30   Donnelly family tombstone at Lucan.

32   Cover, *A Suit of Nettles*. Porcupine's Quill, 2010.

40   James Reaney emblem poem: 'The Riddle', 1969.

48   *The Donnellys* tour poster for the NDWT Company, 1975.

66   Vesta matchbox.

69   Photograph of Sharon Temple by Bruce Forsythe.

78   Branwell, an engraving by Jim Westergard from *A Suit of Nettles*. Porcupine's Quill, 2010.

94   Butterfly party favour, handmade by James Reaney, 1947.

95   Drawing by James Reaney from *Twelve Letters to a Small Town*. Ryerson, 1962.

98   'Near Fraserburg, Fall 1985,' watercolour by James Reaney.

100   Hood ornament on a 1934 Triumph. Photograph by Martin Garfinkel.

107   James Reaney, Bicycle with wheels of Queen Anne's Lace, from *Twelve Letters to a Small Town*. Ryerson, 1962.

151   James Reaney, self-portrait as a 'Rural Dandy.'

156   Masonic ornament from Farmer, Little & Co. typographic specimen book. New York, 1879.

166   Tim Inkster photo of part of a case of monotype once used by James Reaney.

167 Type case from James Reaney, *The Boy With an Я in His Hand*.
Macmillan, 1965.

168 bpNichol, 'The Complete Works,' from *An H in the Heart*.
McClelland & Stewart, 1994.

169 James Reaney, from 'Animated Film,' 1983.
Cover, James Reaney issue, *Essays on Canadian Writing* 24–25
(Winter–Spring 1982–83).

170 Reaney's signature on my copy of *Twelve Letters to a Small Town*.
Ryerson, 1962.

172 James Reaney, 'Boehme's diagram of the first six days
of creation.'

174 Rhoda Kellogg gestalts from *Analysing Children's Art*.
National Press Books, 1969.

178 Tim Inkster photo of James Reaney's Nolan proof press.

185 Map of Souwesto from *The Box Social and Other Stories*.
Porcupine's Quill, 1996.

192 Phil Hall, 'Reaney & I go for a ride in his carriage
pulled by my white porcupines.'

192 James Reaney, coach from *Twelve Letters to a Small Town*.
Ryerson, 1962.

196 Gerald Squires, 'St. Francis Receiving the Stigmata.'
Acrylic on canvas, 1988.

200 William Blake, 'Good and Evil Angels Struggling For Possession
of a Child.' Pen and ink and watercolour on paper, 1793.

210 James Reaney at the farm near Stratford, Ontario, Summer 1979.
Photograph by Lester Kohalmi.

222 Poster for an NDWT production of *The Dismissal*, 1977.

245 Jack Chambers, 'The Poet,' from Jack Chambers and
James Reaney, *The Dance of Death at London, Ontario*.
Alphabet Press, 1963.

Acknowledgments

This book began as the tenth annual James Reaney Memorial Lecture, delivered during WordsFest in London, Ontario on November 2, 2019. I thank James Stewart Reaney and Susan Wallace for recommending me, and Josh Lambier, WordsFest organizer, for inviting me. I'm grateful to Susan Reaney for help in dating and identifying some of her father's visuals. Thanks also to James Stuart and Susan for permission to reproduce their Barker Fairley portrait of James Reaney, photography by Victor Aziz.

Thanks for their friendship and their books to Robin van Löben Sels and Donald Kalsched, Jungian psychotherapists who divide their time between Maine and Newfoundland. Thanks to Marshall Soules for sending me nothing in Wallace Stevens's 'The Snow Man.' Ray Fennelly's photographic expertise is gratefully acknowledged. Martin Garfinkel (Roadside Gallery roadsidegallery.com, 320 Main Street, Carbondale, CO 81623, USA) kindly made available his gorgeous photo of a hood ornament. The photo of Sharon Temple is by Bruce Forsythe, and was generously shared. Thanks to Ken Sparling for indispensable copy-editing.

Don McKay is my faithful and valuable first reader. As has been the case with his responses to previous books, this one profited immensely from his wide range of interests, especially, these days, in various sciences and in intersections between those sciences and poetry and other literary forms. Deeply considered responses from Sean Kane have been most welcome and most helpful.

Beth Follett, of Pedlar Press, was my publisher for many years. Had she not been winding down the operation of Pedlar, this book would also have been hers. Though no longer my publisher, she is still in my corner and I thank her, with love, for her love and her dedication.

If not Pedlar, then why not the wonderful alternative of The Porcupine's Quill? I thank Tim Inkster for his interest in the book, and for his encouragement to keep as many of the visuals as possible, for his fine work in making them look great and for his striking cover design.

———————

Permissions:

Oxford University Press for Jay Macpherson, 'The Anagogic Man' and 'The Third Eye.'

Brick Books for Colleen Thibaudeau, 'This Elastic Moment' and James Reaney, 'Wild Flora of Elgin County,' poem 'u' of 'Brush Strokes Decorating a Fan' and 'I know a book.'

House of Anansi Press for Dennis Lee, 'The Mystery' and 'noth.'

Dundurn Press for James Reaney, 'The Alphabet' as it appeared in Selected Shorter Poems (Dundurn Press, 1999) and 'The St. Nicholas Hotel as it appeared in The Donnellys (Dundurn Press, 2008).

Ellie Nichol for bpNichol, 'The Complete Works.'

Gail Squires and Copyright Visual Arts/Droits d'auteur Arts visuels for 'St Francis Receiving the Stigmata,' 1988, Gerald Squires. Copyright Visual Arts-CARCC, 2021.

Sheila Curnoe and SOCAN for Greg Curnoe, 'The Vision of Dr. Bucke, 1964, Art Gallery of Ontario © Estate of Greg Curnoe / SOCAN 2021.

Bidgeman Images (https://bridgemanimages.com) for 'Good and Evil Angels Struggling for Possession of a Child.'

———————

James Reaney on the Grid is dedicated to Benjamin Michael Christopher Hogan Basha, son of Holly Hogan and Mike Basha, step-son of Michael Crummey, brother of Arielle and Robin Hogan. Ben was nineteen when he died suddenly of an epileptic seizure in 2019.

Ben would have been eight or nine when I first began exchanging Christmas presents with his family. That first year, or the second, I had something tiny for Ben. I don't now remember what it was, but I remember wrapping it, then putting it in a little box and wrapping that, then putting that in a larger box and wrapping that, and so on and on, boxes growing larger and larger, until appearances would have suggested that Ben's present was huge. It was partly the fun had by the rest of the family while watching Ben open his gift, open his gift, open his gift … that inspired me to make Ben an unusual Christmas present from then on. Because I love that whole family.

So from then on I either made or assembled something strange, usually out of things I happened to have on hand, like any good bricoleur. Ben took to finding something adequately weird for me, as well, and a close relationship that he would probably have called interesting developed between us. I call it loving. I won't bother listing all the one-of-a-kind foolish fabrications, but I will detail one exchange that took us through three years. I keep a special affection for this one.

One year, I asked Holly for a photo of Ben and she sent a slightly smirky school photo. Don't ask me how certain ideas pop up, but I thought to reproduce a reduced version of that photo a dozen times, paste the photos onto wooden discs I sawed off a broom handle, and arrange them for presentation in a slim metal box. Open that box up, as Ben did that Christmas morning, and looking up at him were a dozen copies of his own face in what must have been one of his least favourite portraits. No gift of any kind could have been more useless.

The following year, Ben went me one better. In exchange for I forget what of mine, he had that same photo printed on a T-shirt and two pillowcases.

So the following year, I went him one better. All year, I took T-shirt and pillow cases with me everywhere I went. For photos, I asked acquaintances and strangers to wear the shirt and I arranged the pillow cases on beds and other locations in a wide variety of houses and retail establishments. I had fun for a whole year with this project. I offer just two images: one of the pillow cases on a bed in Champney's East, Newfoundland, the T-shirt on a street in Valparaíso, Chile.

I bought a photo album and filled it with photos of the itinerant T-shirt and pillowcases. Each page of the album accommodated four 4 X 6 photos, above and below, front and back, and between them was a slot into which captions or descriptions could be slid. Not to waste that space, I inserted lines of a non-fiction story that I reprint here, in loving memory of the young man it was written for.

Ben Basha. Credit: Emma McDonald.

Like A Flower. My friend, Al Cottreau, was taking German. He found the language perfectly hilarious and loved to amuse me with it. I still remember some of the sentences he thought were so funny: 'Ich freue mich, Sie kennenzulernen' (I'm very glad to meet you). 'Nehmen Sie da drüben Platz. Es ist sehr bequem' (Sit over there. It's very comfortable). 'Du bist wie eine Blume' (You are like a flower). That's about all the German I ever did learn, except for the odd word like 'krankenschwester' (nurse) and 'ausgezeichnet' (excellent) plus some of the words to 'Die Lorelei.' Where would I have learned those? Not from Al. Probably from my first year French prof, who hosted a kind of international singsong one day of the week at noon.

> Ich weiß nicht, was soll es bedeuten
>
> Daß ich so traurig bin;
>
> Ein Märchen aus alten Zeiten
>
> Das kommt mir nicht aus dem Sinn.

Beautiful! 'Sie kämmt ihr goldenes Haar.' Lovely!

Anyway, one day on the bus back from work at Oliver Mental Hospital that summer, I was sitting with another fellow, a summer replacement like me, when Al's German welled up, along with my natural sense of the absurd, so I turned to my seatmate and said, counting on his ignorance of German, 'Du bist wie eine blume.' But the woman sitting just behind us burst out laughing and there I was, caught, apparently courting another man in German. It was the classic moment of comedy, the old triangle (comic/straight man/witness) nicely arranged, as if by God.

We don't hear nearly enough unexpected stuff. Those of us who can handle the unusual, the weird, the bizarre—irony, non sequitur, pun, etcetera, etcetera—we want more, don't we, more snap in the language, more harlequin surprise in the day-to-day. We want more Samuel Beckett: 'No cliché is so stale, no metaphor so dead,' says Stefan Collini, 'that Beckett can't find a way to make it twitch.'[665] Yes! Less of the quotidian and more, *very much more*, of the twitch. Isn't that what we want, Ben? You know it is.

Notes

Front cover: 'Biddulph Township', 1878. M. Pacey, based on *Illustrated Historical Atlas of the County of Middlesex, Ontario*. H.R. Page & Co., 1878. The map also appears in *The Donnelly Documents: An Ontario Vendetta*, a collection of documents edited and introduced by James C. Reaney.

Page 8: Barker Fairley, *James Reaney*, 1958. Oil on Masonite, 49.5 x 59.7 cm.

1 Northrop Frye, from 'Letters in Canada' (*University of Toronto Quarterly*). *The Bush Garden: Essays on the Canadian Imagination* (Toronto: House of Anansi, 1971), 91.

2 Robert Bringhurst, 'Xiangyan Zhixian'. *Selected Poems* (Kentville, Nova Scotia: Gaspereau Press, 2009), 128.

3 David P. Silcox, *Painting Place: The Life and Work of David B. Milne* (Toronto, Buffalo, London: University of Toronto Press, 1996), xv. Some analogues of this sense of love may be found in Iain McGilchrist's remarks about beauty: 'Our relationship with what is beautiful … is more like longing, or love, a betweenness, a reverberative process between the beautiful and our selves, which has no ulterior purpose, no aim in view, and is non-acquisitive. Beauty is in this way distinguished from erotic pleasure or any other interest we may have in the object. This is surely what Leibniz meant by beauty being a "disinterested love". In fact, so central is this idea that one finds it also in Kant, who spoke of beauty as a "disinterested pleasure", and in Burke, who saw it as a form of "love [that is] different from desire".' *The Master and His Emissary: The Divided Brain and the Making of the Western World* (New Haven and London: Yale University Press, 2009), 445.

4 Roland Barthes, 'The Death of the Author'. *Image, Music, Text*. Essays selected and translated by Stephen Heath (Glasgow: Fontana/Collins, 1977), 146.

5 Northrop Frye, *Anatomy of Criticism: Four Essays* (New York: Atheneum, 1967), 97.

6   James Reaney, *14 Barrels from Sea to Sea* (Erin, Ontario: Press Porcépic, 1977), 34.

7   *Image, Music, Text*, 143.

8   Ibid, 147.

9   Jonathan Culler, *Roland Barthes* (New York: Oxford University Press, 1983), 11.

10   Robert Bringhurst, 'Sunday Morning'. *The Calling: Selected Poems 1970–1995* (Toronto: McClelland & Stewart, 1995), 168.

11   James Reaney, 'The Story Behind *King Whistle!*'. *Brick* 8 (Winter 1980), 61.

12   Gerald D. Parker, *How to Play* (Toronto: ECW Press, 1991), 55.

13   James Reaney, 'An Evening with Babble and Doodle'. *Canadian Literature* 12 (Spring 1962), 40.

14   Stan Dragland, *The Difficult* (St. John's, Newfoundland: Pedlar Press, 2019), 13–14. Not all essayists bother locating the origin of their sources with format based on the *Chicago Manual of Style*. Drop all those numbers out of a text, it's going to look much cleaner and less pedantic. There was a time when I was encouraged to follow the MLA style of citation: author and title of book mentioned in the text, page number in brackets after the quotation, full text in Works Cited at the end. That method has its appeal for those who want their argument self-contained, no spillover into aside, qualification or expansion beyond what the text proper seems meant to hold. But for this meanderthal, notes hold the *promise* of aside, qualification, expansion. Some of the notes might be taken as a sign that the writer didn't know where to call a halt, but I like to think of them as encouraging a look back at the main text: complete as ever this maker could make it, but still an instalment, not even *his* last word. 'The process increasingly becomes,' Phil Hall says about writing a poem, 'to let what one has started have everything it wants, & everything one has, like a stew, & to wait out any later requests, a smidgen of mint / mind, if the tilt-aim is still hungry. I think you are finding something similar,' he goes on, 'in the essay methods you are letting take you, their rolling, accumulative designs.' (email to SD, April 7, 2020). He got that right.

15   Rosemary Sutcliff, *The Mark of the Horse Lord*. Illustrated by Charles Keeping (London, Oxford University Press, 1975), 71.

16   Anna Lowenhaupt Tsing, *The Mushroom at the End of the World: On the*

Possibility of Life in Capitalist Ruins (Princeton and Oxford: Princeton University Press, 2015), viii.

17 Ibid., viii.

18 Milton Acorn, Morley Callaghan, Roch Carrier, Paul Chamberland, Robertson Davies, Selwyn Dewdney, Northrop Frye, Margaret Laurence, Irving Layton, Dorothy Livesay, Jay Macpherson, Hugh MacLennan, Alice Munro, Alden Nowlan, George Ryga (phone interview with James Reaney), F. R. Scott, A. J. M. Smith, Robert Weaver.

19 Reaney refers to this painting in the contributors notes to *Alphabet* 9 (November 1964). He seems not to have been as familiar with Bucke then as he later became: 'Greg Curnoe has recently exhibited at the Mirvish Gallery in Toronto and one of his paintings in progress concerns the fire epiphany in Dr. Charles Buck's [sic] famous book, *Cosmic Consciousness*.' (96)

20 Richard Maurice Bucke, *Cosmic Consciousness: A Study in the Evolution of the Human Mind*. New Introduction by George Moreby Acklom (New York: E. P. Dutton and Company, 1969), 9.

21 James Reaney, Scene 9, 'Jacky the Baptist', in *Antler River*. Unpublished script, Western University Archives. 'Richard Maurice Bucke was anything but an ordinary professional man,' says Acklom. 'He was a matter-of-fact scientist on one side of his brain, but on the other he was a man of highly developed imaginative faculty and endowed with an enormous memory, especially for poetry—of which he knew volumes by heart. His professional career was a distinguished one. In 1876 he was appointed Superintendent of the newly built Provincial Asylum for the Insane at Hamilton, Ontario, and in 1877 of the London (Ontario) Hospital. He became one of the foremost alienists on this Continent, introducing many reforms in procedure which, though considered dangerously radical at the time, are now a matter of everyday method' ('The Man and the Book', *Cosmic Consciousness*, ix).

22 *Antler River*, scene 9.

23 James Reaney, 'David Willson'. *Dictionary of Canadian Biography*, Vol. 9 (Toronto: University of Toronto Press, 1976), 842.

24 William Blake, 'To Thomas Butts, 6 July 1803'. *The Letters of William Blake*. Edited by Geoffrey Keynes (London: Rupert Hart-Davis, 1968), 88.

25 Richard Maurice Bucke, *Cosmic Consciousness*, 9–10.

26 In Part VI, 'Last Words' of *Cosmic Consciousness*, Bucke says 'Many readers, before they have reached this page, will have been struck by the fact that the name of no woman is included in the list of so-called "great cases", and the names of only three in that of "Lesser, Imperfect and Doubtful Instances". Besides these three the editor knows another woman, still living, who is undoubtedly if not a great, still a genuine case. She would not, however, permit the editor to use her experience even without her name, and the case is therefore reluctantly entirely omitted.' Ibid., 365. Bucke doesn't reflect on why he finds so few women to write about. The word 'patriarchy' comes to mind.

27 Ibid., 11.

28 Tim Keane, 'The Unsparing Pages of Francis Bacon'. https://hyperallergic.com/534981. December 28, 2019.

29 James Reaney, 'Author's note from the original production'. *Colours in the Dark* (Vancouver: Talonplays with Macmillan, 1969), 4.

30 Sarah Milroy, 'David Milne and the First World War'. *Canadian Art* (Summer 2014), 56.

31 James Reaney, 'Contributors'. *Alphabet* 9, (November 1964), 96.

32 See James Reaney, 'Serinette'. *Performance Poems* (Goderich, Ontario: Moonstone Press, 1990), 31–32.

33 James Reaney, *14 Barrels*, 40.

34 James Stewart Reaney, *James Reaney*. Profiles in Canadian Drama, General Editor: Geraldine C. Anthony (Toronto: Gage Educational Publishing, 1977), 5.

35 James Reaney, *Sticks & Stones, The Donnellys: Part One*. With Scholarly Apparatus by James Noonan (Erin, Ontario: Press Porcépic, 1975), 71.

36 The research eventually went into James C. Reaney, *The Donnelly Documents: An Ontario Vendetta* (Toronto: Champlain Society, 2004), with a 145 page introduction by Reaney.

37 James Reaney, *Two Plays: Gentle Rain Food Co-op, One Man Masque* (London: Ergo Productions, 2003), 30.

38 Ibid., 31.

39 '"To Flow Like You", An Interview with James Reaney'. Wanda Campbell, *Windsor Review*, Vol. 29, No. 1 (Spring 1996), 21.

40 Imre Salusinszky, 'Interview with Jacques Derrida'. *Criticism in Society: Interviews with Jacques Derrida, Northrop Frye, Harold Bloom, Geoffrey Hartman, Frank Kermode, Edward Said, Barbara Johnson, Frank Lentricchia, and J. Hillis Miller* (New York and London, Methuen, 1987), 17.

41 Ibid., 21–22.

42 James Reaney, *The Dismissal: or Twisted Beards & Tangled Whiskers* (Erin, Ontario: Press Porcépic, 1978), 39.

43 James Reaney, 'Long Poems'. Long-liners Conference Issue, *Open Letter*, Sixth Series, Nos. 2–3 (Summer–Fall 1985), 119.

44 John Beckwith, 'James Reaney and Music'. James Reaney Memorial Lecture, 2016. https://jamesreaney.com.

45 Northrop Frye, *Fearful Symmetry: A Study of William Blake* (Princeton: Princeton University Press, 1969), 118.

46 Ibid., 150.

47 Iain McGilchrist, *The Master and His Emissary*, 434.

48 Ibid., 441.

49 James Reaney, 'Long Poems', 117.

50 Ibid., 123.

51 James Reaney, *A Suit of Nettles* (Toronto: Macmillan of Canada, 1968), 26.

52 Northrop Frye, 'Preface'. *Fearful Symmetry*, viii.

53 James Reaney, 'Vision in Canada?'. *University of Toronto Quarterly*, Vol. 70, number 4 (Fall 2001), 943.

54 James Reaney, 'Editorial'. *Alphabet* 16 (September 1969), 5.

55 Ibid., 4.

56 James Reaney, 'Winnipeg as a Chess Game', 'A Message to Winnipeg' vi. *Poems*. Edited by Germaine Warkentin (Toronto: new press, 1972), 139–140.

57 Jan Zwicky, *The Experience of Meaning* (Montreal & Kingston, London, Chicago: McGill-Queen's University Press), 71.

58 'A Letter from James Reaney: Halloween.' *Black Moss*, Series 2, Number 1 (Spring 1976), 4.

59 Ibid., 7.

60 'My guess is that behind this network of *Alphabet* friends stands an even larger circle of people, just out of sight. I don't know them by name, but I do

know that their presence is extremely important as far as the imaginative life of this country is concerned. Yes, I do know them by name, or at least a year ago I heard a good name for them:—they were called the Identifiers.' James Reaney, 'Editorial', *Alphabet* 18 & 19 (June 1971), 2.

61 James Reaney, 'Editorial.' *Alphabet* 1 (September 1960), 3.

62 James Reaney, 'Long Poems', 124.

63 James Reaney *The Donnelly Documents*, cxliv.

64 James Reaney, *Poems*, 56.

65 James Reaney, *The Killdeer, Masks of Childhood*, edited and with an afterword by Brian Parker (Toronto: new press, 1972), 212.

66 James Reaney, 'Introduction', Ann Cardwell, *Crazy to Kill* (London, Ontario: Nightwood Editions, 1989), 7. Ann Cardwell was the pseudonym of Stratford author Jean Makins Powley. Cardwell was the name of Powley's grandmother. Reaney was related to her through the Cardwells.

67 James Reaney, 'Laputanada', review of Norval Morrisseau, *Legends of My People, The Great Ojibway*. *Alphabet* 13 (June 1967), 101.

68 In the story called 'The Ditch: Second Reading', in *The Box Social and Other Stories* (Erin, Ontario: The Porcupine's Quill, 1996), the narrator refers to the 'Palaeo-Woodland Indians [who] came after the caribou to feed on them and clothe themselves with their skins and told the stories that slowly crystallized themselves into a civilization.' (94) About what he calls the 'Indian Studies' component of his graduate course in Ontario Literature and Culture, Reaney says, 'how can Wallace Stevens say, completely overlooking those who gave his state a name, that "we never had a mythology in Connecticut"? Since it seems unfair to exterminate them while stealing their myths, perhaps this is wise. Still, Jehova came to Ontario like a rapacious Elizabethan settler to Ireland. Surely you have to know who were the gods of your country before your arrival.' 'Canadian Literature and What?' *Canadian Literature* 15 (Winter, 1963), 255. Saying so, Reaney anticipates Robert Jago, 'a registered member of the Kwantlen First Nation, and an enrolled member of the Nooksack Indian Tribe', introducing a *Walrus* magazine project called 'Terra Cognita' in 2020: 'I don't think you should be able to pass yourself off as smart in this country without knowing the Indigenous name of the place you're standing on or its

gods and legends and battles. If the words of Socrates are known to us, then Swaneset's are knowable too. When the Europeans first looked at our country, they called it *terra incognita*—unknown land—and when they arrived, they drew maps, put their names all over it, but never really tried to know it.

That's the idea with this project, and that's why we named it **Terra Cognita**: because we know this land, and you don't know enough about Canada without knowing us, and one good way to get to know us is to read us the way that we want to be writing.' *The Walrus* Newsletter, July 5, 2020. Lest Reaney's irony, above, be misconstrued: he is for acknowledging the myths of Indigenous peoples, and dead set against killing them.

69 *Heroes of Comedy: Barry Humphries.*

https://www.google.com/search?q=heroes+of+comedy+barry+humphries

70 James Reaney, *14 Barrels*, 139–40.

71 James Reaney, 'Invocation to the Muse of Satire'. *A Suit of Nettles*), ix.

72 James Reaney, *14 Barrels*, 105. An allied thought: 'The reason why society pays so little attention to its wise men is not that society consists of criminals or hypocrites, but that it consists of "normal" people who sincerely believe in the superiority of common to uncommon sense.' Northrop Frye, *Fearful Symmetry*, 332.

73 C.H. Gervais & James Reaney, *Baldoon* (Erin, Ontario: The Porcupine's Quill, 1976), 1.

74 Ibid., 2.

75 James Reaney, 'Serinette'. *Scripts: Librettos for Operas and Other Musical Works*. Edited with an introduction by John Beckwith (Toronto: Coach House Books, 2004), 282.

76 James Reaney, 'Introduction.' *Gyroscope* (Toronto: Playwrights Canada, 1983), np.

77 Sonu Shamdasani, 'Liber Novus: The "Red Book" of C.G. Jung'. C.G. Jung, *The Red Book: Liber Novus*, edited by Sonu Shamdasani. Preface by Ulrich Hoerni. Translated by Mark Kyburz, John Peck and Sonu Shamdasani. Philemon Series, a publication in arrangement with the Foundation of the Works of C.G. Jung, Zürich (New York and London: W.W. Norton, 2009), 263.

78 M.C. Richards, *Centering in Pottery, Poetry, and the Person*, second edition (Middletown, Connecticut: Wesleyan University Press, 1989), xvii–xix.

79   James Reaney, *Colours in the Dark* (Vancouver: Talonplays with Macmillan of Canada, 1969), 10.

80   'A Letter from James Reaney', 7. 'In some respects, yes,' says Jan Zwicky, '[the world is] built like a machine, because that's another way of understanding it that appears to be evolutionarily adaptive. But the world is also built like a web of analogies. It is as much a piece of music as it is a pile of lumber.' *The Experience of Meaning*, 50.

81   James Reaney, *Twelve Letters to a Small Town* (Toronto: The Ryerson Press, 1962), 3.

82   James Reaney, 'Long Poems', 124.

83   James Reaney, 'Editorial'. *Alphabet* 2 (July 1961), 1.

84   Margaret Avison, 'Poets in Canada'. *Poetry* Vol. xciv, No. 3 (June 1959), 184.

85   Margaret Avison, 'There are several writers in residence, named or not …' *I am Here and Not Not-There: An Autobiography* (Erin, Ontario: The Porcupine's Quill, 2009), 293.

86   Jean McKay, 'Colleen Thibaudeau: A Biographical Sketch'. *Brick* 5 (Winter 1979), 10.

87   James Reaney, 'The Canadian Poet's Predicament'. A. J. M. Smith, ed. *Masks of Poetry: Canadian Critics on Canadian Verse* (Toronto: McClelland and Stewart, 1962), 111.

88   Guy Birchard, 'Fort Poetry'. *Valedictions: William Hawkins, Ray ('Condo') Tremblay, Artie Gold* (Ottawa: above/ground press, 2019), np.

89   James Reaney, *14 Barrels*, 60.

90   James Reaney, 'An Evening with Babble and Doodle', 43.

91   George Johnston, 'Northrop Frye: Some Recollections and Observations'. *The CEA Critic*, Vol. 42, No. 2 (January 1980), 23.

92   Ibid., 22.

93   Ibid., 23.

94   R. G. Everson, 'Report for Northrop Frye'. *Selected Poems 1920–1970*. Drawings by Colin Haworth (Montreal: Delta Canada, 1970), 37. Mind you, the Frye line is taken out of context. Here is the full passage: 'Literature may have life, reality, experience, nature, imaginative truth, social conditions, or what you will for its *content*; but literature itself is not made out of these things. Poetry

can only be made out of other poems; novels out of other novels. Literature shapes itself, and is not shaped externally: the *forms* of literature can no more exist outside literature than the forms of sonata and fugue and rondo can exist outside music.' (*Anatomy of Criticism*, 97) Any objection to this that sticks will have to go after form, not content.

95 James Reaney, 'Editorial'. *Alphabet* 2 (July 1961), 2.

96 'A Letter from James Reaney', 6.

97 James Reaney, 'July: Catalogue Poems'. *Performance Poems,* 79. Reaney writes in the Editorial to *Alphabet* 3 (December 1961), 'Last issue we printed a whale's backbone—a complete list of the British kings.... Well, it has been ... the backbone of a poem in the past and it may very well be again. It's a table of human elements one should know about.' 3.

98 James Reaney, *Imprecations: The Art of Swearing* (Windsor, Ontario: Black Moss Press, 1984), np.

99 'Though mainly Presbyterian and Plymouth Brethren in background, Reaney's parents were also involved during his childhood with an Independent Gospel Hall and a missionary-oriented Congregationalist church that had not entered Church Union in 1925.' Richard Stingle, 'James Reaney and His Works', 1.

100 James Reaney, 'The Identifier Effect'. *The CEA Critic,* Vol. 42, No. 2 (January 1980), 26–27.

101 James Reaney, 'Gentle Rain Food Co-op'. *Two Plays,* 65.

102 James Reaney, 'The Identifier Effect', 27.

103 Ibid., 28.

104 Northrop Frye, *Fearful Symmetry*, 9.

105 Ibid., 9–10.

106 Ibid., 121.

107 Ibid., 10.

108 Ibid., 11.

109 Ibid., 11.

110 Northrop Frye, *Anatomy of Criticism: Four Essays* (New York: Atheneum, 1967), 3.

111 George Johnston, 'Northrop Frye: Some Recollections and Observations'. *The CEA Critic,* 22.

112 James Reaney, 'Editorial'. *Alphabet* 1 (September 1960), 4.

113 James Reaney, 'Souwesto'. *Performance Poems*, 34.

114 Ibid., 37.

115 James Reaney, 'July: Catalogue Poems'. *Performance Poems*, 79.

116 Ibid., 83.

117 James Reaney, 'Some Critics Are Music Teachers'. Eleanor Cook, Chaviva
Hošek, Jay Macpherson, Patricia Parker, and Julian Patrick, editors, *Centre
and Labyrinth: Essays in Honour of Northrop Frye* (Toronto, Buffalo, London:
University of Toronto Press in association with Victoria University, 1983), 307.

118 James Reaney, 'The Identifier Effect', 30.

119 There are occasions when 'imposition' is proper. In Catherine Ross's 'An
interview with James Reaney' (*Canadian Children's Literature* 29, 1983),
Reaney speaks approvingly of 'what Hope and Alvin Lee did in that series of
readers called *Wish and Nightmare*. It's in a series edited by Frye called *Uses of
the Imagination*. It introduces the child to a carefully spread out version of all
the modes.' (8) I myself would choose some such literary structure for such an
anthology over the random, one-unrelated-thing-after-another. Elsewhere (in
a book called *The Bricoleur and His Sentences*) I have written about a first-year
advanced English course that I taught with Richard Stingle and Donald Hair,
two former students of Frye. (Stingle once told me that even eminent
Professor Frye would be pestered by the old nugget of a question posed by
those students for whom personal results trump actual learning: 'Will this be
on the exam?') English 022 at Western was organized according to the modes,
and it worked beautifully. This was partly because Stingle and Hair were
wonderful teachers; their particular approaches to each text were inspiring. I
was really a student as well as a teacher of that course, and I learned a great deal
from being part of it. I did come to chafe a little under the Frye structure; I
now rather think Frye would have approved of that. The fact that the Reaney-
designed English 138 was *not* structured according to Frye might be taken as
another sign that Reaney was not indebted to Frye for everything.

120 Craig Stewart Walker, *The Buried Astrolabe: Canadian Dramatic Imagination
and Western Tradition* (Montreal and Kingston, London, Ithaca: McGill-
Queen's University Press, 2001), 414.

121 Jay Macpherson, 'Educated Doodle: Some Notes on *One Man Masque*'. Stan
Dragland, ed. *Approaches to the Work of James Reaney* (Toronto: ECW Press,
1983), 70. Reprinted from *Essays in Canadian Writing* 24–25
(Winter 1982–83), 65–99.

122 Barker Fairley, *Portraits*. With a text by the Artist. Edited with an Introduction
by Gary Michael Dault (Toronto, New York, London, Sydney, Auckland:
Methuen, 1981), 39.

123 Ibid., xiii.

124 James Reaney, 'Editorial'. *Alphabet* 4 (June 1962), 3.

125 James Reaney, *Canada Dash, Canada Dot. Scripts*, 79.

126 James Reaney, *14 Barrels*, 65.

127 James Reaney, 'Preface'. *Masks of Childhood*, viii.

128 Margaret Atwood, 'Reaney Collected'. George Woodcock, ed., *Poets and
Critics: Essays from Canadian Literature 1966–1974* (Toronto: Oxford
University Press, 1974), 151.

129 Ibid., 152.

130 James Reaney, 'To the Secret City: From a Winnipeg Sketchbook'.
Queen's Quarterly 61, no. 2 (Summer 1954), 167.

131 Ibid., 174.

132 Ibid., 177.

133 James Reaney, 'Preface'. *Lewis Carroll's Alice Through the Looking Glass*
(Erin, Ontario: The Porcupine's Quill, 1994), 8.

134 'the angel of time': this phrase—odd in the context of keeping a journal—also
appears in Northrop Frye's *The Great Code: The Bible and Literature* (New York
and London: Harcourt Brace Jovanovich, 1981), 198. There it's 'the angel of time
that man clings to until daybreak' (Genesis 32:36). Since there is no 32:36, the
reference should probably be to 32:26, where Jacob wrestles a 'man' to a draw by
holding on all night, thus earning a huge blessing. If Reaney had that Biblical
verse in mind, perhaps he was recommending a metaphorical kind of holding
on: patience. This would involve methodical accumulation of information,
itself insignificant, until the aggregate is seen—or made—to mean something.

135 James Reaney, 'May: Facta'. *Performance Poems*, 67.

136 James Reaney, 'January'. *Performance Poems*, 7.

137 James Reaney, 'Catalogue Poems'. *Performance Poems*, 81.

138 James Reaney, 'Brushstrokes Decorating a Fan'. *Souwesto Home* (London, Ontario: Brick Books, 2005), 22.

139 James Reaney, *Performance Poems*, 7.

140 James Reaney, 'The Granary'. *Performance Poems*, 25.

141 James Reaney, 'The Easter Egg'. *Masks of Childhood*, 22.

142 James Reaney, *Performance Poems*, 81.

143 A brief example: speaking in *14 Barrels from Sea to Sea* about the National Theatre School, Reaney says that 'one thing [it] produces enough of is right-weight lead and ingenue actresses; what it could do with is some character actresses, in other words—more ectomorph and endomorph power, less mesomorph narcissism.' 68

144 James Reaney, *The Donnellys Part III. Handcuffs* (Erin, Ontario: Press Porcépic, 1977), 92.

145 James Reaney, *14 Barrels*, 146. In an essay called 'Cycle', published in *Canadian Drama*, Vol. 2, No. 1 (Spring 1976), Reaney describes an Edmonton workshop based on the four provinces and separate castes of Ancient Eire that was resumed, with refinements, at Mount Allison University in Sackville, New Brunswick.

146 James Reaney, 'Moses', *Souwesto Home*, 53.

147 James Reaney, Introduction, *Gyroscope*, np.

148 James Reaney, 'The Easter Egg'. *Masks of Childhood*, 37. Pondering saints' days sent me to two Reaney books that Richard Stingle gave me in return for teaching one of his classes. He had Reaney inscribe them to me. *The Dance of Death at London, Ontario* ('Happy Odenstag, Stan'), *Twelve Letters to a Small Town* ('Happy St Swithold — Stan!'). Both inscriptions are dated X 24 72: October 24, 1972. Odenstag or Wodenstag is a Wednesday, but who is St Swithold? The Roman Catholic liturgical calendar has Saint Anthony Mary Claret on October 24; Anglicans have no saint for that day. Well, St. Swithold shows up in Shakespeare's *King Lear* and *MacBeth* as a queller of nightmares. In *The White Goddess*, a book Reaney knew, Robert Graves says that Shakespeare substituted Swithold for Odin, so there is that connection. Others say Swithold is a misreading of Withold and Withold is a corruption of St.

Vitalis, whose day is April 27. I'm left with a puzzle as to what Reaney may have been thinking by inscribing *Twelve Letters* as he did, but I'm fascinated by where the trail leads: to entirely unexpected mythological and literary places. The inscribed copy of *Twelve Letters* is somehow missing its twelfth letter. Would that be why Reaney gave me a copy of the 2002 facsimile edition of the book, this one inscribed 'for Stan ♥ from Jamie ** May 2 (Beltaine I day after) 2002.'

149 James Reaney, 'The Wild Flora of Elgin County'. *Souwesto Home*, 33.

150 Diana Beresford-Kroeger, *To Speak for the Trees: My Life's Journey from Ancient Celtic Wisdom to a Healing Vision of the Forest* (Toronto: Random House Canada, 2019), 3.

151 James Reaney, 'Souwesto Theatre: A Beginning'. *Alumni Gazette* (Spring 1976).

152 James Reaney, 'David Willson', 842.

153 Ralph Cunningham, 'A Note on David Willson's Temple'. *Alphabet* 9 (November 1964), 39–40.

154 James Reaney, *Canada Dash, Canada Dot. Scripts*, 134.

155 'Topless Nightmares, being a dialogue with himself by James Reaney'. *Halloween* 2, an occasional theatrical newsletter edited by James Reaney (London, Ontario: James Reaney, 1976), 8.

156 'Names & Nicknames'. *Apple Butter & Other Plays for Children* (Vancouver: Talonbooks, 1973), 101.

157 *Canada Dash, Canada Dot. Scripts*, 104–105.

158 James Reaney, 'Cutting Up Didoes'. *University of Toronto Quarterly*, Vol. 61, No. 3 (Mar. 1992), 373.

159 Ibid., 375.

160 James Reaney, 'Vision in Canada?'. *University of Toronto Quarterly*, Vol. 70, No. 4 (Oct. 2001), 938.

161 James Reaney, 'Introduction', *Scripts*, 10.

162 'Three Versions of a Press Conference in Vienna'. *C. G. Jung Speaking: Interviews and Encounters*. Edited by William McGuire and R. F. C. Hull. Bollingen Series xcvii (Princeton: Princeton University Press, 1977), 44.

163 James Reaney, *14 Barrels*, 22–23.

164 James Reaney, *Ignoramus* (Vancouver: Talonbooks, 1978), 14.

165 Ibid., 11.

166 Ibid., 5.

167 James Reaney, *Take the Big Picture* (Erin, Ontario: The Porcupine's Quill, 1986), 120. 'Given without notes, the Frye lectures in tone rather reminded me at the time of the piano performances of Glenn Gould; a Manitoba friend once remarked that the latter's way of playing Bach made you "think"; so with the Frye lectures. The energetic drive to clarity makes the listener feel new unused mental muscles swing into action, but never to the point of bafflement. The drive forward is not too clear, but just clear enough. "Consequently" constructions I recall being used a great deal; at the end there was always a paradox that kept you unravelling until the next lecture next week.' 'Identifier Effect', 29.

168 Ibid, 121.

169 James Reaney, 'Cutting Up Didoes,' 376.

170 James Reaney, 'Identifier Effect,' 26.

171 Ibid., 26.

172 James Reaney, 'Some Critics Are Music Teachers,' 299.

173 James Reaney, 'Editorial.' *Alphabet* 17 (December 1969), 3.

174 Ross Woodman, *James Reaney*. Canadian Writers Number 12, New Canadian Library (Toronto / Montreal: McClelland and Stewart, 1971), 39–40.

175 James Reaney, *Souwesto Home*, 23.

176 Branwell, for example, the 'hero' of *A Suit of Nettles*. For most, Branwell is the most obscure member of the amazing Brontë family, his three sisters, Emily and Charlotte in particular, having achieved lasting literary fame. Branwell was a writer too, and also something of a painter. He made a portrait of himself and his sisters but didn't like the way he turned out, so painted over his image. He is and is not there, having left a ghostly trace of himself between two sisters. That's just about how he figures in literary history. But Reaney has read the 'thousands and thousands of words' of the Angrian saga created by the Brontë youngsters, Charlotte and Branwell especially, and has written about the juvenilia in an article called 'The Brontës: Gothic Transgressor as Cattle

Drover', in Kenneth W. Graham, ed., *Gothic Fictions: Prohibition /
Transgression* (New York: AMS Press, 1989), 230. The Branwell he quotes has
real stylistic verve. 'Although Charlotte … can provide a few,' Reaney remarks
about one memorable passage, 'this must be the most mind-boggling
moment in all of the youthful writings, even more so when the reader
remembers that it is written by a fifteen year old, and that it antedates not only
Monty Python, Tony Hancock, and the Goon Show, but also Borges, Nabokov,
and the *nouvelle vague*.' 235. (Jay Macpherson also has an article in the Graham
volume.) Reaney included Brontë juvenilia on a graduate course he offered at
Western University. Branwell is a poet in Reaney's play, *Zamorna! And the
House by the Churchyard*. Clearly, the Branwell in *A Suit of Nettles*
is an homage.

177 James Reaney, *A Suit of Nettles*, 30–31.

178 James Reaney, *Poems*, 190.

179 James Reaney, 'The Shivaree'. *Scripts*, 211.

180 'The Kings of Britain: a tentative list drawn from Milton and Spenser'.
     Alphabet 2 (July 1961), 92–97.

181 James Reaney, 'Three Desks'. *Masks of Childhood*, 176.

182 Alvin A. Lee, *James Reaney* (New York: Twayne Publishers, 1968), 152.

183 James Reaney, *Performance Poems*, 75.

184 Ibid., 82.

185 James Reaney, *Colours in the Dark* (Vancouver: Talonplays
     with Macmillan of Canada, 1969), 17.

186 Ibid., 91. The 'Motif Chart' Craig Stewart Walker has made for *Colours in the
     Dark* (Colour, Subtitle, Day, Letter, Flower, Special symbol, Astral body,
     Religious song, Secular song) is a useful digest of listable materials assembled
     for making the play. *The Buried Astrolabe*, 51.

187 James Reaney, *A Suit of Nettles*, 31.

188 Jesper Hoffmeyer, *Signs of Meaning in the Universe*. Translated by Barbara J.
     Haveland (Bloomington & Indianapolis: Indiana University Press, 1993), 36.

189 James Reaney, *Baldoon*, 117–118.

190 Ibid., 118.

191 Ibid., 119.

192 James Reaney, *Imprecations: The Art of Swearing*
(Windsor, Ontario: Black Moss Press, 1984), 7.

193 Ibid., 13.

194 James Reaney, 'Editorial'. *Alphabet* 8 (June 1964), 5.

195 Jay Macpherson, 'Preface'. *Listen to the Wind* (Vancouver:
Talonbooks, 1972), vii.

196 *Wacousta!* (Toronto, Victoria: Press Porcépic, 1979), 22.

197 Ibid., 23. Cree dramatist Tomson Highway was a member of the cast and
taught the other cast members Cree words during the workshops.

198 John Beckwith, 'James Reaney and Music'.

199 James Reaney, 'Taptoo!'. *Scripts*, 303.

200 Ibid., 312–313.

201 James Reaney, *Wacousta!*, 44.

202 James Reaney, 'Taptoo!', *Scripts*, 313–314.

203 Jan Zwicky, *The Experience of Meaning*, 58.

204 James Reaney, *Poems*, 185.

205 James Reaney, 'Wacousta Workshops: an Overview', *Wacousta!*, 157.

206 Having found out that I was working on Reaney, Robert Shipley gave me a call.
He was hoping to make contact with others currently engaged with the man
who had changed his life, since he wanted to write something himself by way
of tribute. He told me how he came to participate in the Listener's Workshop,
and I asked if I could mention it. In response, he wrote 'The Jamie Effect,' and
sent it to me on May 26, 2020. I quote from it with his permission.

207 Alice Munro, 'Epilogue: The Photographer'. *Lives of Girls and Women*
(New York: McGraw-Hill Ryerson, 1971), 210.

208 David McFadden, *A Trip Around Lake Erie* (Toronto: Coach House Press, 1980) 11.

209 Mary Dalton, *Edge: Essays, Reviews, Interviews* (Windsor, Ontario: Palimpsest
Press, 2015), 56. In *Red Ledger*, her fourth book of poetry (Montreal: Signal
Editions, 2006), Dalton published an eleven-poem sequence called 'Reaney
Gardens', riffing on 'Shakespearean Gardens', eleventh letter in *Twelve Letters
to a Small Town*. Where Reaney's titles for brief prose snippets set in Stratford,
Ontario come from Shakespeare plays, Dalton's are drawn from Reaney
poems and plays and are set in St. John's, Newfoundland.

210 James Reaney, 'A Letter from a Playwright Who Once Attended Your High School'. *Brick* 8 (Winter 1980), a special issue featuring *King Whistle!*, a play about the Stratford Strike of 1933, by James Reaney, with 'The Story Behind *King Whistle!*', 61.

211 James Reaney, 'The Story Behind *King Whistle!*', 50–52.

212 James Reaney, 'A Letter from a Playwright', 61.

213 Tim Inkster, 'The Iconography of James Reaney: An Anecdotal Bibliography'. *The Devil's Artisan* 75 (Fall/Winter 2014), 32.

214 Frank Davey, 'Wonderful, Wonderful'. Review of *Twelve Letters to a Small Town*. *Canadian Literature* 17 (Summer 1963), 82–83.

215 Iain McGilchrist, *The Master and His Emissary*, 450.

216 Northrop Frye, *Fearful Symmetry*, 42–43.

217 D.I. Brown, 'A Brief History of *Alphabet* magazine'. *The Devil's Artisan* 71 (Fall/Winter 2012), 43.

218 James Reaney, *Performance Poems*, 55.

219 Ibid., 59.

220 Ibid., 58.

221 Ibid., 57.

222 'The term "Southern Ontario Gothic",' says Tim Inkster, 'comes from an interview Graeme Gibson conducted with Timothy Findley that appeared in Gibson's *Eleven Canadian Novelists* (1973) in which Findley acknowledged similarities between his own novel *The Last of the Crazy People* and stylistic elements endemic to the familiar Southern Gothic of William Faulkner or Eudora Welty.' 'The Iconography of James Reaney', 36.

223 James Reaney, 'The Car'. *The Box Social and Other Stories*, 59.

224 Ibid., 68.

225 Ibid., 72.

226 James Reaney, *Poems*, 84.

227 Ibid., 84.

228 Nathan Heller, 'Driven: life in the automobile era'. *The New Yorker* (July 29, 2019), 25.

229 *A Suit of Nettles*, 22.

230 Ibid., 23.

231 Ibid., 24.

232 James Reaney, *14 Barrels*, 82.

233 James Reaney, *Performance Poems*, 72.

234 James Reaney, *Wacousta!*, 61.

235 James Reaney, 'Topless Nightmares', 3.

236 Ibid., 4–5.

237 Apparently I can be as cranky as Reaney. But something in me is also called to backpedal—not to take back what I said, but to go on and say what else I sometimes find myself thinking. For instance: though I'm often bored with much radio programming, I admire the resourcefulness that keeps on, day after day after day, finding the content. Even when there's very little in it, there it is, week after month after year. Also, just by being there, radio and television stand ready to relay useful public information in an era of plague like COVID 19. There are times when I'm not judgmental about all the dull routine in contemporary life. ('Fine weather we're having.' 'You betcha.') At such times I feel more tolerant, not holier than thou, not smarter than you, more a member of my society as a whole, less a critic of the life I'm in. Also lazier. I wouldn't be able to stand myself if all I did was go along with whatever's going. I do have to take some care not to let any inclination to fit in deny the stranger in me. That alien is the true citizen; he might occasionally have something useful to say. But the other needs a voice too. He may be the one to mention that what in Albert Camus' novel *The Plague* holds Algerian society together while people are dying is boring old unfeeling bureaucracy. It keeps on functioning because it's so good at plain old going through the motions. What if the glue of society were invisible and entirely banal: structures neither good nor evil, just there? By golly, there'd be *some* good in them.

238 *14 Barrels*, 35.

239 James Reaney, *Antler River*. Unpublished script. Western University Archives. Iain McGilchrist: 'I would contend that a combination of urban environments which are increasingly rectilinear grids of machine-made surfaces and shapes, in which little speaks of the natural world; a worldwide increase in the proportion of the population who live in such environments, and live in them in greater degrees of isolation; an unprecedented assault on the natural world,

not just through exploitation, despoliation and pollution, but also more subtly, through excessive "management" of one kind or another, coupled with an increase in the virtuality of life, both in the nature of work undertaken, and in the omnipresence in leisure time of television and the internet, which between them have created a largely insubstantial replica of "life" as processed by the left hemisphere—all these to a remarkable extent have realized this aim, if I am right that it is an aim, in an almost unbelievably short period of time.' *The Master and His Emissary*, 387.

240   James Reaney, *Take the Big Picture*, 25.

241   James Reaney, *Gentle Rain Food Co-op*, 17–18.

242   James Reaney, *Twelve Letters to a Small Town*, 31.

243   *Alphabet* 1 (September 1950), 3.

244   Ibid., 32.

245   James Reaney, *The Dismissal*, 39.

246   Gerald Parker, 'The integral versus the fractional: Reaney's *The Dismissal*'. *Brick* 7 (Fall 1979), 17.

247   James Reaney, 'Author's Note'. *The Dismissal*, 4.

248   James Reaney, *The Dismissal*, 11.

249   James Reaney, 'Sleigh Without Bells'. *The Box Social and Other Stories*, 142.

250   Ibid., 142.

251   James Reaney, 'Editorial'. *Alphabet* 6 (June 1963), 75.

252   James Reaney, *Colours in the Dark*, vi.

253   Northrop Frye, 'Conclusion to a *Literary History of Canada*.' *The Bush Garden: Essays on the Canadian Imagination* (Toronto: House of Anansi, 1971), 249.

254   James Reaney, *Night Blooming Cereus. The Killdeer & Other Plays* (Toronto: Macmillan Company of Canada, 1962), 202.

255   James Reaney, *Canada Dash, Canada Dot. Scripts*, 150.

256   James Reaney, 'Introduction'. Isabella Valancy Crawford, *Collected Poems*. Literature of Canada, Poetry and Prose in Reprint, Douglas Lochhead, General Editor (Toronto & Buffalo: University of Toronto Press, 1972), xx.

257   *Alphabet* 10 (July 1965), 51–57.

258   Ibid., 203.

259 Jay Macpherson, 'The Anagogic Man'. *The Boatman and Other Poems* (Toronto: Oxford University Press, 1968), 56.

260 James Reaney, *Poems*, 133.

261 Ibid., 133.

262 Ibid., 133.

263 James Reaney, *A Suit of Nettles*, xxi.

264 James Reaney, 'To the Secret City', 177.

265 James Reaney, *The Influence of Spenser on Yeats*. Quoted in Thomas Gerry, *The Emblems of James Reaney* (Erin, Ontario: The Porcupine's Quill, 2013), 26.

266 James Reaney, 'To Flow Like You', 14.

267 Sean Kane, email to the author, March 29, 2021.

268 Ibid.

269 Sean Kane, email to the author, March 15, 2021.

270 James Reaney, 'Editorial'. *Alphabet* 4 (June 1962), 3.

271 James Reaney, 'Names & Nicknames'. *Apple Butter & Other Plays for Children*, 101.

272 James Reaney, 'Horses, Buggies and Cadillacs'. Bruce Meyer and Brian O'Riordan, *In Their Words: Interviews with Fourteen Canadian Writers* (Toronto, Buffalo, London, Sydney: House of Anansi, 1984), 65.

273 James Reaney, 'Wacousta Workshops: An Overview'. *Wacousta!*, 120.

274 'Preface,' *Listen to the Wind*, viii.

275 Ibid., viii.

276 *Wacousta!*, 116.

277 James Reaney, 'Introduction', *The Death and Execution of Frank Holloway or The First Act of John Richardson's* Wacousta. *Jubilee* No. 4. (Wingham, Ontario: Jubilee Press, 1978), 3.

278 *14 Barrels*, vii. 'Mouth horseshoe' needs a word of explanation. Near the end of *Sticks & Stones*, the Donnelly barn having been burned down the previous night and an incriminating horseshoe having been found on the scene, James Donnelly meets one of his enemies, Tom Cassleigh, on the road. Cassleigh tries to convince Donnelly that he and his sons should join the Catholic side in the local conflicts. Donnelly rebuffs him. He notices that Cassleigh's horse has a new shoe. Well, he just happens to have that lost shoe in his possession and tempts Cassleigh off his wagon to retrieve it. Reaching for where Donnelly has

tossed it, Cassleigh gets his shoulder jammed in the spoke of his own wagon wheel. 'Why,' says Donnelly, 'you caught your arm trying to reach for the horseshoe; here I'll put it a bit closer. I'll jam it right into your mouth, Cassleigh. Bite onto it, there.' (153) Humiliating an enemy is a sure way to confirm his hatred, but Donnelly's last words in this scene are 'Donnellys don't kneel.'

279 James Reaney, *14 Barrels from Sea to Sea*, vii.

280 Craig Stewart Walker, *The Buried Astrolabe*, 56–57.

281 Phil Hall, 'Abuse'. *Niagara & Government* (St. John's: Pedlar Press, 2020), 75.

282 In *The Bricoleur and His Sentences*.

283 James Reaney, *Wacousta!*, 35.

284 James Reaney, 'A letter from James Reaney', 5.

285 'Vision in Canada?', 943.

286 James Reaney, 'Search for an Undiscovered Alphabet'. *Canadian Art* 98, Vol. 22 (September/October 1965), 41.

287 Reaney, 'The Condition of Light: Henry James's *The Sacred Fount*'. *University of Toronto Quarterly*, Vol. 3, No. 2 (January 1962), 141.

288 Leona Gom, 'Wood Wide Web — after reading *The Hidden Life of Trees*, by Peter Wohlleben'. *62 Billionaires…* (North Vancouver, BC: The Alfred Gustav Press, 2020), 10.

289 James Reaney, 'The Canadian Imagination'. *Poetry (Chicago)* Vol. 94, No. 3 (June 1959), 187. This essay, one of a group of pieces about Canadian poetry, is ostensibly a review of the nine books of Canadian poetry listed at the beginning. Except for a glance at Ralph Gustafson's *The Penguin Book of Canadian Verse*, Reaney never touches those books. Instead, he addresses his American readers with what he thinks they ought to know about the subject in his title. 'So this is what the Canadian literary landscape looks like to me:' he concludes, 'a giant critical focus [Northrop Frye] with some mythopoeic poets trying to live up to it. So exciting is all this to me that I am afraid I have not had any time for the poetry books mentioned above' (188).

290 Jesper Hoffmeyer, *Signs of Meaning in the Universe*, 129.

291 James Reaney, 'The Canadian Imagination', 188.

292 Victoria Pitts-Taylor, 'Mattering, Feminism, Science, and Corporeal Politics'.

Victoria Pitts-Taylor, ed. *Mattering: Feminism, Science, and Materialism* (New York and London: New York University Press, 2016). 2.

293 Ibid., 4.

294 Stephanie Clare, 'On the Politics of "New Feminist Materialisms"'. *Mattering*, 68.

295 Don McKay, '[ ] or Iconostalgia.' *All New Animal Acts: Essays, Stretchers, Poems* (Kentville, Nova Scotia: Gaspereau Press, 2020), 131.

296 *Signs of Meaning in the Universe*, 94. 'The whole essence of the sign process is that the decentralized units at tissue or cell level can interpret their own environment and act accordingly.' (94) This is not the place to detail how Hoffmeyer has arrived at that essence. I recommend the very reader-friendly account in his book.

297 James Reaney, 'Ontario Culture and—What?', *Canadian Literature* 100 (Spring 1984), 256.

298 Ibid., 256.

299 Ibid., 255.

300 Iain McGilchrist, *The Master and His* Emissary, 269. McGilchrist quotes Diels's translations of fragment IX and fragment X, 123.

301 James Reaney, 'Ontario Culture and—What?', 253.

302 James Reaney, 'An ABC to Ontario Literature and Culture'. *Black Moss* 2nd Series, No. 3 (1970), 2.

303 Ibid., 254.

304 Alice Munro, 'Wild Swans'. *Who Do You Think You Are?* (Toronto: Macmillan of Canada, 1978), 63.

305 Jesper Hoffmeyer, *Signs of Meaning in the Universe*, 31.

306 Don McKay, '[ ] or Iconostalgia', 122.

307 Suzanne Simard, 'How trees talk to each other'. Ted Summit, June 2016. https://www.ted.com/talks/suzanne_simard_how_trees_talk_to_each_other?.

308 Robert Bringhurst, *The Ridge*, preprint edition for limited circulation (Winter Harbour: In Finibus Mundi, 2021), 52.

309 James Reaney, *The St. Nicholas Hotel, Wm Donnelly Prop.* (Erin, Ontario: Press Porcépic, 1976), 25.

310 Ibid., 26.

311 Ibid., 27–29.

312 'The Story Behind *King Whistle!*', 51–52.

313 Anna Lowenhaupt Tsing, *The Mushroom at the End of the World*, vii.

314 Ibid., viii.

315 Ibid., vii.

316 Ibid., viii.

317 Ibid., 3.

318 Ibid., viii.

319 'A Letter From James Reaney', 4.

320 Jesper Hoffmeyer, *Signs of Meaning in the Universe*, 133.

321 Margaret Avison, *I Am here and Not Not-There: An Autobiography*, 142.

322 Ibid., 141.

323 Ibid., 141.

324 Ibid., 210.

325 Iain McGilchrist, *The Master and His Emissary*, 171.

326 Ibid., 170.

327 Pat Barker, *Regeneration* (New York: Penguin Plume, 1991), 241.
     Ellipses are Barker's.

328 Ibid, 241–242.

329 Cormac McCarthy, *The Stonemason: A Play in Five Acts*
     (New York: Vintage International, 1995), 97.

330 Ibid., 9–10.

331 Catherine Ross, 'An Interview with James Reaney', 6.

332 Northrop Frye, *Fearful Symmetry*, 328.

333 Ibid., 87.

334 Jane Bennett, *Vibrant Matter: a political ecology of things* (Durham and
     London: Duke University Press, 2010), 4.

335 Ibid., ix.

336 Ibid., xvi.

337 Don McKay, 'Thorax', *Paradoxides: Poems* (Toronto:
     McClelland & Stewart, 2012), 42.

338 Loren Eiseley, 'Paw Marks and Buried Towns', *The Night Country: Reflections
     of a Bone-hunting Man*. Illustrated by Leonard Everett Fisher (New York:
     Charles Scribner's Sons, 1971), 81.

339 Loren Eiseley, 'The Coming of the Giant Wasps'. *All the Strange Hours: The Excavation of a Life.* Illustrations by Emanuel Haller (New York: Charles Scribner's Sons, 1975), 249.

1) In a poem called 'The Maya' (*Another Kind of Autumn.* Woodcuts by Walter Ferro [New York: Charles Scribner's Sons, 1977], 23–24), Eiseley repeats this perhaps ironic call to worship—at least to acknowledge—the mystery of existence. In both essay and poem he is referring to one of three Mayan calendars, the one known as Long Count with its tally of the number of days that had elapsed since the mythological date of creation. It was set to reach the end of a 1,872,000-day-long period in 2012. Certain non-Mayans expected the world to end in December of that year. Instead, another cycle began, though with few Mayans there to witness it. '[T]ime was the god' for the Maya, Eiseley writes. To salute time, they erected markers of 'wrought stone'.

> It is all
>
> a secret of the zeros unfolding.
>
> Behind, nothing,
>
> before, nothing.
>
> Worship it, the zero, and at intervals
>
> erect the road markers
>
> the great stelae
>
> with the graven numbers.

The poem recalls Shelley's 'Ozymandias', but without the irony of 'Look on my Works, ye Mighty, and despair!'—the boast of a king whose whole civilization lies in ruins. Time has swept away that vaunted power. It has taken Mayan civilization as well, if not all Mayans. Eiseley marks the brevity of their individual lives and the decline of their civilization, but he also sees them taking the long view, well knowing that they were humanly subject to time. That perspective would make sense to an anthropologist acquainted with the world of 'primitive' man.

2) The Great Golden Digger Wasp (*Sphex ichneumoneus*) digs an almost vertical burrow, with cells radiating off it for storage of prey. The wasp unerringly finds a cicada or grasshopper or cricket to paralyze, carries it back to

the burrow, drags it in, covers the burrow up. Videos of these operations may be viewed online. The wasp repeats the process four times, laying one egg in each cell. The prey nourish the wasp larvae, which become pupae, which eventually mature into Sphex wasps, which dig their way out and find a cicada or grasshopper or cricket to paralyze. 'These wasps, and their assorted brethren, the tarantula killers,' says Eiseley, 'present in miniature several of the greatest problems in the universe.' (*All the Strange Hours*, 244) Their behaviour is not accounted for by the theory of evolution. 'The fearsome operations of these wasps depend upon an uncanny knowledge of the location of the nerve centers of their prey in order to stun, not kill the creature. The larvae, also, must possess an instinctive knowledge of how to eat in order to prolong the life of the paralyzed body which they devour' (*All the Strange Hours*, 247–248).

340 Loren Eiseley, 'The Mind as Nature'. *The Night Country*, 220.

341 James Reaney, *Poems*, 122.

342 Joseph Donahue, *Wind Maps I-VII* (Northfield, Massachusetts: Talisman House, 2018), 135.

343 James Reaney, *A Suit of Nettles*, 9.

344 William Maurice Bucke, *Cosmic Consciousness*, 10.

345 Margaret Atwood, 'Fifties Vic'. Northrop Frye: a Tribute. *The CEA Critic*, Vol. 42, No. 1 (November 1979), 20.

346 James Reaney, 'Counterpoint of Meaning'. Review of John Ayre, *Northrop Frye: A Biography*. booksincanada.com/article_view.asp?id=2362.

347 George Bowering, *George Bowering Selected: Poems 1961–1992*. Edited by Roy Miki (Toronto: McClelland & Stewart, 1993), 64–65.

348 'A Letter from James Reaney', 2.

349 James Reaney, *14 Barrels*, 71.

350 James Reaney, 'The Condition of Light', 136.

351 Ibid., 138.

352 Ibid., 136.

353 James Reaney, 'The Wacousta Process', *Wacousta!*, 8.

354 Ibid., 159.

355 James Reaney, 'Production Notes', *Listen to the Wind*, 117.

356 James Reaney, 'Ten Years at Play'. George Woodcock, ed. *The Sixties: Canadian*

Writers and Writing of the Decade (Vancouver: University of British Columbia Publication Centre, 1969), 59.

357 Ibid., 59.

358 James Reaney, 'Preface', *Masks of Childhood*, vi.

359 James Reaney, 'The Condition of Light', 144.

360 James Reaney, 'Author's Preface', *Performance Poems*, 3.

361 Northrop Frye, *Fearful Symmetry*, 93–94.

362 Patricia Ludwick, 'One Actor's Journey with James Reaney'. *Approaches to the Work of James Reaney*, 133.

363 Ibid., 134.

364 Tom Smart, 'The Visual Art of James Reaney'. *The Devil's Artisan* 82 (Spring/Summer, 2018), 9.

365 Jean McKay, 'Interview with Keith Turnbull'. *Approaches to the Work of James Reaney*, 159.

366 Patricia Ludwick, 'One Actor's Journey', 136.

367 Jean McKay, 'Interview with James Reaney'. *Approaches to the Work of James Reaney*, 148.

368 James Reaney, 'Ten Years at Play', 60.

369 'A Letter from James Reaney', 3–4.

370 Northrop Frye, *Anatomy of Criticism*, 313–314.

371 William Blake, 'Jerusalem'. *The Complete Poetry & Prose of William Blake*. Newly Revised Edition. David V. Erdman, ed. Commentary by Harold Bloom (New York: Anchor Books/Random House, 1988), 185.

372 Catherine Ross, 'An Interview with James Reaney', 10.

373 Ibid., 10.

374 Ibid., 13.

375 Ibid., 13.

376 Ibid., 23

377 James Reaney, 'Editorial', *Alphabet* 2 (July 1961), 2.

378 James Reaney, 'Editorial', *Alphabet* 5 (December 1962), 3.

379 Ibid., 3.

380 *The Bicameral Review*, Claremont, Ontario (Supersummer Issue, 1988), 2.

381 *Alphabet* 5 (December 1962), 2.

382   *The Bicameral Review*, 2.

383   Tom Smart, 'The Visual Art of James Reaney', 49.

384   Brian Bartlett, ed. *The Essential James Reaney* (Erin, Ontario: The Porcupine's Quill, 2009), 8.

385   James Reaney, *The Killdeer & Other Plays*, 26.

386   James Reaney, *The St. Nicholas Hotel*, 33.

387   Ibid., 32.

388   Ibid., 35–36.

389   Ibid., 36.

390   Ibid., 36–37.

391   Ibid., 37–38.

392   James Reaney, *Sticks & Stones*, 152.

393   Northrop Frye, *Anatomy of Criticism*, 72.

394   *Ibid.*, 115.

395   Dante, *The Banquet*. Translated by Christopher Ryan. Stanford French and Italian Studies 61 (Saratoga, California: ANMA Libri, 1989), 43.

396   Northrop Frye, *Anatomy of Criticism*, 119.

397   James Reaney, *Poems*, 121.

398   James Reaney, *Twelve Letters*, 15.

399   James Reaney, *Poems*, 121.

400   James Reaney, *Souwesto Home*, 17.

401   James Reaney, *Poems*, 103.

402   James Reaney, *Performance Poems*, 7.

403   James Reaney, *Twelve Letters*, 10.

404   Ibid., 16. The janitor 'from my collegiate days' was still fascinating Reaney as late as 2005. A poem called 'Janitor' in *Souwesto Home* ends this way:

> You shuffler & sweeper who opened, who shut,
>
> Kept the rain, wind, mud, snow out,
>
> And us, inside, warm & dry.
>
> Doorkeeper, in some strange way,
>
> You caretaker, though you were
>
> Neither principal nor teacher,

You secretly governed the school.

We often dreamt of you,

Our most remembered educator. (64)

405 James Reaney, *Colours in the Dark*, 16.

406 C. G. Jung, *The Red Book*, 264.

407 Ibid., 16.

408 Ibid., 38

409 James Reaney, *The Killdeer & Other Plays*, 204.

410 Ibid., 204.

411 Ibid., 221.

412 Ibid., 221.

413 Ibid., 221.

414 Ibid., 223.

415 James Reaney, *The Boy with an Я in His Hand*, 48.

416 Rhoda Kellogg, *Analyzing Children's Art* (Palo Alto, California: National Press Books, 1969), 49.

417 Ibid., 64.

418 James Reaney, 'Search for an Undiscovered Alphabet', 38–39.

419 Ibid., 40.

420 Margaret Avison, 'Perspective'. *Always Now: The Collected Poems*, Volume One (Erin, Ontario: The Porcupine's Quill, 2003), 31–32.

421 James Reaney, 'Search for an Undiscovered Alphabet', 41.

422 Ibid., 41.

423 Rudolph Arnheim, *Visual Thinking* (Berkeley: University of California Press, 1977), 134.

424 Gerald D. Parker, *How to Play*, 151.

425 Quoted in *How to Play*, 143.

426 *Alphabet* 9 (November 1964), 34.

427 Rhoda Kellogg, *Analyzing Children's Art*, 159.

428 James Reaney, *The Real Foundation for the Spree: The Working Poet in the Contemporary World of Poetry & Criticism* (St. John's: Memorial University of Newfoundland, 1978), 11–12.

429 C.G. Jung, 'On the Frontiers of Knowledge'. *C.G. Jung Speaking*, 421.

430 James Reaney, *The Real Foundation for the Spree*, 12. Reaney is going his own way in the latter part of this passage, but still echoing a point that Kellogg makes: 'The child's idea of art collides head-on with the typical formulas adults have passed down from one generation to another. Watchful and well-meaning teachers who coax young children to draw real-life objects are not being helpful; indeed, their efforts may stifle the pride, the pleasure, the confidence so necessary to the growth of a creative spirit.' Rhoda Kellogg with Scott O'Dell, *The Psychology of Children's Art* (New York: CRM Random House, 1967), 17.

431 *Analyzing Children's Art*, 64.

432 C.G. Jung, *Memories, Dreams, Reflections*. Aniela Jaffe, ed. Clara Winston and Richard Winston, trans. (New York: Vintage Books, 1989), 196. Jung also wrote about mandalas in his 1944 book, *Psychology and Alchemy*.

433 James Reaney, 'David Willson', 842.

434 C.G. Jung, 'On the Frontiers of Knowledge'. *C.G. Jung Speaking*, 414.

435 C.G. Jung, *The Red Book*, 207.

436 C.G. Jung, 'Everyone Has Two Souls'. *C.G. Jung Speaking*, 57.

437 C.G. Jung, 'The Importance of Dreams'. Carl G. Jung, M.L. von Franz, Joseph L. Henderson, Jolande Jacobi, Aniela Jaffé, *Man and His Symbols*. Introduction by John Freeman (New York: Dell, 1964), 44.

438 Tim Inkster, 'The Iconography of James Reaney', 23.

439 D.I. Brown, 'A Brief History of *Alphabet* Magazine', 44.

440 James Reaney, *14 Barrels*, 82.

441 James Reaney, *Poems* 185–186.

442 William Blake, 'Milton: A Poem in 2 Books'. *The Complete Poetry and Prose of William Blake*, 95–96.

443 Richard Stingle, 'James Reaney and His Works'. *Canadian Writers and Their Works*, Poetry Series, Vol. 7 (Toronto: ECW Press, 1990), 195.

444 'Editorial', *Alphabet* 4 (June 1962), 3.

445 James Joyce, *A Portrait of the Artist as a Young Man*. Text, criticism, and notes, edited by Chester G. Anderson (New York: The Viking Press, 1964), 15.

446 James Reaney, *The Box Social and Other Stories*, 43.

447 Ibid., 43.

448 Ibid., 43.

449 Ibid., 44.

450 James Reaney, *Souwesto Home*, 47.

451 Jan Zwicky, *The Experience of Meaning*, 92.

452 Terry Pratchett and Neil Gaiman, *Good Omens: The Nice and Accurate Prophecies of Agnes Nutter, Witch* (London: Corgi Books, 1990), 45.

453 'The Gospel According to St. Luke', 'The New Testament of Our Lord and Saviour', *Holy Bible* (Cleveland and New York: World Publishing Company, 1962), 72.

454 Northrop Frye, *The Great Code*, 161.

455 Dante, *The Banquet*, 45.

456 Ibid., 52.

457 Jacob Boehme, *The Aurora*. Translated by John Sparrow, edited by C. J. Barker and D. S. Hehner (London: John M. Watkins, James Clarke & Co, 1914), 124.

458 I had written 'bullshit filter' before reading, in Iain McGilchrist's *The Master and His Emissary* (193), of the 'role of the right hemisphere [of the brain] as "bullshit detector".' Well, why not go to the mental source? Like metaphor and other linguistic subtleties, irony is decoded by the right hemisphere.

459 C. G. Jung, 'On the Frontiers of Knowledge', 413.

460 James Reaney, *Performance Poems*, 75.

461 Ibid., 72.

462 James Reaney, *Take the Big Picture*, 40.

463 James Reaney, *Gentle Rain Food Co-op*, 24.

464 According to Les Kohalmi, with whom Reaney 'traded gardening tips and anecdotes', the co-op was a mine of material that might have been more fully exploited: 'Jamie's gardening anecdotes were tangential, being mostly about the food co-op where a large part of Jamie's harvest ended up. Jamie regaled me with stories about the eccentric characters, escapades, politics and intrigues at the co-op.

'I pestered Jamie for years: "Jamie, this is fantastic material. You have to write about it." His answer after a brief silence and meditation was always,

"Oh, I don't know." It took a very long time but he finally turned the material into *The Gentle Rain Food Co-op*. Jamie's reluctance to use the co-op experiences was most likely concern over offending fellow co-op members. I was a bit disappointed in the final product. The finished play was gentle compared to the anecdotes. I wish I had been able somehow to record the anecdotes as told. Jamie and Colleen were both spellbinding oral artists as well as exceptionally talented writers.' Les Kohalmi, e-mail to the author, May 17, 2021.

465 James Reaney, *Performance Poems*, 78.

466 Phil Hall, *Niagara & Government*, 11.

467 Original drawing sent to the author by Phil Hall.

468 Terry Pratchett and Neil Gaiman, *Good Omens*, 13.

469 Ibid., 40.

470 Ibid., 84.

471 Homer, *The Odyssey*. A new verse translation by Albert Cook (New York: W. W. Norton, 1967), 157–158.

472 Jeanette Winterson, *Christmas Days: 12 Stories and 12 Feasts for 12 Days* (New York: Grove Press, 2016), 252.

473 Jane Siberry (with K. D. Lang), 'Calling All Angels'. *Until the End of the World*, Warner Records, 1991.

474 Margaret Laurence, *The Stone Angel*. New Canadian Library No. 59 (Toronto: McClelland & Stewart, 1964), 3–4.

475 Ibid., 146.

476 Ibid., 179,

477 Ibid., 304.

478 Donald Kalsched, 'Wrestling with Our Angels: Inner and Outer Democracy in America Under the Shadow of Donald Trump'. Thomas Singer, ed. *Cultural Complexes and the Soul of America: Myth, Psyche, and Politics* (London and New York: Routledge, 2020), 53.

479 Robin van Löben Sels, *Shamanic Dimensions of Psychotherapy: Healing through the Symbolic Process* (London and New York: Routledge, 2020), 46.

480 Tate, London / Art Resource, New York.

481 See Donald Kalsched, *Trauma and the Soul: A psycho-spiritual approach to human development and its interruption* (London and New York: Routledge, 2013), 53 ff.

482 Robin van Löben Sels, *Shamanic Dimensions*, 124.

483 James Reaney, *Colours in the Dark*, 83.

484 In his essay, 'Kids and Crossovers', Reaney outlines the kind of 'submerging of individual identity' required for participation in the kind of plays he is writing. What is needed, he says, is 'FAMILIES. Many parents fall by the wayside; so do their infants and I rather imagine that some of the would-be actors I met who were so extremely un-cooperative had missed out somewhere along the line on the enormous amount of touching and playing with a father and mother figure that does lay the groundwork for a social personality. What I am arguing here is that some helpless, defenseless being's need for love can change you into a more lovable being; grotesquely simple as this sounds, and it is strange how the creators of the isms that divide us into intellectual camps do not seem to have been around babies much (Sartre? Friedrich? Jesus? Karl? Thoreau? Augustine?), it just might be simple enough to be the seed for some new insight into theatre.' *Canadian Theatre Review*, 10 (Spring 1976), 28, 29.

485 Robin van Löben Sels, *Shamanic Dimensions*, 97.

486 James Reaney, 'An Evening with Babble and Doodle', 40.

487 Ibid., 39.

488 Robin van Löben Sels, *Shamanic Dimensions*, 62.

489 'Vision in Canada?', 942.

490 Ross Woodman, *James Reaney*, 39.

491 *Canada Dash, Canada Dot, Scripts*, 139–140.

492 James Reaney, 'An Evening with Babble and Doodle', 41.

493 Northrop Frye, *Fearful Symmetry*, 267–268.

494 Donald Kalsched, 'Wrestling with our Angels', 55.

495 Ibid.

496 James Reaney, 'A Letter from James Reaney', 4.

497 Robin van Löben Sels, email to SD March 20, 2020.

498 Colleen Thibaudeau, 'This Elastic Moment'. *The Artemesia Book: Poems Selected and New* (London, Ontario: Brick Books, 1991), 80.

499 James Reaney, 'The Third Eye: Jay Macpherson's *The Boatman*'.
    Canadian Literature 3 (Winter 1960), 24.

500 James Reaney, ' "Your Plays Are Like Movies—Cinemascope Ones." '
    Canadian Drama, No. 1 (Spring 1979), 40.

501 Ibid., 33.

502 Jacob Boehme, *The Way to Christ*. Translation and Introduction by Peter Erb.
    Preface by Winfried Zeller (New York: Paulist Press, 1978), 6.

503 James Reaney, *Performance Poems*, 54.

504 Ibid., 65.

505 James Reaney, *A Suit of Nettles*, 43.

506 Jacob Boehme, *The Aurora*, xx.

507 Jacob Boehme, *Six Theosophic Points and Other Writings*, with an
    Introductory Essay, 'Unground and Freedom', by Nicholas Berdyaev.
    Translated by John Rolleston Earle (Ann Arbor:
    The University of Michigan Press, 1971), v.

508 James Reaney, 'Serinette', *Scripts*, 293.

509 Jan Zwicky, *The Experience of Meaning*, 5.

510 Ibid., 21.

511 James Reaney, *The Dismissal*, 39.

512 Loren Eiseley, 'Strangeness in the Proportion'. *The Night Country*, 142.

513 C. G. Jung, 'On the Frontiers of Knowledge'. *C. G. Jung Speaking*, 420.
    Robin van Löben Sels's book, *Shamanic Dimensions of Psychotherapy*,
    sent me to this interview with Jung.

514 C. G. Jung, 'Three Versions of a Press Conference in Vienna'.
    C. G. Jung Speaking, 45.

515 Iain McGilchrist, *The Master and His Emissary*, 116.

516 'From Charles Baudouin's Journal: 1934'. *C. G. Jung Speaking*, 79.

517 James Reaney, *The Dismissal*, 38.

518 Ibid., 38–39.

519 D. I. Brown, 'A Brief History of *Alphabet* Magazine', 72.

520 Ibid., 73.

521 Jan Zwicky, *The Experience of Meaning*, 20.

522 Ibid., 20.

523 Joanne McNeil, 'Search and Destroy', from *Lurking: How a Person Became a User. Harper's Magazine* (February 2020), 11.

524 Ibid., 14.

525 Marshall Soules, 'Surveillance Capitalism Pandemic'. Review of Shoshana Zuboff, *The Age of Surveillance Capitalism: The Fight for a Human Future at the New Frontier of Power* (New York: Hachette Book Group, 2019). *New Explorations in Culture and Communication*, Vol. 1, No. 2 (August 2020), 215. https://jps.library.utoronto.ca/index.php/nexj/article/view/35084.

526 Andrew Marantz, '#Winning: Brad Parscale used social media to sway the 2016 election. He's poised to do it again.' *The New Yorker* (March 9, 2020), 55.

527 Susanne M. Sklar, *Blake's Jerusalem as Visionary Theatre: Entering the Divine Body* (Oxford: Oxford University Press, 2011), 1.

528 Ibid., vii.

529 James Reaney, *A Suit of Nettles*, 12.

530 Ibid., 15.

531 Ibid., 16.

532 Ibid., 16. The slightly odd thing here, at least to me, is 'drunken' Noah. This refers to Genesis 9:20–21: 'And Noah began to be an husbandman, and he planted a vineyard:/ And he drank of the wine and was drunken; and he was uncovered within his tent.' Younger son Ham saw his father naked and told his brothers Shem and Japhet (or Japheth) about it. They knew to walk into the tent backwards and cover their father with a blanket, sight unseen. There must have been some sort of prohibition against seeing Dad with nothing on. I don't see how Ham could be blamed for what must have been an inadvertent encounter (the Bible doesn't explain such things), but Noah didn't like it and there were consequences for Ham. He was still to be one of the generations of Noah, but Noah decreed that Canaan, his nation, would be subservient to those of his brothers. 'Drunken' seems like a red herring in Reaney's passage. Was it just a two-syllable word required to round out the metre?

533 Ibid., 16.

534 Craig Stewart Walker, *The Buried Astrolabe*, 29. The reference is to Northrop Frye, *Anatomy of Criticism*, 121.

535 C.G. Jung, 'On the Frontiers of Knowledge', 417.

536   Ibid., 417.

537   Ibid., 417.

538   Ibid., 419. Robin van Löben Sels relates a story, very like this, of another cure, not of patient by analyst, but of troubled five-year-old Shelley Alhanati by an uncle. The child was so deeply introverted in her extroverted Greek family, and so disturbed by a move from New York to Athens, that she all but went into hiding and retreated into a silence to which most of her family was impervious. 'One day, however, an uncle came over to meet Shelley for the first time, and he did something different. As usual, everything was loud and intense, and as usual, Shelley was hiding behind a tree on the balcony. The following is Shelley's report of the incident: "My uncle came over, sat down near me, picked up a toy bird, played with it silently, and then went home without ever having said a word to me. For a long time after that, I would talk only to him. I instinctively knew, by the quality of his presence, that he would find me through the interior of his own heart. Paradoxically, the message I got by his silence was that he would value my words. So I felt safe to speak. Neither of us could have articulated what the problem was, why I wasn't talking, but on another level, in an invisible, silent way, we were understanding each other."' (Shelley Alhanati, 'To Die and to Grow.' *Psychoanalytic Review;* New York, Vol. 91, Issue 6 Dec. 2004; Robin van Löben Sels, *Shamanic Dimensions*, 111)
      This fascinating story is told to illustrate how a child might be a shaman-soul. It doesn't say anything more about the uncle. I'm curious about him. Who was he, outside of this anecdote? What made him understand the need for wordless communication in this particular case?

539   Ibid., 419.

540   Jan Zwicky, *The Experience of Meaning*, 156.

541   'Vision in Canada?', 942.

542   *The Experience of Meaning*, 160.

543   Ibid., viii.

544   Iain McGilchrist, *The Master and His Emissary*, 209.

545   Ibid., 128.

546   Ibid., 206.

547   James Reaney, *One Man Masque, Two Plays*, iv.

548 *The Bicameral Review*, 2.

549 Iain McGilchrist, *The Master and His Emissary*, 206.

550 Ibid., 233.

551 Ibid., 3.

552 William Blake, 'Auguries of Innocence', *The Complete Poetry & Prose*, 490.

553 James Reaney, 'Vision in Canada?', 939.

554 Ibid., 938.

555 Ibid., 939.

556 Grace Paley, *The Collected Stories* (New York: Farrar, Straus and Giroux, 1994), 338.

557 Mary Midgley, 'Preface to the Routledge Classics Edition', *Science and Poetry* (London and New York: Routledge, 2006), ix.

558 Ibid., x.

559 Ibid., xi-xiii.

560 Jesper Hoffmeyer, *Signs of Meaning in the Universe*, 131. Hoffmeyer brings together so many threads that it seems a little strange that Simard's research is missing. If she had shown up in his book, I think he would have had less difficulty (see p. 140) in working the semiosis of trees into his scheme of things.

561 Iain McGilchrist, *The Master and His Emissary*, 141.

562 'Three Desks,' *Masks of Childhood*, 154.

563 Ibid., 156.

564 James Reaney, *The Dismissal*, 15.

565 Anna Lowenhaupt Tsing, *The Mushroom at the End of the World*, 285.

566 James Reaney, *The Killdeer*, 81.

567 James Reaney, *The Dismissal*, 27.

568 James Reaney, *Colours in the Dark*, 67.

569 Ibid., 67.

570 James Reaney, 'Editorial', *Alphabet* 1 (September 1960), 3.

571 James Reaney, *Colours in the Dark*, 69.

572 C. G. Jung, *Psychology and Alchemy*. Translated by R. F. C. Hull. 270 illustrated (London: Routledge & Kegan Paul, 1953), 101.

573 James Reaney, *Colours in the Dark*, 70.

574 Ibid., 70.

575 James Reaney, 'Vision in Canada?', 945.

576 James Reaney, *Lewis Carroll's Alice Through the Looking Glass*, 9.

577 Ibid., 12.

578 'Some Notes on the Text', ibid., 130.

579 Northrop Frye, 'Preface'. *Fearful Symmetry*, viii.

580 Elizabeth Strout, *Olive, Again* (New York: Penguin Viking, 2019), 114–116.

581 Jan Zwicky, *The Experience of Meaning*, 6.

582 Ibid., 7.

583 Ibid., 50.

584 James Reaney, 'The Real Foundation for the Spree', 11.

585 Dennis Lee, 'The Mystery'. 'SoCool', *Heart Residence: Collected Poems 1967–2017* (Toronto: House of Anansi, 2017), 161.

586 Dennis Lee, 'admire', *testament: Poems 2000–2011* (Toronto: House of Anansi, 2012), 26.

587 Northrop Frye, 'Royal Bank Award Address, September 1978.' *The CEA Critic*, Vol. 42, No. 2 (January 1980), 5.

588 See Raffi Khatchadourian, 'The Trash Nebula: Millions of man-made artifacts are circling Earth. Will one of them cause a disaster?' *The New Yorker* (September 28, 2020).

589 Jesper Hoffmeyer, *Signs of Meaning in the Universe*, 89.

590 Dan Kaufman, 'The Last Stand: How Suffering Farmers May Determine Trump's Fate' *The New Yorker* (August 17, 2020).

591 Tad Friend, 'Value Meal: Impossible Foods wants to save the world by inventing a better burger'. *The New Yorker* (September 30, 2019), 42.

592 James Reaney, *Sticks & Stones*, 137.

593 Gerald Parker, 'The key word … is "listen": James Reaney's "sonic environment".' *Mosaic* Vol 14, No. 4 (Fall 1981), 9.

594 Ibid., 11.

595 Ibid., 11.

596 Ibid., 11–12.

597 James Reaney, *14 Barrels*, 42.

598 *Sticks & Stones*, 161.

599 James C. Reaney, 'Introduction'. *The Donnelly Documents*, xvii.

600 Ibid., lxxxv.

601 James Reaney, *Souwesto Home*, 60. In a passage from Reaney's early story called 'Memento Mori', already quoted, Loyal is the big reader who lives in the books he reads: 'Real life! What was that? No, the real life for Loyal was not in the world of things, although he, with book in hand or pocket, managed to help his father on the farm quite well enough; no, the real life was in the kingdom of shadows in the small, much thumbed library, and in the mushroom-and-Indian pipes mental landscape that found its nourishment in the chlorophyll of writers, most of them long since dead.' *The Box Social and Other Stories*, 44. Major John Richardson, author of *Wacousta* 'never seems to have forgotten that reality is only one side of a border river, a river that can expand into lakes as big as seas and takes leaps like thousands of snow white tigers.' Author's Notes, *Wacousta*, 6. Reaney hopes that Baldoon will convey 'the sense that out of the past comes a world where the laws of atheism, progress and materialism suddenly break down. Surely it is a good thing that they do break down occasionally to let in some terror and some mystery. This is a story from our own deep past and our own Lake St. Clair fen country which should add a feeling of there being more depths and heights to existence than our present-day usually discovers.' *Baldoon*, 119.

602 Grace Paley, *The Collected Stories*, 383.

603 James C. Reaney, 'Introduction', *The Donnelly Documents*, cxliv.

604 James Reaney, *Sticks & Stones*, 46.

605 Ibid., 46–47.

606 James Reaney, *Wacousta!*, 38.

607 Wanda Campbell, 'To Flow Like You', 18. In 'A letter from James Reaney', this 'theory' takes different but related form: '[O]ne of the reasons I am interested in STORY theatre particularly for *The Donnellys* is that I was told the Vigilante versions when about eight years old; the particular story-teller in question is just one of about eight people in our neighbourhood (the Little Lakes near Stratford) who could and still can really talk about the past of that tiny but stubborn canton; I like to think sometimes that the feeling of

village with traditions worth talking about probably comes from the fact that the Huron Road couldn't go straight though the Paff-Jones lake, but had to take a bend, a bend surveyed by the way with the help of the same surveyor who appears in the early scenes of *Sticks & Stones*. Such a crook in the road produced a sense of place and around this stories can collect' (5).

608 William Blake, 'The Marriage of Heaven and Hell'.
      The Complete Poetry & Prose, 38.

609 James Reaney *Souwesto Home*, 27.

610 Jean McKay, email to the author, April 14, 2020.

611 email to the author, May 8, 2020.

612 James Reaney, *The Donnelly Documents*, liv.

613 Ibid., xlvii.

614 James Reaney, *Souwesto Home*, 51.

615 James Reaney, *Handcuffs*, 95.

616 Ibid., 56.

617 James Reaney, *Sticks & Stones*, 66.

618 James Reaney, *Handcuffs*, 79.

619 Ibid., 80.

620 James Reaney, *The Donnelly Documents*, 259.

621 Ibid., 150.

622 James Reaney & Jack Chambers, *The Dance of Death at London, Ontario* (London: Alphabet Press, 1963), 6.

623 Ibid., 26.

624 Ibid., 32.

625 James Reaney, *A Suit of Nettles*, 51.

626 Northrop Frye, *The Great Code*, 117.

627 James Reaney, *Listen to the Wind*, 117

628 'A Letter from James Reaney', 9.

629 Thomas Hardy, *Selected Poems*, edited by Richard Willmott (Oxford: Oxford University Press, 1992), 8.

630 Ibid., 8.

631 Jesper Hoffmeyer, *Signs of Meaning in the Universe*, 53.
      Hoffmeyer is citing biologist Joan Hall-Craggs.

632 Thomas Hardy, *Tess of the D'Urbervilles*. Edited by Juliet Grindle and Simon Gatrell (Oxford: Clarendon Press, 1983), 542.

633 Dennis Lee, 'hope', *testament*, 75.

634 Jay Macpherson, *The Boatman*, 7.

635 W. H. Auden, 'In Memory of W. B. Yeats'. *Selected Poems* (London: Faber and Faber, 1968), 41.

636 John Metcalf and Leon Rooke, eds. *The Second Macmillan Anthology* (Toronto: Macmillan of Canada, 1989), 208.

637 Don McKay, 'Sleeping Places', *Paradoxides*, 80. McKay's poems in this and other books are influenced by the *Tao Te Ching*, where one reads that 'The myriad creatures in the world are born from Something, and Something from Nothing.' Lao Tzu, *Tao Te Ching*, XL. Translated and with an introduction by D. C. Lau (London: Penguin Books, 1963), 47. In the title poem of *Paradoxides*, a levelling of previously unequal fields of meaning is envisioned: unwrite the human; read the script of nature, as in a trilobite spotted on a hike. There it was, 'sprawling in the shale—bold, declarative, big as my hand and just as complicated. It seemed the shale had suddenly broken into literacy, publishing one enigmatic pictograph from a secret alphabet. Suddenly it was refusing relegation to raw material. Suddenly it was demanding to be read.' ('Cephalon', 40).

638 Ibid., 31.

639 Ibid., 32.

640 Wallace Stevens, 'The Snow Man.' *The Collected Poems of Wallace Stevens* (New York: Alfred A. Knopf, 1974), 10.

641 Ibid., 10.

642 Anne Carson, 'Variations on the Right to Remain Silent'. *A Public Space*, Issue 7 / 2008.

643 Charles Simic, 'The Point'. *Return to a Place Lit by a Glass of Milk* (New York: George Braziller, 1974), 33–34.

644 C. G. Jung, *The Red Book*, 231. Here is a milder way of referring to the 'murder' of explanation. It might be called objectifying: '*An object is a thing that has been removed from its party line of rhizomes, hyphae, and roots, and treated to public scrutiny—framed, analyzed, experimented upon, known.*' Don McKay, 'Thingamajig', *Paradoxides*, 55.

645 Don McKay, '[   ] or Iconostalgia', 136.

646 Ibid., 119.

647 Jorge Luis Borges, *Labyrinths: Selected Stories & Other Writings*. Edited by Donald A. Yates & James E. Irby. Preface by Andre Maurois (New York: New Directions, 1964), 63.

648 Ibid., 65.

649 Christina Baillie & Martha Baillie, *Sister Language* (St. John's: Pedlar Press, 2019), 38.

650 Ibid., 17.

651 John Cage, *Silence* (Middletown Connecticut: Wesleyan University Press, 1961), 8. 'Venturing home from outer space,' writes Robin van Löben Sels, 'the Russian cosmonaut Aleksei Leonov tells us that what struck him most was a silence so vast and deep that he began to hear his own body—his heart beating, his blood pulsing, the rustle of his muscles moving over each other—unlike any silence on earth. Feeling "struck" is a sensate, *feeling* term, as if Leonov's description is suggesting that the silence of space enabled him—hearing and feeling himself *alive*—to rediscover his "original" embodiment.' *Shamanic Dimensions*, 166–167.

652 Ibid., 8.

653 Simone Weil, *Waiting On God*. Translated by Emma Craufurd. Foreword by Malcolm Muggeridge (London: Routledge and Kegan Paul, 1951, 2010), 82.

654 Iain McGilchrist, *The Master and His Emissary*, 386.

655 Jesper Hoffmeyer, *Signs of Meaning in the Universe*, 38.

656 Ibid., 66.

657 Ibid., 49.

658 Ibid., 112.

659 Ibid., 131.

660 Ibid., 137.

661 Dennis Lee, 'galore', *testament*, 128.

662 Dennis Lee, 'noth'. Ibid., 56.

663 Though it's worth mentioning that a 'noth' appears in the thought of Martin Heidegger. Heidegger's fundamental question is: Why is there something rather than nothing? Plenty of commentary, pro and con, has picked at that

opening and its elaboration. One whole branch of philosophy, logical positivism or logical empiricism, wants nothing to do with 'airy' ontological thinking of that sort. Here is a brief anti-Heidegger piece by Michael Inwood called 'Does the Nothing Noth?' (The Royal Institute of Philosophy Supplements, Vol. 44, 1999; published online by Cambridge University Press, January 8, 2010): 'In 1929 Heidegger gave his Freiburg inaugural lecture entitled "What is Metaphysics?". In it he announced: *Das Nichts selbst nichtet,* "The Nothing itself noths" (or "nihilates", or "nothings"). This soon earned Heidegger fame as a purveyor of metaphysical nonsense. In his 1931 paper, "Overcoming of Metaphysics through Logical Analysis of Language" Rudolf Carnap charged Heidegger with the offences of the whole metaphysical genre. His sentence has the same grammatical form as the sentence "The rain rains" — a sentence which Carnap, or at least his translator, regarded as a "meaningful sentence of ordinary language". But this harmless guise conceals severe logical blemishes. Heidegger treats the indefinite pronoun "nothing" as a noun, as the "name or description of an entity". (When he says "The nothing noths" he surely does not mean "There is nothing that noths" or "It is not the case that anything noths".) He introduces the meaningless word "to noth". He implies, and later affirms, the existence of the nothing, when the "existence of this entity would be denied in its very definition". If all this were not enough, the sentence is meaningless, since it is neither analytic, nor contradictory, nor empirical. It is metaphysics, and metaphysics seriously damages our spiritual health.'

Heidegger was venturing beyond metaphysics, so this distorts his thought. I'm no metaphysician, myself, but I find that last sentence laughable. Taking nothing seriously, as I do, and willing to entertain assertions that nothing may noth, as I am, I'm no logical positivist either. But, you ask, are you taking nothing *seriously* or taking *nothing* seriously? Well, I reply, both. I like the play (both wiggle room and recreation) in the sentence. Ambiguity. A tiny, illogical, enjoyable zap of mental energy.

And it's interesting that, in *Hunger Mountain: A Field Guide to Mind and Landscape* (Boston & London: Shambhala, 2012), David Hinton asks

Heidegger's fundamental question after being deflected from Western thinking by a lifetime of preoccupation with ancient Chinese poetry and thought. Following Lao Tzu, he says 'the Cosmos is divided into two fundamental elements: "Absence" or "Nonbeing" … and "Presence" or "Being" …. Presence is simply the empirical universe, which the ancients described as the ten thousand living and nonliving things in constant transformation; and Absence is the generative void from which this ever-changing realm of Presence perpetually emerges, though it should not be conceived in a spatial sense….' (16) The empirical universe (Presence) itself is not simple. Just to think of its existence brings the mind up short, because 'what could be more overwhelmingly mysterious than Presence, than the fact that it exists, that there is something rather than nothing.' (28) As for generative absence, 'For as far back as the eye can see, that pregnant emptiness at the heart of things has been a woman dancing, her swirling movements enhanced by foxtails streaming out from her hands….' (104). This is nothing *doing*.

664 Dennis Lee, 'hang-', *testament*, 34.

665 There was no footnote in the story I gave to Ben, but here is the citation for those who wish to pursue it: 'Review of *The Letters of Samuel Beckett, Vol. 14: 1966–89*,' *London Review of Books*, Vol. 38, no. 23 (December 2016).

Index

Arnheim, Rudolph 173, 296

Atwood, Margaret 62, 140, 279, 293

Avison, Margaret 48, 49, 51, 132, 133, 171, 227, 276, 291, 296

Bach, Johann Sebastian 76, 282

Bacon, Francis 28, 272

Barker, Pat 134, 291

Barthes, Roland 17, 18, 19, 21, 269, 270

Bartlett, Brian 152, 295

Beatles, The 77

Beckwith, John 35, 76, 86, 93, 273, 275, 284

Bennett, Jane 137, 138, 220, 291

Beresford-Kroeger, Diana 68, 121, 281

Berry, Chuck 77

Birchard, Guy 50, 276

Blake, William 13, 26, 27, 35, 36, 37, 39, 41, 51, 52, 54, 55, 56, 60, 68, 77, 88, 92, 93, 113, 114, 147, 156, 159, 183, 184, 188, 199, 200, 202, 212, 213, 219, 225, 227, 228, 240, 248, 262, 271, 273, 294, 297, 302, 304, 307

Boehme, Jacob 27, 172, 173, 189, 205, 206, 207, 262, 298, 301

Bowering, George 141, 293

Bringhurst, Robert 9, 19, 81, 82, 127, 251, 269, 270, 290

Bucke, Richard Maurice 25, 26, 27, 28, 29, 36, 124, 140, 164, 207, 261, 264, 271, 272, 293

Campbell, Wanda 33, 240, 272, 306

Cardwell, Ann 42, 43, 274

Chambers, Jack 91, 245, 246, 262, 307

Clare, Stephanie 122, 290

Cossey, Ralph 97

Crawford, Isabella Valancy 79, 110, 111, 287

Cunningham, Ralph 68, 70, 174, 281

Curnoe, Greg 23, 25, 26, 73, 91, 174, 191, 261, 264, 271

Dalton, Mary 91, 284

Dante Alighieri 159, 189, 295, 298

Davey, Frank 33, 93, 94, 285

Derrida, Jacques 33, 34, 36, 37, 47, 273

Donahue, Joseph 140, 293

Duncan, Sara Jeanette 24

Dylan, Bob 77

Eiseley, Loren 123, 138, 139, 208, 209, 291, 292, 293, 301

Everson, R.G. 52, 276

Exley, Bill 73

Fairley, Barker 61, 261, 263, 269, 279

Favro, Murray 73

Ferron, Jacques 73

Fleming, Allan 10, 14, 175, 261

Frye, Northrop 9, 18, 33, 34, 35, 36, 37, 39, 44, 48, 49, 51, 52, 54, 55, 56, 57, 58,
    59, 60, 61, 62, 75, 76, 82, 88, 96, 109, 110, 120, 121, 127, 128, 137, 140, 141,
    144, 147, 159, 160, 171, 188, 202, 212, 214, 216, 227, 228, 231, 232, 238, 247,
    269, 271, 273, 275, 276, 277, 278, 279, 282, 285, 287, 289, 291, 293, 294, 295,
    298, 300, 302, 305, 307

Galbraith, John Kenneth 24, 25

Gerry, Thomas 13, 94, 170, 288

Greer, Germaine 43

Hall, Phil 119, 191, 192, 193, 262, 270, 289, 299

Heller, Nathan 101, 285

Hicks, Edward 109

Hirsch, John 174

Hoffmeyer, Jesper 121, 122, 123, 132, 220, 257,258, 283, 289, 290, 291, 304, 305,
    308, 309

Hulme, T.E. 113

Inkster, Tim 93, 177, 178, 179, 185, 261, 262, 264, 285, 297

James, Henry 120, 121, 143, 144, 289

Johnston, George 51, 52, 56, 276, 277

Joyce, James 36, 147, 297

Jung, C. G. 45, 72, 163, 174, 176, 177, 190, 199, 201, 209, 214, 215, 225, 254, 275, 281, 296, 297, 298, 301, 303, 304, 308

Kane, Sean 114, 263, 288

Kelley, Thomas P. 29

Kellogg, Rhoda 170, 174, 175, 176, 177, 262, 296, 297

King, Stephen 99

Lee, Alvin A. 13, 77, 278, 283

Lee, Dennis 36, 116, 231, 249, 259, 264, 305, 308, 309, 310, 311

Lessing, Doris 94

Lewis, Jerry Lee 75, 76

Loretto, Teri Rata 59

Ludwick, Patricia 145, 146, 294

Macpherson, Jay 56, 60, 61, 84, 110, 111, 115, 116, 140, 160, 205, 249, 264, 271, 278, 279, 283, 284, 288, 301, 308

McCarthy, Cormac 136, 291

McFadden, David 91, 284

McGilchrist, Iain 35, 134, 216, 218, 220, 257, 269, 273, 285, 286, 290, 291, 298, 301, 304, 309

McKay, Jean 19, 49, 51, 116, 241, 276, 294, 307

McLuhan, Marshall 51, 104, 109

Meeker, Howie 83

Miki, Roy 33, 293

Miller, Orlo 25, 29

Milne, David 15, 28, 29, 124, 171, 269, 272

Milton, John 77, 79, 113, 183, 221, 283, 297

Morrisseau, Norval 43, 274

Munro, Alice 90, 91, 125, 271, 284, 290

Neatby, Hilda 74

Nichol, bp 168, 169, 262, 264

Ondaatje, Michael 36, 51

Parker, Gerald D. 13, 20, 108, 173, 235, 270, 287, 296, 305

Pitts-Taylor, Victoria 121, 289, 290

Pratchett, Terry 149, 188, 193, 298, 299

Purdy, Al 91

Reaney, James 1, 4, 11 12, 13, 15, 16, 17, 18, 19, 20, 22, 23, 24, 25, 26, 28, 29, 30, 31,
33, 34, 35, 36, 37, 38, 39, 40, 41, 42, 43, 44, 45, 46, 47, 48, 49, 50, 51, 52, 53,
54, 55, 56, 57, 58, 59, 60, 61, 62, 63, 64, 68, 69, 70, 71, 72, 73, 74, 75, 76, 77,
78, 79, 80, 81, 82, 83, 84, 85, 86, 87, 88, 89, 90, 91, 92, 93, 94, 95, 97, 98, 99,
101, 102, 103, 104, 106, 107, 108, 109, 110, 111, 112, 113, 114, 115, 116, 117, 119,
120, 121, 123, 124, 125, 127, 128, 131, 132, 136, 139, 141, 142, 143, 144, 145, 146,
147, 148, 149, 150, 151, 152, 156, 159, 160, 161, 162, 164, 165, 166, 167, 168, 169,
170, 171, 172, 173, 174, 175, 176, 177, 178, 179, 180, 183, 184, 185, 187, 188, 189,
190, 191, 192, 193, 199, 201, 203, 204, 205, 206, 207, 208, 210, 211, 213, 214,
216, 217, 218, 219, 220, 221, 222, 223, 224, 226, 227, 228, 229, 230, 231, 232,
233, 234, 235, 236, 237, 238, 239, 240, 241, 244, 245, 246, 247, 248, 249, 250,
255, 257, 258, 259, 260, 261, 262, 263, 264, 269, 270, 271, 272, 273, 274, 275,
276, 277, 278, 279, 280, 281, 282, 283, 284, 285, 286, 287, 288, 289, 290, 291,
292, 293, 294, 295, 296, 297, 298, 299, 300, 301, 302, 304, 305, 306, 307
'A Letter From James Reaney' 53, 120, 273, 276, 277, 285, 289, 291, 293, 294,
300, 306, 307
'A Message to Winnipeg' 38, 41, 112, 273
'A Trip to the Globe Theatre' 190
'Brush Strokes Decorating a Fan' 64, 161, 264, 280
'Catalogue Poems' 53, 58, 64, 277, 278, 280
'Entire Horse (Poems Written About the Donnellys)' 241
'Klaxon' 99
'Little Lake District (Where I Was Born) Poems' 240
'Memento Mori' 184, 306
'Near Tobermory, Ontario' 80
'Pigeon's Necks' 206
'Search for an Undiscovered Alphabet' 120, 170 289, 296
'Serinette' 29, 272
'Some Critics Are Music Teachers' 58, 76, 278, 282
'Ten Years at Play' 146, 293, 294
'The Alphabet' 87, 89, 164, 165, 180, 183, 184, 264

'The Canadian Poet's Predicament' 49, 276

'The Ghost' 139, 141, 159

'The Influence of Spenser on Yeats' 54, 96, 288

'The Riddle' 40, 261

'The Upper Canadian' 42

'The Wild Flora of Elgin County' 67, 127, 264, 281

'To the Secret City: From a Winnipeg Sketchbook' 62, 279

'Topless Nightmares' 70, 281, 286

14 Barrels From Sea to Sea 16, 18, 43, 50, 102, 117, 235, 270, 272, 275, 276, 279, 280, 281, 286, 288, 289, 293, 297, 305

A Suit of Nettles 10, 11, 32, 33, 36, 37, 43, 59, 60, 64, 74, 75, 77, 78, 94, 95, 101, 113, 140, 183, 187, 206, 213, 247, 261, 273, 275, 282, 283, 285, 288, 293, 301, 302, 307

All the Bees and All the Keys 76

Alphabet 13, 14, 29, 37, 41, 43, 47, 53, 68, 77, 80, 88, 97, 104, 107, 109, 111, 115, 125, 150, 152, 165, 168, 174, 175, 177, 179, 184, 211, 224, 230, 248, 260, 261, 271, 272, 273, 274, 276, 277, 278, 279, 281, 282, 283, 284, 285, 287, 288, 294, 296, 297, 301, 304

Antler River 25, 73, 104, 146, 235, 271, 286

Apple Butter 146, 281, 288

Baldoon 81, 235, 275, 283, 306

Canada Dash, Canada Dot 54, 61, 69, 70, 71, 73, 110, 202

Colours in the Dark 46, 54, 64, 66, 76, 80, 90, 109, 159, 163, 173, 174, 200, 224, 225, 235, 248, 257, 272, 276, 283, 287, 296, 300, 304

Gentle Rain Food Co-op 33, 83, 106, 191, 272, 277, 287, 298, 299

Geography Match 75, 82

Gyroscope 46, 50, 235, 237, 248, 275, 280

Halloween 141, 273, 281

Handcuffs 31, 117, 156, 235, 236, 243, 280, 307

Ignoramus 74, 75, 282

Imprecations: The Art of Swearing 75, 83, 187, 248, 277, 284

King Whistle! 19, 44, 51, 91, 92, 173, 235, 270, 285, 291

Listen to the Wind 66, 80, 84, 111, 116, 143, 146, 173, 235, 247, 284, 288, 293, 307

Names & Nicknames 69, 70, 115, 117, 281, 288

Night Blooming Cereus 110, 164, 187, 201, 236, 287

One Man Masque 50, 60, 64, 66, 72, 159, 162, 183, 217, 247, 272, 279, 303

Performance Poems 53, 57, 58, 64, 65, 80, 97, 144, 187, 190, 272, 277, 278, 279, 280, 283, 285, 286, 294, 295, 298, 299, 301

Serinette 29, 45, 70, 207, 272, 275, 301

Shivaree 80, 283

Souwesto! 57, 58

Sticks & Stones 30, 31, 117, 157, 235, 239, 243, 272, 288, 295, 305, 306, 307

Take the Big Picture 25, 73, 75, 105, 106, 147, 148, 191, 282, 287, 297

Taptoo! 86, 110, 284

The Box Social and Other Stories 46, 54, 95, 149, 185, 247, 262, 274, 285, 287, 298, 306

The Boy with an Я in His Hand 147, 148, 150, 167, 169, 262, 296

The Dance of Death at London, Ontario 245, 262, 280, 307

The Dismissal 44, 83, 108, 173, 208, 221, 222, 224, 235, 262, 273, 287, 301, 304

The Donnelly Documents 16, 241, 244, 269, 272, 274, 306, 307

The Donnellys 12, 16, 29, 31, 39, 43, 46, 47, 48, 54, 59, 60, 61, 63, 64, 89, 114, 118, 147, 149, 153, 173, 229, 234, 235, 237, 238, 239, 241, 243, 259, 261, 264, 272, 280, 306

The Easter Egg 67, 144, 280

The Killdeer 42, 152, 223, 235, 274, 287, 295, 296, 304

The Red Heart 42, 54, 76, 95, 99

The St. Nicholas Hotel 18, 31, 128, 129, 154, 235, 264, 290, 295

The Sun and the Moon 235

Three Desks 44, 66, 80, 83, 220, 221, 283, 304

Twelve Letters to a Small Town 46, 66, 93, 95, 107, 159, 160, 162, 187, 192, 261, 262, 276, 280, 281, 284, 285, 287, 295

Wacousta! 44, 70, 85, 86, 89, 102, 116, 119, 146, 173, 240, 284, 286, 288, 289, 293, 306

Zamorna! and the House by the Churchyard 80, 283

Reaney, James Stewart 13, 24, 29, 57, 263, 272

Richards, M.C. 46

Richardson, John 42, 70, 143, 288, 306

Roffey, Peggy 49

Ross, Catherine 148, 278, 291, 294

Shipley, Robert 89, 90, 284

Simard, Suzanne 125, 126, 127, 129, 131, 220, 290, 304

Smart, Tom 145, 152, 294, 295

Somers, Harry 29

Spenser, Edmund 77

Stingle, Richard 13, 59, 183, 225, 277, 278, 280, 297

Sutcliffe, Rosemary 20, 270

Thibaudeau, Colleen 24, 49, 50, 51, 152, 168, 179, 204, 264, 276, 300

Tsing, Anna Lowenhaupt 21, 121, 131, 223, 270, 291, 304

Turnbull, Keith 59, 146, 173, 294

Walker, Craig Stewart 60, 117, 214, 278, 283, 289, 303

Watson, Sheila 53

Webb, R.K. 150

Weeney, James 151, 152, 217

Weil, Simone 257, 309

Whitman, Walt 25, 27, 110, 171, 231

Willson, David 26, 28, 29, 44, 68, 70, 97, 110, 120, 124, 177, 207, 271, 281, 297

Wohlleben, Peter 121, 289

Woodman, Ross 13, 77, 282, 300

Yost, Elwy 83, 187

Zwicky, Jan 38, 81, 82, 87, 187, 188, 208, 211, 214, 215, 216, 218, 220, 230, 273, 276, 284, 298, 301, 303, 305